D1594387

JAMES D. TRACY is a member of the Department of History at the University of Minnesota.

If Machiavelli typifies the 'realist' side of political thought in Renaissance Europe, the 'moralist' side of the argument is best represented by Erasmus. To date, Erasmus' thought has been approached almost exclusively from the vantage point of perennial issues in political philosophy, as if a professional scholar could not be expected to know or care much about actual historical events. This book attempts to fill this gap by focusing on Erasmus' political opinions, that is, his comments on wars, princes, and statesmen of the period. An effort is made to determine whether his views did or did not represent a reasonable sifting of information made available to him.

Professor Tracy demonstrates that Erasmus' views on politics were developed not only from his Christian and humanist principles but also from an informed interest in and knowledge of the day-to-day workings of politics in the Low Countries. Erasmus' assessments of major events were often of such a kind as may still plausibly be defended. Even his errors of judgment have a certain interest for the reader, since in some instances they reflect not only the cultural prejudices of a humanist but also political attitudes prevalent in the Low Countries: to a greater extent than has thus far been realized, Erasmus was a Netherlander.

Tracy's approach provides interesting new perspectives on several of Erasmus' writings, notably the *Panegyricus*, the adages added to the *Chiliades* in 1515, the *Institutio principis christiani*, the *Querela pacis*, and the letters written during 1516 and 1517, and grounds them in the political realities of the sixteenth century. It enlarges our view of Erasmus' thought and broadens our understanding of the intellectual and political history of Renaissance Europe.

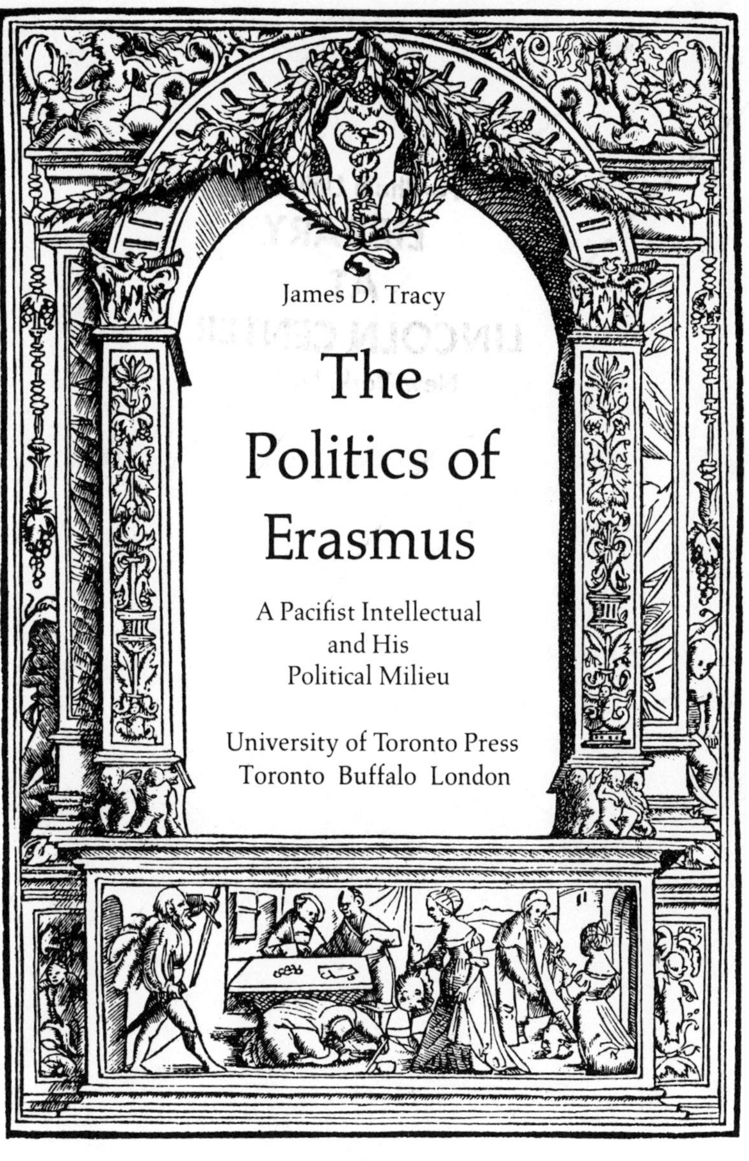

James D. Tracy

The Politics of Erasmus

A Pacifist Intellectual and His Political Milieu

University of Toronto Press
Toronto Buffalo London

Toronto Buffalo London
Printed in Canada

Library of Congress Cataloging in Publication Data

Tracy, James D.
The politics of Erasmus.

(Erasmus studies; 3)
Bibliography: p.
Includes index.
1. Erasmus, Desiderius, d. 1536 – Political and social views. I. Title. II. Series.
PA8518.T7 320.5'092'4 77-20697
ISBN 0-8020-5393-9

The decorated border on the cover and titlepage is from Erasmus *Institutio principis christiani* (Basel: Froben 1518) and is by Hans Holbein the Younger.

FOR NANCY

Contents

Acknowledgments

To the Guggenheim Foundation I am indebted for a Fellowship (1972/3) for a year of research which, though pointed in a different direction, also opened new perspectives on a project then already in hand. Two scholars in Louvain, Professors Jozef IJsewijn and Georges Chantraine, SJ, were gracious in encouraging a foreigner's temerity in still uncharted areas of Low Countries history. Two Minnesota friends and colleagues, Professor David O. Kieft of the University of Minnesota and Dr Louis M. DeGryse, gave the manuscript a careful and judicious reading at an early stage. More recently, Professors De Lamar Jensen of Brigham Young University and James K. McConica of the Pontifical Institute for Mediaeval Studies have made some very pertinent and helpful criticisms. Finally, my research could not have been completed without the able assistance of Joan Fagerlie and the Inter-Library Loans staff of the University of Minnesota Library, and the manuscript itself has been much improved by the painstaking editorial work of Margaret Parker at the University of Toronto Press. To all those mentioned I should like now to express my appreciation, while reserving for my own account such weaknesses in the book as may still be discerned.

Publication of this book has been made possible by a grant from the Humanities Research Council of Canada, using funds provided by the Canada Council, and by grants from the University of Toronto and the Publications Fund of the University of Toronto Press.

THE POLITICS OF ERASMUS

Introduction

WHEN KING CHARLES VIII OF FRANCE led his army across the Alps in 1494, he touched off a sixty-year struggle with Spain – soon to become part of the Habsburg Empire – for hegemony in Italy. As contemporaries looked on in fascination and horror, warfare was practised on a scale unprecedented in medieval European experience. The magnitude of this conflict, together with its resemblance to the power politics of more recent times, led scholars, not too many decades ago, to begin their treatment of the 'modern' period of European history with the Wars of Italy. Nowadays it is not so evident that the 'Middle Ages' came to an end in 1494, nor that the kings whose armies clashed in Italy were 'new monarchs.' Yet it remains clear that monarchs involved in the struggle for Italy were able to mobilize their nations' resources for war in a manner never attained by their predecessors.[1] Changes in the scope of warfare often provoke, as they did on this occasion, new departures in reflection about war and the state. Thus J.R. Hale gives expression to a long and still respected tradition of scholarly opinion when he finds that 'widespread and continuous interest in war as an object of study, rather than simply as a phenomenon to glorify, deplore, justify, or chronicle, begins in the sixteenth century.'[2]

Men of political acumen in Italy were stunned by the apparent helplessness of their governments before the advancing might of 'barbarian' princes from beyond the Alps. Niccolò Machiavelli, embarking on a lonely and desperate path, sought to strip from the minds of statesman compatriots all moral or religious preconceptions that might impede comprehension of the pure dynamics of power.[3] Another Florentine, Francesco Guicciardini, came in the end to believe that the survival of a state depended not upon a rational ordering of its internal constitution, but upon the flux of external events, a sequence comprehensible not by logic, but only by history.[4] North of the Alps men complained – boldly as one could when speaking words that kings might hear – that distant campaigns in Italy had no connection with the interests of their own *patria*, whether it be France, England, or the Netherlands. While Thomas More made sport of princely notions of military glory, Erasmus lamented that Christian Europe had learned to surpass pagan Rome only (he thought) in the magnitude and barbarity of its wars.[5]

Machiavelli and Erasmus are often cited to point up the contrast between two different sixteenth-century approaches to the problem of endemic war, that of the 'realists' and that of the 'moralists.' For Machiavelli it was in the nature of power to expand. The fact the thoughts of an honourable prince turned to war thus required no particular explanation, nor inquiry as to motivation.[6] The very idea that a monarch's appetite for glory might be restrained entailed, it seems, one of those moral presuppositions which stood in the way of a genuine, hence politically responsible, understanding of power. For Erasmus, on the other hand, any discussion of political decisions had to begin with the moral question of motive. He believed the lust for conquest could be traced to false, pagan notions of honour and glory cherished by princes and their noble courtiers. Conversely, a genuine Christian education would help curtail man's violent tendencies. If the Gospel were truly preached, the Christian people would be spared many wars.[7]

In the last century, perhaps especially in the era of great power conflict in Europe from 1870 to 1914, students of the Renaissance period gave much attention to rivalries between states.[8] Machiavelli, long encumbered by the censure of moralists, was admired both for his unvarnished description of power politics and for his recognition of the fact that power is the precondition of liberty.[9] From this perspective Erasmus must be judged naive, since he viewed the question of power squarely within that moral framework from which Machiavelli had set it free. In more recent times, however, the condition of endemic warfare, which Machiavelli assumed, may not appear so natural or inevitable as it did fifty or a hundred years ago. Although wars continue to rage around the globe, the dream of stability through a balance of powers – a dream which to Italians of Machiavelli's generation was a lost idyll of the past[10] – may seem once more to lie within human grasp. Accordingly, while some still view Erasmus as a 'cerebral moralist' remote from ordinary human passions, hence from any comprehension of politics, others now regard him as a voice of sanity crying out in the wilderness of a war-torn epoch.[11]

These divergent views reflect in part a deeper division over fundamental questions concerning the nature of man. Is there a human 'instinct' of aggression, as some would now argue – be it the 'death wish' (*thanatos*) of Freud's later writings or the 'territorial imperative' of Konrad Lorenz – or is the disposition to violence, as Erasmus himself might argue, a product of human culture, hence subject to change?[12] Even granting that some capacity for anger or hostility is somehow 'natural' to man, should this human trait be construed in terms of Freud's *thanatos* or in terms of the *thumos* ('spirit') of Plato and Aristotle, which is viewed as a source of creativity and of emotional richness as well as of violence, a companion to *eros* rather than its enemy?[13] These issues, while too profound ever to be resolved, are nonetheless implicit in many discussions of Eramus' writings on war and peace. The historian, recognizing that his topic is thus linked to problems inaccessible to his (perhaps to any) scholarly discipline, can best be of service not by attempting to pronounce some ultimate judgment, but merely by clarifying the thought of those who, like Erasmus, have contributed significantly to the debate.

For Erasmus' political thought much valuable work has already been done, most recently in Professor Herding's careful editions of his *Panegyricus* and *Institutio principis christiani*. Many of the relevant classical and Christian sources for these works and for *Querela pacis* have been uncovered, and the novelty of Erasmus' religious arguments for peace has been convincingly demonstrated.[14] But political thought must be distinguished from what may be called political opinion. The former deals with timeless issues or *topoi* (commonplaces) inherited from the political speculation of the ancients, such as the question as to which form of government is best.[15] What one thinks about transient conflicts of one's own time, or about the men who make policy – such as the great nobles of the Netherlands – falls rather under the category of political opinion. For purposes of describing Erasmus' thinking on war and peace, the latter is often more instructive than the former. When he says, for example, that popular *consensus* should be a check on the prince's war-making power, it is useful to know that the concept of *consensus* has a long history, but perhaps more pertinent to inquire how he views the relationship between kings and their Estates in the early sixteenth century.[16] Moreover, while the perennial *topoi* in political thought present issues that can never be answered, one can make judgments about the soundness of political opinions. Just as one might assess Erasmus' work as a New Testament scholar,[17] one can assess his concrete perceptions of political life by asking what his sources were, and whether the conclusions he formed represent a reasonable sifting of available information. If one cannot determine whether Erasmus' pleas on behalf of peace were ultimately naive or prophetic, one can at least determine how well he understood the process by which governments entered into war or peace.

Work in Renaissance intellectual history always requires a grasp of the classical and medieval traditions, but seldom a knowledge of sixteenth-century politics. Hence there have been many studies of Erasmus' political thought, but few of his political opinions. The political background for those of his works dealing *ex professo* with matters of state – for *Querela pacis* (1517) and, to a lesser extent, for the *Panegyricus* (1504) and *Institutio principis* (1516) – has often been noted.[18] But little or no attention has been given the political commentary scattered elsewhere in his writings, particularly in some of the essays he added for the 1515 *Adagia*[19] and in his *Epistolae*. The private political opinions of sixteenth-century scholars are usually not well documented, since a prudent man did not readily commit them to paper. Thomas More was privy to many secrets of state, but was also very careful about editing his correspondence, so that few references to concrete political events can be found in his extant writings. Fortunately for the historian, however, Erasmus sometimes permitted himself to be 'too licentious in committing words to paper about kings' in private correspondence, as an influential friend in the Low Countries once had occasion to admonish him.[20] This is particularly true of some unpublished letters to intimate friends which P.S. Allen discovered in a manuscript copy in the Town Library of Deventer.[21] These other sources, permitting one to follow the course of Erasmus' views over the years, are of great intrinsic interest, and can also further illumine particular passages in his explicitly 'political' works.

Finally, more attention must also be given to the specific national matrix of Erasmus' political opinions. Despite his claim to be a citizen of the world, despite sentimental ties to England,[22] home of his dearest friends, his political views and his closest contacts with statesmen were often those of a Netherlander, or, as one might say in the sixteenth century, a 'Burgundian' from the 'landen van herwarts over.'[23] When he speaks of abuses of royal power, his most biting comments are reserved for the Emperor Maximilian's rule in the Netherlands. His frequent contention that princes will sometimes 'collude' with each other to oppress their peoples by war could perhaps be ignored, were it not for the fact that he resolutely applies this conception of princely perfidy to the interpretation of a local conflict in Holland in 1517. To trace the full development of Erasmus' political opinions, with particular attention to the Netherlands background, will thus be the purpose of this study.

Ideally, one might wish to measure Erasmus' political opinions against some accepted standard perception of contemporary political realities. Indeed, just as there are accepted principles of philological common sense which might be used to evaluate his New Testament scholarship, there are a few generalizations about the evolution of the early modern state which most historians now accept, and which accordingly might be set against the views of Erasmus.[24] But no man can fairly be faulted for lacking the wisdom that comes only with hindsight. Moreover, on specific issues there usually is no commonly accepted interpretation. A.F. Pollard portrays Cardinal Wolsey as an ambitious careerist indifferent to moral considerations; J.C. Scarisbrick and Jocelyne Russell present him as a man genuinely concerned for the peace of Christendom. Scarisbrick and Russell, in fact, cite the favourable views of Erasmus and More as an argument for their interpretation of Wolsey's diplomacy.[25] Obviously one cannot reverse the argument and use Scarisbrick's opinion as a yardstick for measuring the truth or falsity of Erasmus' perceptions about contemporary diplomacy. The distinction that can be made is not between true and false, but between opinions held by reasonable and well-informed contemporary observers and opinions which must be described as biased or ill-informed.

Even a relative criterion of this kind is, however, difficult to find for events connected with the Low Countries. The period between the last of the Valois Dukes of Burgundy and the outbreak of the Revolt of the Netherlands (1476–1564) has been neglected by Belgian and Dutch historians. There has been no comprehensive survey of the reign of Charles v in the Netherlands (1515–55) since the work of Alexandre Henne in the 1860s, which covered only what is now Belgium. The history of the reign of Charles's father, Archduke Philip the Fair (1494–1506), has quite simply not been written. Netherlands statesmen of the period are no less important or controversial than their French or English counterparts, but much less is known about them. Guillaume de Croy, Lord of Chièvres, has a fair claim to being considered the arbiter of European diplomacy during the period of Erasmus' closest connection with the court in Brussels (1516–17); to some he has seemed a masterful diplomatic strategist and a loyal protagonist of the national interest, to others a greedy and fumbling aristocrat corrupted by French bribes. Unfortunately, Erasmus' few but significant comments about Chièvres cannot be illumined by a rich secondary literature like that which surrounds the figure of Wolsey.[26] Most often it will be possible to make do with what is available. But in one case (chapter 4) it will be necessary to beg the reader's indulgence for some independent investigation of problems in Netherlands history.

The chronological limits for this study are set by Erasmus' active, face-to-face contacts with court life and men of state. From 1493 to 1495, and again from 1503 to 1504 and from 1515 to 1517, he enjoyed the patronage of leading Netherlands statesmen. His withdrawal from court in 1517 cut him off from the inner councils of government in the Netherlands, though he still maintained a lively contact with friends around Wolsey and Henry VIII, and with certain princes of the Holy Roman Empire. But after he migrated to Basel in 1521, he communicated with men in high places only by occasional correspondence.[27] Moreover, the Reformation came more and more to dominate his view of world events. Luther's revolt, coupled with the ominous violence of his enemies, seemed to pose a graver threat to the peace of Christendom than the mere ambition of princes. The story of Erasmus' strictly political opinions can thus conveniently be concluded in 1521.

A final problem concerns the sixteenth-century humanist movement, the intellectual context for Erasmus' thought. One must not attribute to all humanists a common philosophy, much less a common political ideology.[28] Some humanists, for example, lamented the linguistic plurality of Christian Europe and yearned for a world monarchy; others, including Erasmus, even while professing citizenship in a *Respublica christiana*, were deeply suspicious of the notion of a supranational empire.[29] But humanists did tend to share a common set of intellectual preoccupations or universe of discourse. Furthermore, for reasons which remain obscure, but which may amount to nothing more than the peculiar confidence felt by pioneers of the spirit, and the licence which a literate society permits them, the great Northern humanists of Erasmus' generation were far more forthright in speaking about political and ecclesiastical abuses of the day than were their (generally less illustrious) predecessors or successors. Not all humanists questioned the military ambitions of their princes – most probably did not – but among those who did, humanists were prominent.[30] For these reasons, a comparative discussion of political views among humanists of this generation would be fruitful and instructive; it would illumine the specific character of each man's thought and demonstrate the possibilities for political diversity within the same intellectual movement. Robert T. Adams and Ines Thürlemann have pointed to significant parallels between the views of Erasmus and those of Colet, More, and the self-exiled Spaniard Juan Luis Vives.[31] For Erasmus' perception of events in the Low Countries another humanist friend, Cuthbert Tunstall, English envoy to the court at Brussels, will be of particular importance.

But perhaps the most interesting comparison to be made is that between Erasmus and his great French contemporary Guillaume Budé. Among early sixteenth-century humanists, only Budé could compete with Erasmus in his standing as an intellectual pioneer. Furthermore, Budé's political views are nearly as accessible as those of Erasmus. Just as Erasmus wrote an *Institutio principis christiani* for King Charles in 1516, Budé wrote *De l'institution du prince* for Francis I in 1519. Erasmus was rather free in speaking his mind about contemporary wars in his 1515 *Adagia*; so was Budé, as he later reminded Erasmus, in the long digressions in his 1515 *De asse*. Broad areas of agreement between the two men make more interesting the divergence of their political views. Making appropriate comparisons between Erasmus and Budé will not do justice to the rich variety of opinion among the many humanists, in four or five national traditions, who wrote on the events of their own time during this period. But it will suggest both the broader context and the special character of Erasmus' political opinions.

ONE

Erasmus and the Burgundian National Party

THE ISSUES WHICH DOMINATED Lowlands politics during Erasmus' mature years stemmed in good measure from the bitter legacy of Charles the Rash, last of the Valois Dukes of Burgundy. Having strained the nation's resources to finance an ambitious campaign of conquest, Charles ended in failure, squandering his life and his remaining resources in a futile assault on the town of Nancy in Lorraine (1476). Thereafter the French king, Louis XI, seized what he could of his rival's possessions, notably the Duchy of Burgundy. In the Low Countries, the Estates General were less concerned to defend the Burgundian inheritance than to dismantle the engines of centralized government which Charles had created; Mary of Burgundy, Charles's daughter and heiress, was forced to grant a 'Great Privilege,' restoring near full autonomy to each of the major provinces.[1]

But Mary also gave her hand in marriage to Maximilian, son of the Habsburg emperor, Frederick III, who hoped both to regain the territories absorbed by France and to resume the centralizing aims of Charles the Rash. Following Mary's untimely death in 1482, Maximilian, as a foreigner, was doubly exposed to censure for his efforts to renew Charles's unpopular policies. Opposition quickly fanned into open rebellion, particularly in the southern provinces, which dreaded war with France. Maximilian found support, however, among the powerful Croy family in the south,[2] and among several noble houses with lands concentrated in northern Brabant – the Bergens, the Nassaus, and the Egmonds – all of whom rose to new prominence because of their allegiance to Maximilian during the civil wars of the 1480s. Eventually Maximilian's German mercenary captains carried the day, and those who had stood by him could be rewarded. John of Bergen's second son, Henry, Bishop of Cambrai and soon to become Erasmus' patron, was named Chancellor of the Order of the Golden Fleece in 1493, making him the ranking ecclesiastic at court, entitled to a place of honour in the regency council for Maximilian's son, Philip.[3]

In short succession, Maximilian made peace with France, permitted Philip to be declared of age (1494), and succeeded his own father as Holy Roman Emperor in Germany (1495). But since he still had grievances against France,[4] which portended war, the embers of factional conflict in the Netherlands were rekindled. This time the Croy family, francophile by tradition, joined the opposition. Philip's council, led by his former tutor, Francis Busleiden, and by Guillaume de Croy, Lord of Chièvres, thwarted more than one of Maximilian's plans.[5] Philip did agree (1496) to the marriage with Joanna of Castile that his father had arranged. But he and his council defied the emperor in the crucial matter of the Duchy of Guelders. This complex of lands, lying astride all important branches of the Rhine, had been conquered by Charles the Rash in 1473. But in 1492 Charles of Egmond, scion of the old ducal house, returned to power with French help and strong local support. Henceforth France, through her new ally, could pressure the Netherlands by raids from Guelders or, worse still, by closure of the rivers to commerce. While Maximilian was determined to recover a territory he had once possessed, the 'national party' in Philip's council – Chièvres, Busleiden, and others – shared the extreme reluctance of the Netherlands Estates to provoke war with Guelders. In 1498 Archduke Philip went so far as to permit French troops to cross Netherlands soil to reinforce strongholds in Guelders against a possible attack by Maximilian.[6]

Meanwhile, the Bergens, Nassaus, and Egmonds continued faithful to the emperor. The ports of northern Brabant, Antwerp and Bergen, had prospered in the fifteenth century largely because of a flourishing trade with England. Hence noble families of the region, like the Bergens, cultivated ties with the English court[7] and did not find it difficult to support Maximilian's projects for war against France.[8] At Philip's court, however, the position of the imperial loyalists was deteriorating. Once Philip's wife, Joanna, became heiress to Castile (1500), the archduke required even closer ties with France. Just prior to Philip's departure for an extended visit to Castile, Chièvres and Busleiden negotiated a marriage alliance with France on terms very favourable to the latter (Treaty of Lyons, 1501).[9] Maximilian's friends could not withstand the francophile drift of Netherlands policy; in 1502 Henry of Bergen and his brother, John, were sent home in disgrace from Castile after a quarrel with Busleiden.[10]

From his court at Innsbruck, Maximilian raised objections to the Treaty of Lyons and called once more for an invasion of Guelders.[11] Since Philip was to return from Castile by way of Innsbruck, there were fears lest Maximilian persuade him to change his course, fears reflected in the *Panegyricus* with which Erasmus greeted the archduke when he appeared before the Estates of Brabant upon his return. But the death of Joanna's mother, Isabella of Castile, persuaded even Maximilian to seek friendship with France (Treaty of Blois, 1504). Since this treaty included a French promise to withdraw protection from Guelders, Philip reciprocated by joining his father in an assault on Guelders. The campaign had to be cut short, however, because of a new and threatening alliance in 1505 between France and Ferdinand of Aragon, Philip's father-in-law. The archduke departed in haste for Castile, where, having taken possession of his wife's inheritance, he was fatally stricken by sweating sickness in 1506.[12] Philip's premature death robbed the Netherlands of its first and last 'natural prince' of the Habsburg line. His elder son, Charles, though reared in Flanders, would be swept off to the wider horizons of Spain before crossing the threshold of manhood.

Some time in 1493, Erasmus 'escaped' his monastery at Steyn in Holland to join the retinue of the Bishop of Cambrai, Henry of Bergen. Henry, expecting to be called to Rome for a cardinal's hat, required a good Latinist to accompany him, but he already had in his retinue an Italian humanist, Petrus Santeranus. Why he should require also the services of an obscure if learned monk is thus something of a puzzle. Although Erasmus says in the *Compendium vitae* that he came to Henry's notice 'by chance' (*per occasionem*), it seems he had been angling for patronage through Utrecht, where Bishop David of Burgundy ordained him on 25 April 1492. Erasmus may have impressed the bishop, since he was, he says, one of but three candidates found worthy of ordination. Erasmus' recounting of one of the bishop's *bons mots*, which probably dates from the summer of 1493, suggests he was in Utrecht at that time also. If so, Bishop David may have presented him to one or more of the distinguished emissaries then in Utrecht, each of whom hoped to induce the Utrecht chapter to elect as coadjutor bishop the candidate favoured by his prince. Since Archduke Philip's representative was his chief councillor, Francis Busleiden, it is possible that Maximilian sent to Utrecht *his* most prominent ecclesiastical supporter in the Netherlands, Henry of Bergen. Thus it is at least possible that Erasmus did not come to Henry's notice entirely 'by chance.'[13]

Accompanied by his 'family,' Henry travelled constantly between Bergen, Cambrai, and the court in Brussels;[14] he and they were doubtless present, for example, at Philip's *joyeuse entrée* as Duke of Brabant. In scattered writings from this period, Erasmus complains about court life and mores,[15] but gives no hint of curiosity about political questions.[16] For example, although the cause of monastic reform was dear to the hearts of Erasmus' friends in the cloister, he never alludes to Henry of Bergen's intervention at Egmond Abbey (in Holland) against the reformist party of monks supported by the Egmond family.[17] In recalling, at a later date, how Bishop David of Burgundy – the prelate who ordained him to the priesthood – refused to accept a coadjutor bishop for his diocese of Utrecht, Erasmus relishes the bishop's turn of phrase, but omits, either from prudence or from lack of interest, all reference to the political context of the incident.[18] He was too eager to pursue his studies, too frustrated by a courtier's lack of leisure,[19] to take an interest in affairs of state. In 1495 he obtained from his patron leave of absence and some financial support to study theology at the University of Paris.

After several years of study in France and England – years of great importance for his intellectual development – Erasmus revisited the Netherlands in 1501 in search of further patronage. The Bishop of Cambrai had continued all the while to send him money, but not in sufficient quantity to permit a life in keeping with Erasmus' conception of his dignity as a scholar.[20] Meanwhile, his friend James Batt, schoolmaster in Bergen, had obtained a post as tutor for Adolph of Veere, grandson of Anthony, Grand Bastard of Burgundy.[21] Although linked to the opposition to Maximilian in the 1480s, the Grand Bastard had for some years been allowed to live in peace with his daughter-in-law and grandson in Tournehem castle, near St Omer.[22] Anthony of Bergen, brother of Erasmus' patron and Abbot of St Bertin in St Omer, was a frequent guest at Tournehem. Erasmus' incessant pleading with Batt to intercede with Lady Veere on his behalf seemed finally to promise some result. To strengthen his case, Erasmus dispatched well-phrased letters to the abbot, Lady Veere, and the Grand Bastard's illegitimate son Nicholas.[23] Leaving Paris in May, and stopping first to pay his respects to Henry of Bergen in Brussels, Erasmus arrived at Tournehem in July,[24] only to find the household under a pall of suspicion. In January the Order of the Golden Fleece had required the Grand Bastard to return his collar of membership. Shortly thereafter he and Lady Veere were placed under house arrest at Tournehem, and Nicholas was imprisoned.[25] Although apparently forewarned about Nicholas' imprisonment, Erasmus had walked into an awkward situation: 'The situation there was such that I could neither enter into a conversation with her [Lady Veere] without extreme danger, nor take my leave without incurring grave suspicion.'[26] He soon removed, however, to the abbot's monastery in St Omer.[27]

Given the abbot's connections with Tournehem, Erasmus' quest for patronage from Lady Veere was not incompatible with his obligations to Henry of Bergen. But in Brussels, shortly before his visit to Tournehem, the bishop had accused him of 'ingratitude.' P.S. Allen refers the accusation to Erasmus' habit of complaining to friends about his patron's stinginess.[28] Contemporary political alignments suggest in addition a more recondite explanation. Some months earlier, while residing for a time in Orléans, Erasmus had met Francis Busleiden's brother Jerome. In July of 1501 he heard that Jerome was planning a trip to Italy, a land which Erasmus himself dreamed of visiting: '[Jerome] values aspiring scholars and has not too poor an opinion of my intellectual gifts. If I had not been so totally inept when I was in your part of the world [Orléans], I should surely have found some loophole through which I could penetrate the defences of his friendship.' Although he apparently did not see Jerome again until his return from Italy (1503), Erasmus seemed to expect patronage from his brother. When Francis died (August 1502) he lamented the passing of the man 'in whom lay my highest hope.'[29] In 1501–2 Henry of Bergen's family waged a losing struggle with Francis Busleiden and others for influence at court. One cannot be sure that patronage conventions of the period would require a scholar to pay heed to who his benefactor's enemies were. Jerome Busleiden, for example, was on good terms with Jacobus Anthonisz, Henry's vicar-general.[30] But years later, when seeking employment for a friend, Erasmus apparently found that a scholar who had enjoyed Busleiden patronage was not acceptable to the Bergens.[31] Hence if it did come to Henry's notice that Erasmus was even thinking of forming ties with the Busleidens, he might well accuse him of disloyalty or 'ingratitude.' How much Erasmus himself knew about court politics is open to question, since he had been out of the country for some time; the way he blundered into Tournehem castle at an awkward moment indicates, if anything, a certain political innocence. He may have seen in Jerome Busleiden simply a wealthy man of scholarly inclinations who truly 'valued aspiring scholars.'[32]

One circumstance suggests, however, that even at this time he was not in sympathy with the political views represented by the Bergens. In 1500 Jacobus Anthonisz, Vicar-General of Cambrai, presented the bishop with a tract, *De precellentia potestatis imperatorie*, exalting the imperial crown. Although doubtful of his own learning, and hence promising a collection of 'opinions woven together' rather than an original work, Anthonisz endeavoured to refute the anti-imperial views of the Florentine humanist scholar Leonardo Bruni (d. 1441).[33] Just as peace and justice are best secured through a single ruler, Anthonisz argues, so in ancient times 'it seemed good to place individual [principalities] under a single principate which the Greeks call *monarchia* and we *imperium*.'[34] But many who might agree thus far would still argue that the present kings of France and England are in no sense subject to the Holy Roman Emperor. To meet this objection, Anthonisz cites Dionysius the Areopagite's description of the nine choirs of angels, each of whom receives its power and splendour from those above; in like manner 'all temporal power is derived from the emperor, like a streamlet from a river.' Thus 'the kings of France and England and Spain ought by right [*de jure*] to obey the emperor, even if by chance they do not obey him in fact [*de facto*].' Long disregard of the emperor's rights *de jure* makes no difference, for 'lesser princes' cannot exempt themselves from imperial authority by prescriptive right. For good measure Anthonisz adds a quotation from the fourteenth-century Italian jurist Bartolus of Sassoferrato: 'If anyone should say the emperor is not universal lord and monarch, he would be a heretic, for he would speak against the determination of Holy Mother Church and against the Gospel, "For there went forth a decree from Caesar Augustus to take a census of the whole world."'[35] This form of exegetical reasoning could be applauded by Henry of Bergen, a 'faithful zealot of the Holy Roman Empire,'[36] if not by one who, like Erasmus, was embarked on a study of New Testament Greek.

After his disagreeable interview with Henry of Bergen in June 1501, Erasmus agreed to take Anthonisz' work back with him to Paris for publication, apparently in return for Anthonisz' intervention with the bishop on his behalf.[37] If the bishop did doubt Erasmus' loyalty, he might have been satisfied by his promotion of a book upholding the imperial cause. But from Tournehem Erasmus apologized to Anthonisz because 'my servant, after repeated and careful instructions, left your distinguished book behind [in Brussels].' Over a year later, after the bishop himself had died, Erasmus did contribute a prefatory letter for the first edition of Anthonisz' tract. He complimented the author for exalting in such a way as 'to keep clear of any commitment to a faction' the power which God had willed 'should, next to his own, be mightiest of all in the affairs of states.' But his praise of the book was so faint as to constitute a warning to learned readers: 'Like a busy bee that flies about everywhere, you seem to me with the most amazing persistence to have overlooked no book that could yield you some honey, though I would that you had exercised more choice and also a little restraint.'[38] Erasmus can be expected to have disapproved of works of this type – a scholastic compendium of legal and theological opinions. But it is also possible he was unwilling to endorse Anthonisz' extreme imperialist conclusions. Before the year was out he would be working on a project not calculated to please the emperor or his Netherlands partisans.

In 1502 Erasmus settled in Louvain. Although he hoped, in this university town, to devote himself exclusively to study, the learned men among whom he lived were not strangers to political life. John Paludanus, his host, had formerly been at court. His 'neighbour,' Philibert Naturel, Provost of Utrecht Cathedral, was often employed on diplomatic missions.[39] Through Paludanus, Erasmus was commissioned by September 1503 to prepare a Latin oration to welcome the archduke upon his impending return from Spain.[40] Paludanus and Jerome Busleiden introduced him to Nicholas Ruistre, Bishop of Arras, an important member of Philip's council.[41] Ruistre was present when Erasmus delivered his *Panegyricus* as part of the ceremony by which the Estates of Brabant welcomed Philip in the ducal court in Brussels on the feast of the Epiphany, 1504. Although one doubts that Philip understood Latin, Erasmus claims the prince was visibly pleased to hear himself praised.[42] In February he published a revised version, 'interweaving various things in many places.'[43]

Erasmus' opinion of the *Panegyricus* varied over the years. Shortly after publication he professed to be displeased by it, perhaps because learned friends felt he flattered the prince more than was necessary.[44] In later years he thought it a work of serious moral character, expressing, if more guardedly, the same high doctrine of the Christian prince's responsibilities which is to be found in his *Institutio principis* of 1516.[45] The work itself provides ample basis for such contrary evaluations. As Otto Herding points out, it blends, not always harmoniously, two distinct literary genres, the classical oration in praise of the emperor (the 'panegyric') and the medieval treatise on princely duties ('mirror of princes').[46] What Herding calls the 'panegyric elements' of the work reveal in unmistakable terms the contrast between what Erasmus felt obliged to say at this stage in his career and what he felt free to say later. For example, Philip's ceremonious departure from Brussels is described in terms he would later characterize as proper to foolish popular beliefs about kingship: 'Accompanied by a splendid procession of court nobles, you stood out by so far [*sic procul eminebas*] as the day-star outshines the other lights of heaven.'[47] While *Institutio principis* attacks aristocratic culture at its root, the *Panegyricus* is lavish in praise of Philip as one who fulfils traditional Burgundian ideals of chivalry: 'For who among the nobles of the sword is swifter of foot than you, more agile in leaping, more firm in combat, better at bending the bow, or more practised in pursuing game with sure shafts, more knowledgeable in wielding a pike or experienced in smiting with the sword, or more learned at riding in a horse race?' Philip sits a horse as nobly as Alexander the Great, he is terrible as Achilles to his enemies, he will be glorious in war as were his ancestors, the Valois dukes.[48] Erasmus does, to be sure, endeavour to persuade the archduke – as was conventional in humanist literature – that true *gloria* is gained more from virtuous deeds than from conquest in battle.[49] But in places the *Panegyricus* seems more like the work of a courtier than of a man who was, as Erasmus then described himself, an aspiring theologian.[50] It may indeed be that he was in this work practising to become a courtier. The dedicatory epistle to the *Panegyricus* contains a statement to the effect that the archduke, when paying Erasmus for his labours on the oration, 'offered much besides if I should wish to join his entourage at court.' This phrase was added in 1516 when the *Panegyricus* was reissued as a companion piece to the *Institutio principis* which Erasmus had been commissioned to write in his new capacity as honorary councillor to Prince Charles. In 1504 too there apparently had been some question of finding suitable instruction for Charles, though he was then only three: 'For already (as I hear) you [sc. Philip] are looking about in order to choose from the entire fatherland some man accomplished in morals and in letters, to whose bosom you may entrust your children, still of tender age, for the purpose of instructing them in those disciplines worthy of a prince.' This passage could be read as an advertisement of the author's availability for the position. If there was talk in 1504 of involving Erasmus with the education of Philip's children, it would help account for his later assimilation of the *Panegyricus* to the *Institutio principis*.[51] In any event, whatever the nature of Philip's offer, Erasmus decided not to accept.

Erasmus' flattery of Philip is such that he asks 'if anyone be so much a Brutus or a Cato or a Cassius that he will not willingly permit all things to be lawful to such a prince.'[52] Yet in its character as a 'mirror of princes' the *Panegyricus* also expounds a traditional medieval constitutionalism in which all things are clearly not lawful even to the best of princes. Erasmus mentions – only, of course, to dismiss it as groundless – a fear among Philip's Netherlands subjects lest their prince be 'corrupted' by his sojourn in the Spanish kingdoms, 'where there is very much of dominion and servitude, and very little of liberty and equality.'[53] By contrast, Brabant's strong tradition of limited government, guarded by the provincial Estates before which Erasmus spoke, was incorporated in the *joyeuse entrée* of each new ruler, to which Erasmus alluded in addressing Philip: 'You do not think it *lèse-majesté* if someone questions you in word. Rather, you rejoice to be reminded of your obligation and of the oath by which you bound yourself in accepting your principate [i.e. as Duke of Brabant].'[54] Further assertions that the prince is subject to law may be pointed against extreme imperialist theories of the type expounded by Anthonisz.[55] But it is worth noting that in Brabant, even jurists tied to the imperial party did not necessarily construe *imperium* to mean absolute rule. Nicholas Everardi, Henry of Bergen's chancellor and (later, at least) a friend of Erasmus, tempered his high conception of princely authority with an insistence that the prince keep faith with his subjects: just as the Lord God keeps His Covenant, so Philip as Duke of Brabant must observe each of the clauses of his *joyeuse entrée*.[56] Erasmus' general views on the nature of government would thus have seemed perfectly conventional to his audience.

Specifically in regard to questions of war and peace, the *Panegyricus* is both more original and more partisan. One particularly long section recounts the evils of war in great detail, while the unfavourable contrast between civil and military *gloria* recurs throughout.[57] At times the arguments are of a conventional nature, perhaps even distasteful to Erasmus himself. Although he did not believe human destiny was 'fated' (*fatalis*) in the stars,[58] he apparently had been told that Philip put faith in his astrologers, for he repeatedly describes the archduke as endowed with a 'fatal force' for making peace among men and nations.[59] Clerical listeners who had read St Augustine may have found something familiar in the statement that *imperium* – the power of command, military and civil – is, for Christians, 'not a matter of outward splendour ... but a public function,'[60] ordained not for conquest but for the public good. But one passage departs from the traditional Christian doctrine of limited war, anticipating later writings like the *Querela pacis*: since war is the fountain of so many evils, 'I would make bold to assert that for the pious prince it is far better to accept a peace, however unjust, than to take up even the most just war.' For the Christian prince 'not only believes there is "a divinity mindful of justice," but knows that he must one day render most strict account for every least drop of human blood.'[61] Yet even when he gives utterance, as he does here, to a profound religious conviction,[62] Erasmus' thought in the *Panegyricus* is never wholly divorced from a political context. For the passage goes on to say that the Christian prince, rather than be the cause of bloodshed, will agree not to press this or that territorial claim; and it would not require an active imagination among Erasmus' hearers to refer this general injunction to Maximilian's perennial and troublesome claims to Burgundy and Guelders. Elsewhere, describing Philip's stay with Maximilian, Erasmus reminds him of the 'great agreement among authors' that, after God, *pietas* is owed first to *patria*, not to *pater*. Another passage complains bitterly of the (German) mercenary soldiers which were quartered on the civilian population,[63] and which would form the backbone of Maximilian's forces in the event of war with France. Finally, as Herding has noted, the enthusiasm with which Erasmus praises the archduke for making peace with France is itself evidence of a certain political tendency.[64] The *Panegyricus* clearly reflects current apprehension, at court and in the Estates, lest Maximilian had persuaded Philip to undertake war against France or Guelders. It is, as Vittorio di Caprariis has said, the document of a policy.[65]

But it is also the document of a faction. Erasmus' original informants included imperial partisans like Philibert Naturel and Floris of Egmond, son of Frederick, Lord of Ijselstein. Naturel was Maximilian's candidate (against Nicholas Ruistre, who was supported by Philip) to succeed Henry of Bergen as Chancellor of the Golden Fleece.[66] The Holland branch of the Egmond family had long been faithful to the emperor. To his friend Willem Hermans, still in the cloister at Steyn, Erasmus boasted of his acquaintance with Floris of Ijselstein, scion of a house famous in Holland and known also for its championship of monastic reform:

> Come now, would it cost you so much trouble to encourage the friendly attitudes of men like those with a short letter? Floris van Egmont has won all his battles, and returned victorious from Spain, Savoy, France, and Germany with such credit that he has, by himself alone, not merely eclipsed but positively extinguished the renown won by all his ancestors; I shall include a passage in praise of him in my panegyric. You would do well to congratulate him in a letter or, as I should prefer, a poem; I shall see that he receives it, and at my own hands too.[67]

In the printed *Panegyricus*, however, Ijselstein is not mentioned. Praise of this staunch imperialist would doubtless not have pleased Ruistre, to whom the book is dedicated. Instead there is a eulogy of the late Francis Busleiden, which Erasmus added at the suggestion of Paludanus.[68] In these two cases, then, he took his cues from the court faction whose policies he advocates in the *Panegyricus*. But he seems not to have given equal weight to all components of the 'national' party. In one place – a passage so uncharacteristic for Erasmus that it may be assumed to have been suggested by his patrons – he observes that, like children who honour their parents, princes who faithfully respect the rights and property of the clergy are promised not merely a heavenly reward, but also longevity and prosperity in this life.[69] Elsewhere he attacks certain 'very stupid men' at court who tell the prince he is above the laws, and who bid him to ignore the contrary advice of those whom they call mere 'philosophers and scholasticals.' From the *Panegyricus* one might thus gain the impression that the party of reason and restraint at court was 'clerical' in both senses of the term – men of the cloth and men of the robe. Given Erasmus' connections with Paludanus and Ruistre, this emphasis is not surprising. What is worthy of note is that powerful noblemen among the 'national' party, like Chièvres, are nowhere mentioned.[70]

Not long after the *Panegyricus* was delivered, while Erasmus was living in Louvain,[71] Philip agreed to join Maximilian in an invasion of Guelders. Although Erasmus in the *Panegyricus* credits 'philosophers and scholasticals' with wise and moderate counsel, it was, according to an anonymous source, 'two noble men' on Philip's council who argued for peace, while 'two gentlemen of low birth, and of the long robe,' persuaded the archduke to go to war; these men 'well knew they would be like the baker who puts bread in a hot oven and remains outside, for they could send noble men off to war while remaining at home in their houses.'[72] Erasmus perhaps knew who the 'long robes' were and he was probably disappointed by the new direction in Philip's policy. But his decision to migrate to England (1505) was prompted by scholarly and personal considerations. Although English patrons might not support him so well as Philip could, there were 'five or six men in London profoundly versed in Latin and Greek, and I doubt if Italy itself contains such good ones at this moment.'[73] For this reason Erasmus was to spend some of his happiest years in England.

TWO

The Eagle of Empire: A Bird of Prey

❧

CHARLES VIII OF FRANCE (1483–98), son of Louis XI, was in youth content to emulate his father's prudent expansion of royal influence; provinces grown too independent were brought to heel, by force if necessary.[1] As he grew to manhood, however, the king dreamed of distant conquest in Italy, where a century-old claim to the *Regno* of Naples had recently been willed to the French crown. Discouraged by his father's advisers from undertaking such grand schemes, Charles preferred the counsel of an Italian prince, the Duke of Milan, who, for private reasons, urged him to make good his claim to Naples.[2] By 1492 the decision was made. Once the quiescence of France's rivals had been purchased by treaty, Charles crossed the Alps in 1494, the first of four successive French monarchs who were to lead armies into Italy.[3]

The fruits of Charles's invasion, crowned initially with success, were lost when the French army, decimated by sickness, began a painful homeward journey in 1495. But Louis XII (1498–1514) determined to succeed where his predecessor had failed. As he had been Duke of Orléans before ascending the throne and thus heir, through his family, to an ancient claim to Milan, he selected the Lombard Duchy as his objective. The same Duke of Milan who once sought French intervention was now expelled by the French (1498), and Louis XII returned home in triumph. Four years later he invited Ferdinand of Aragon to join in a partition of Naples. But the wily Ferdinand first induced his cousin, the reigning monarch of Naples, to retire to a monastery in Aragon, then instructed his brilliant general, Gonsalvo de Cordoba, to drive the French from the kingdom.[4]

Having occupied Milan and Naples, the great powers turned their attention to the Republic of Venice, greatest of the still independent states of Italy, and one whose territorial gains in recent decades had attracted widespread jealousy. The Treaty of Blois in 1504 provided for a joint invasion and partition of Venetian territory by France and the emperor. Pope Julius II (1503–13), angered by Venice's recent occupation of towns in Romagna, added his name to the treaty in exchange for a pledge of their return.[5] As the Venetians themselves anticipated, the planned assault was not carried out, owing to divisions between Louis XII and Maximilian. But Julius II, taking advantage of the prevailing uncertainty in Italian affairs, gathered an army and subjugated to his control two important cities of the Papal States, Perugia and Bologna; among the crowd which saw the armour-clad pontiff make his triumphal entry into Bologna in November 1506 was Erasmus, then just arrived in Italy. In 1507, when Maximilian announced his intention to attack the French in Milan, nominally still a fief of the empire, the pope urged him instead to renew the alliance with France against Venice. Maximilian's disastrous invasion of the Veneto (spring 1508) – resulting in the occupation of some imperial territories by Venice – made him more receptive to an alliance with France. Meanwhile his daughter, Margaret of Austria, had concluded that peace with France was the only means to cut off French military aid to the Duke of Guelders, whose hostile incursions into the Netherlands her government was unable to prevent. She therefore summoned the major powers – including Spain and England – to Cambrai, where a league against Venice was concluded in December 1508. Julius II adhered to the league in April of 1509.[6]

The armies of the League of Cambrai badly defeated the Venetians at Agnadello, and the allies occupied several major towns of the Venetian *terraferma*. But the league's initial successes played into the hands of Venetian diplomacy, since other coalition partners began to fear a French predominance. In England Henry VIII had just succeeded to the throne (April 1509) at the age of eighteen. From his father he inherited a group of councillors who eschewed further English involvement in continental wars with France.[7] But the Venetian ambassador, Andrea Badoer, reported that the young king was eager for military glory in a war against England's traditional enemy. Badoer claimed credit for the appointment of Christopher Bainbridge, a resolute foe of France, as royal proctor in the papal court.[8] Bainbridge actively furthered the idea of a league against France[9] and was instrumental in negotiating the settlement between Julius II and Venice in February 1510 which was a precondition for any such coalition.[10] A few months later Bainbridge received a temporary setback when Henry, prompted by generous French subsidies, entered into a new treaty of peace with Louis XII.[11] But proponents of a coalition against France did not lose hope. Julius II, newly embroiled in conflict with the Duke of Ferrara, a French client, was eager for English support. While Ferdinand of Aragon believed Henry might be drawn into war by appealing to his Christian duty to defend the pope,[12] the young English king was himself far from passive. Reportedly reluctant (with good reason) to embark on a major venture with Ferdinand of Aragon as his chief ally,[13] he sought to include the emperor as well. Maximilian, who needed French support to maintain his territorial gains in the Veneto, had to be won back to his former enmity against France. Hoping to obtain the desired result through the co-operation of Margaret of Austria, Henry secretly promised (January 1510) English military aid in the event of further war between Guelders and the Netherlands. Bolstered by this assurance, Margaret contrived to thwart her father's instructions for a negotiated settlement with Guelders. By the fall of 1511, Maximilian's Netherlands provinces, now supported, as promised, by an English expeditionary force, were again at war with France's ally, the Duke of Guelders.[14] Meanwhile Louis XII made his enemies draw together by encouraging a group of dissident cardinals, who summoned a General Council of the Church to meet in Pisa in September 1511.[15] Negotiations in England were for a time delayed when it was learned that the papal nuncio, Hieronimo Bonvisi, was in French pay and had contravened his instructions from Julius.[16] But in Rome, on October 4, representatives of Ferdinand, Maximilian, and Julius formally signed a treaty of alliance; owing to a delay in the arrival of their commission, the English representatives did not sign until November 13.[17] Thus was born the Holy League.

By separate treaty, an English force was dispatched to Spain in 1512 to assist in a planned expedition against Gascony. Instead, the English camp opposite Bayonne merely served to occupy the attention of French forces while the Duke of Alba conquered the Spanish portion of the Kingdom of Navarre, whereupon the English were politely sent home.[18] After this lesson in statecraft Henry was all the more eager to prove the might of English arms by arranging with Maximilian an expedition against northern France. Still reluctant to break entirely with France,[19] the emperor required further inducements. Henry first promised to pay for a Swiss army to invade the Duchy of Burgundy,[20] then agreed that the Habsburg Netherlands could remain neutral in the war against France.[21] Maximilian did not finally commit himself to join Henry on the field of battle until he learned that the Swiss had expelled the French from Milan.[22] Meanwhile Julius II had died (February 21), and his successor, Leo x (Giovanni de'Medici), was known to be cool to the prospect of war with France.[23] Nonetheless Henry pressed forward. He crossed to Calais in July, in the wake of an army of between 30,000 and 40,000.[24] When Maximilian finally appeared in person to volunteer his services as commander-in-chief, the army invested the strategic fortified town of Thérouanne.[25] A French relief column was put to rout (Battle of the Spurs, August 16), with the capture of many French nobles.[26] Thérouanne soon capitulated, and its fortifications were razed.[27] The army then moved on to Tournai, which, being poorly defended, would have surrendered at once, save that Henry insisted on a siege.[28] Having thus enlarged the English pale around Calais by the addition of Thérouanne and Tournai, the king returned to England.

Although Henry hoped to renew the campaign in the following spring,[29] his coalition partners had other ideas. Ferdinand had gained what he wanted from the Holy League, while Maximilian had gained nothing. Thus when Ferdinand and Louis xii concluded a peace treaty in March 1514, Maximilian quickly adhered to it.[30] Meanwhile Leo x had sent peace proposals to England by a special envoy, Gian Pietro Caraffa, instructing him to rely on the advice of two members of the royal council known to favour peace, Thomas Wolsey, Bishop of Lincoln, and Richard Foxe, Bishop of Winchester.[31] Dissatisfied with Caraffa's progress, the pope sent another emissary. Count Lodivico Canossa, arriving in June, was told to contact the humanist Andrea Ammonio, who, besides being close to Wolsey and Foxe, was an intimate friend of Erasmus and More.[32] A French envoy arrived at the same time, ostensibly to treat of the release of hostages taken at the Battle of the Spurs, but in fact to conduct negotiations which resulted in the Treaty of London of August 1514: peace was sealed by the marriage of Henry's younger sister, Mary, to the ageing Louis xii.[33] Thus by the end of his reign in December 1514 Louis xii had gained a bride, but had lost Milan and two French towns as well. His successor, Francis i, would soon begin his reign with a glorious reconquest of Milan, thus launching still another cycle of war.

The often-told story of Erasmus' stay in Italy (1506–9) need not be repeated here.[34] Most important for present purposes is his reaction to the warlike policies of Julius ii. As is clear from a letter to Jerome Busleiden, two days after the event, the conquering pope's triumphal entry into Bologna on 15 November 1506 filled him with profound disgust:[35] 'For at this moment studies are remarkably dormant in Italy, whereas wars are hotly pursued. Pope Julius is waging war, conquering, leading triumphal processions; in fact, playing Julius to the life.'[36] In contrast to many humanists, Erasmus regarded Caesar not as a glorious but as a 'most pestilent' leader; while Cicero interpreted Caesar's melancholy as the sadness of a great soul with no higher peaks to scale, Erasmus took it to mean that the conqueror was tormented by 'shades of those he slew, always flitting before his eyes.'[37] Busleiden, whose brother had been prominent in the anti-imperial party in the Netherlands, would understand the import of his comparison of pope and Caesar.[38] In Rome some two years later, while Julius was deciding whether or not to adhere to the League of Cambrai, Erasmus was asked – by whom he does not say – to prepare draft speeches for and against war with Venice. He duly produced both speeches, though he says he laboured more on the speech against war, which he afterwards kept among his papers.[39] But once Julius had decided on war, Erasmus prudently avoided even the appearance of sympathy for Venice. He refrained from accepting a promising invitation to the residence and library of Cardinal Grimani, the present Palazzo di Venezia, until just after an embassy from the cardinal's native city arrived in Rome to discuss peace terms.[40]

In the summer of 1509 he left Rome for England, where his friends promised that the new king, Henry VIII, would provide for him handsomely. There Erasmus could speak his mind more freely. *The Praise of Folly* (*Moriae encomium*), written some time during his residence in Thomas More's house in Bucklersbury (1509–11),[41] has a comment on war-making churchmen which plainly alludes to the seventy-year-old pontiff's strenuous march against Bologna: 'Here you may even see doddering old men display the vigour of a youthful spirit, and not be deterred by expenses, nor fatigued by trials, nor in any way stricken in conscience if they must overturn laws, religion, peace, and all humanity.'[42] In Paris, where *Moriae encomium* was published in the summer of 1511, he penned a satirical poem which makes the comparison with Caesar more vehement and explicit:[43]

> [Caesar] too was once *pontifex maximus*,
> He too arrived at tyranny by a path of crime,
> Pleasing to him, no less than you,
> Was faith broken for the sake of power.
> He scorned the gods; in this too you are Julius.
> The whole world he churned with blood,

Battle and gore; here too you are another Julius.
That you be Julius wholly one thing alone
Is lacking, that another Brutus should befall you.

In the case of Julius II, Erasmus may for a moment have flirted with the doctrine of tyrannicide.[44]

Returning once more to England, where he was to spend the next three years in Cambridge, preparing a new *Adagia* and other scholarly projects,[45] Erasmus seemed for a time sympathetic to France, the pope's enemy, even though it was fast becoming the enemy of his host country as well. In Cambridge he depended for news of 'French and Italian affairs' on his close friend Ammonio, who, as secretary first to Foxe and then to Wolsey, had access to information reaching the king's council.[46] In November 1511 he greeted Ammonio's report that a coalition (the Holy League) was about to be formed against France with an assessment of Italian affairs that might well have been made by a French partisan: 'But pray suppose the French are driven out of Italy, and then reflect, please, whether you prefer to have the Spaniards as your masters, or the Venetians, whose rule is intolerable even to their own countrymen. Priests are something that princes will never put up with; and yet they will never be able to agree among themselves because of the more than deadly feuds between their factions. I fear Italy is to have a change of masters, and, because she cannot endure the French, may have to endure French rule multiplied by two.'[47] Ammonio himself apparently thought Erasmus was pro-French.[48] If he was, however, he soon made his usual adjustment to the sentiments of those among whom he lived.[49] Ammonio, though willing to joke about Julius II, had connections with the della Rovere family, and hoped for advancement in papal service.[50] Thus Erasmus probably agreed to Ammonio's description of the Council of Pisa as 'schismatic.'[51] At one point he accepted an invitation from Bishop John Fisher of Rochester to accompany him to the rival council which Julius II had summoned to meet in the Lateran, though in the end Fisher did not go.[52] After the Battle of the Spurs in August 1513 Erasmus could even join with English friends and patrons in ridiculing the 'unwarlike Gauls.' In a letter to Thomas Ruthall, for example, he spoke of French 'civility' in yielding to the English.[53] But this retreat from an earlier francophile tendency did not betoken any change in his attitude toward Julius II. Events in Italy grieved him, he told Ammonio, 'not from love of the Gaul, but from hatred of war.'[54] One of the most vehement of contemporary attacks on the warlike pontiff, the satirical dialogue *Julius exclusus e coelo*, for which it can no longer be denied that Erasmus was at least partly responsible, was probably composed before he left England in the summer of 1514.[55]

As one who dreamed of making the New Testament ethic more effective in men's lives, Erasmus would naturally be horrified by the spectacle of a pope donning armour to lead his armies against Christian cities.[56] Indeed, given his firm belief in the purely spiritual character of Christ's Kingdom, one might ask whether he did not, like some medieval thinkers, regard the very existence of a Papal State as a moral contradiction.[57]

The question is in fact touched on in the 1515 adage 'Sileni Alcibiadis,' which is one of the most concise and emphatic statements of Erasmus' convictions concerning the opposition between worldly power and faith in Christ.[58] Civil dominion, he says, 'should be refused' by bishops or popes, 'even if it be handed over.'[59] Moreover, in terms that may be reminiscent of contemporary complaints about the maladministration of the Papal States, he remarks that 'while the cities of lay princes flourish in wealth, buildings, and inhabitants, towns ruled by priests stagnate and fall into ruins.'[60] Elsewhere he lectures the popes on the spiritual character of their office: 'If Christ openly denied that His kingdom is of this world, do you think it fitting that the successor of Christ should not merely accept worldly rule, but even campaign for it, and, as they say, leave no stone unturned on its behalf?'[61] Here he distinguishes between the fact of civil dominion by a pope and an attempt to increase it; the latter is plainly immoral, the former may or may not be.[62] The same distinction seems implied a bit further on when he asks how Christ's doctrine of not resisting evil can be preached by a pope 'who stirs up the world with tempests of war for the sake of his authority over a small town, or for a tax on salt-works?'[63] The examples point to Julius II, since Romagna, the occasion for Julius' quarrel with Venice, was a province of small towns and an important source of salt.[64] Julius violated Christ's doctrine, then, by going to war over Romagna. But Erasmus refrains from saying the pope was unfaithful to Christ by the mere act of accepting the temporal dominion bequeathed from the past. Fundamentally he was not of a visionary temper; he did not expect history to be undone. Yet one suspects he did not fully grasp the moral dilemma of the Renaissance papacy: if the popes were not to accept some powerful prince as protector, they must have a state; if they were to have a state, it must be defended. In this respect, Julius II, who made conquests for the Papal States rather than for his relatives, has been called the saviour of the papacy.[65] But this was a logic Erasmus could not accept. Recognizing that lay princes must defend their states against attack, he could not, it seems, grant the same right to one who called himself Vicar of the gentle Christ. Rather than defend his state, as Julius did, Erasmus appears to say the pope should rejoice in its diminution, trusting not in human power but in God. There were, in other words, cases in which a Christian churchman must renounce his legitimate power, rather than struggle to preserve it.[66] In the end, Erasmus was, if not visionary, radical in his perception of the moral demands made by faith in Christ.

This perspective would in itself suffice to account for a deep suspicion of Julius II and his motives. Yet there is much in Erasmus' view of Julius that is not required by strict allegiance to the Gospel ethic. One must recognize, in other words, that Erasmus' personal contacts in Italy and France included many who then or formerly served the pope's enemies.

In Bologna, where he stayed for some months (1506–7), his best friend was the humanist Paolo Bombasio, who had been an ardent partisan of the Bentivoglio, the ruling family ousted by Julius.[67] He next went to Venice, where he resided during the period in 1508 when the pope and other princes were attempting to organize a coalition against the Adriatic Republic.[68] As is clear from what appears to be an outline of the anti-war speech he composed in Rome, Erasmus was quite familiar with arguments the Venetians might employ in their quarrel with the pope over Romagna.[69] While he was in Paris a few years later, supporters of Louis XII were endeavouring to rally support for the Council of Pisa.[70] Fausto Andrelini, a friend from Erasmus' student days in Paris in the 1490s, had lately been in the service of Cardinal Georges d'Amboise (d. 1510), who had been Julius' rival for the tiara in 1503 and was an early architect of the anti-papal council. In 1511 Fausto was composing propaganda tracts for king and council.[71] While in Paris Erasmus saw 'a play, written by some Spaniard and translated into French,' directed against the pope.[72] He also had 'long and familiar conversations' with the learned humanist Jacques Lefèvre d'Etaples, perhaps at the monastery of St Germain des Prés, where Lefèvre was then staying.[73] Lefèvre's patron, Guillaume Briçonnet, Bishop of Lodève and Abbot of St Germain, was the son of the cardinal of the same name who was a sponsor of the Council of Pisa. Erasmus later named Louis XII and the younger Briçonnet among his own patrons.[74]

Not surprisingly, then, the picture of Julius that emerges from Erasmus' writings is wholly partisan. Giovanni Bentivoglio, whom

Julius expelled from Bologna, was, despite his ability as a ruler, hated by many of his subjects.[75] But *Julius exclusus* describes him as a just prince to whom the citizens clung 'tenaciously.'[76] Julius lowered taxes in order to gain favour with his new subjects. For governance of the city and the countryside, he caused a senate to be chosen, which functioned as the council of the papal legate, and which had more autonomy than similar bodies under the Bentivoglio. But in one of the *Adagia* for the 1515 edition Erasmus seems to blame Julius directly for the new government's fiscal exploitation of the peasantry: 'When I was in Bologna, Julius having by now gained authority over the city, I saw peasants of extreme poverty, whose entire wealth consisted of two oxen – for by the labour of these they sustained their families – forced to pay a tax of one ducat per ox.'[77]

He also represented Julius as the prime mover in contemporary diplomatic combinations. Hearing that a coalition was to be formed against France, he wrote Ammonio, 'I have no one against whom to turn my anger, unless it be that circumcised [in Greek] *physician of the High Priest*,' that is, the Jewish doctor reported to have restored the pope to health. Later he referred to the 'Julian tuba' which had roused Europe to war in 1512.[78] In *Julius exclusus* the pope boasts of having organized the League of Cambrai as well as the Holy League: 'Today there is not one of the Christian kings whom I have not incited to arms, having broken, torn up and scattered all the treaties by which they had been most carefully reconciled among themselves.'[79] Here too, Erasmus overstates the case. Scholars are, to be sure, divided as to Julius' role in organizing the League of Cambrai. As Luigi Simeoni points out, the text of the Treaty of Cambrai closely follows proposals made to Maximilian by the papal legate, Cardinal Carvajal. But Carvajal himself was excluded from the deliberations at Cambrai. Maximilian and Margaret of Austria, as pointed out above, each had motives quite independent of papal wishes, the one desiring an alliance against Venice, the other an alliance with France. F. Seneca rightly concludes that this complex diplomatic background 'attenuates' Venetian claims that Julius II bore the major responsibility for organizing the League of Cambrai.[80] The same holds true for the Holy League against France three years later, which was due to initiatives from Aragon and England as well as from Rome. Erasmus' sceptical reaction to an English proclamation of November 1512, justifying the alliance on the grounds that the French king sought to undermine papal authority, shows he was not taken in by royal propaganda.[81] Rather, he was himself, in regard to Julius II, a propagandist. For the pope who made war on Christians in the name of Christ, no amount of vilification was excessive.[82]

If contacts in Italy and France contributed to his rather jaundiced view of Julius II, Erasmus was able to form a more balanced picture of contemporary diplomacy from highly placed friends and patrons in England. Still influential in the young king's council were several men who had guided his father's policies during a period when England eschewed involvement in continental wars: William Warham, Archbishop of Canterbury, Richard Foxe, Bishop of Winchester, and Thomas Ruthall, Bishop of Durham. To these names must be added Thomas Wolsey, Bishop of Lincoln, a rising star in Henry's entourage.[83] All four were sympathetic to the new learning. Through close friends in England – More, Colet, and Ammonio – Erasmus made the acquaintance of each, dedicating scholarly works to them and, at least in the case of Warham, benefiting from their generosity as patrons.[84] He was also on good terms with the humanist Richard Pace,[85] Bainbridge's secretary in Rome, and with Christopher Fisher, who had come from Rome in 1510 on an embassy from the pope.[86] Robert T. Adams suggests that Erasmus and his humanist friends knew little of Henry's secret diplomacy in 1510–11.[87] But as one who had friends in the Netherlands, he can hardly have been ignorant of the expeditionary force Henry sent against Guelders in 1511. A chance comment in *Lingua* (1525), telling how the war party in the king's council made good use of Hieronimo Bonvisi's treachery (November 1511), shows he knew of discussions within the council and shared the view of those who hoped war might be prevented.[88]

Although it was, as Erasmus thought, the 'magnates' in council who encouraged Henry's bellicose disposition,[89] those who favoured humanist learning did not necessarily work for peace. Foxe, who was later to support Leo X's peace initiative, was reported by the Aragonese ambassador in 1510 to favour an alliance against France.[90] Richard Pace was for some time an ardent proponent of war with France.[91] But two[92] of Erasmus' friends and patrons did speak out clearly against the war, at the risk of incurring royal displeasure. On 6 February 1512, Archbishop Warham departed from his announced theme in a convocation sermon and preached on the evils of war, which, he said, God permitted only to chastise men's sins. Warham was subsequently beset by his suffragan bishops (including Foxe and Wolsey) in a legal quarrel over the disposition of testamentary cases, a dispute he interpreted as contrived to drive him from the king's favour.[93] With war preparations actively under way a year later, John Colet, in a sermon before the court, 'preached wondrously on the victory of Christ,' and showed 'how difficult it is to die a Christian death, and how few undertake war except out of greed or hatred.' Thereafter the king found it necessary to take Colet aside for some further discussion on the concept of the just war.[94] Most of Erasmus' published comments about contemporary wars are subsequent to the sermons of Warham and Colet. It may safely be assumed that he gathered from his English friends not only information, but also courage.

After leaving England in 1514, Erasmus could express some of his thoughts about Henry VIII. In 'Scarabaeus aquilam quaerit,' the most important of the short political tracts composed for his 1515 *Adagia*, he alluded to Henry in commenting on Horace's description of how young predator birds are driven from the nest by their love of fighting: 'Those regions will better understand this figure of speech, who have experienced how many evils befall them from untamed impulses of this sort on the part of young princes.'[95] Far from recognizing peace as a religious imperative, Henry took with him on his French campaign twelve great siege cannon christened for the twelve apostles.[96] Even *Julius exclusus* portrays the English as 'a particularly fierce nation, eager for war,' while Henry is described as 'truly juvenile, that is, inquiet and warlike.'[97] Nonetheless Henry was unique among ultramontane princes of his generation in having had a humanistic education. In the company of his friend Thomas More, Erasmus met the future king as a boy of nine in 1499, and composed for him a Latin ode.[98] Richard Pace relates that Erasmus in later years carried about with him in a memento box a Latin letter from Prince Henry informing him of King Philip's death in 1506.[99] He seems to have thought of Henry as that jewel among men, a prince formed in the spirit of humane letters. Not even Henry's campaign in 1513 could destroy this favourable prejudice. Wolsey was quartermaster for the English army, and his secretary, Ammonio, kept Erasmus posted on events in the field. He knew, for example, that Maximilian, not Henry, had been responsible for the 'ignoble' decision to raze Thérouanne.[100] This may account for his later willingness to tell Henry he conducted the campaign with moderation.[101] If stories were told of how Henry decided to attack Tournai in a fit of pique, Erasmus transferred them to his own prince, the Emperor Maximilian.[102] Even while recognizing that the young English king thirsted for military glory, Erasmus did not censure him as he did Julius II.

The real counterpart to his view of Julius II was his image of Leo X as a peacemaker. He doubtless had some understanding of papal peace efforts early in 1514, since he knew that Gian Pietro Caraffa, whom he had met on a visit to London, was not making progress.[103] How much Erasmus' highly placed friends may have told him is put in some doubt by an incident that occurred in June. Ammonio invited him to dine with a mysterious and courtly Italian visitor, to whom Erasmus freely gave his opinion as to what the pope should do to bring peace. Only afterwards did Ammonio reveal that they had just dined with the papal nuncio, Count Lodovico Canossa.[104] It should be noted, however, that Erasmus' advice seems to correspond to a recent shift of emphasis in papal letters to England,[105] as if he had gleaned some hint of the papal diplomatic initiative. In any case, after hostilities were concluded, Erasmus believed that Pope Leo, together with the new French king, Francis I, had been chiefly responsible for peace: 'We have seen the hearts of princes, transformed as if by divine power, zealous to bend all effort toward peace and concord, and this by the special agency of Pope Leo ... and Francis King of France.'[106] Peace became possible if the princes, and especially the pope, were men of good will. In a letter of March 1514 Erasmus articulated a new version of the traditional medieval view of the pope's role as mediator among Christian states:

> If the dispute is mainly about the question who exercises sovereignty, what is the need of so much bloodshed? For it is not the people's safety that is at stake, but merely whether they ought to call one person or another their ruler. There are popes and bishops and men of discretion and honour through whom petty issues of this kind can be resolved without conducting incessant wars and throwing Heaven and earth alike into confusion. It is the proper function of the Roman pontiff, of the cardinals, bishops, and abbots, to settle disputes between Christian princes; this is where they should wield their authority and reveal the power they possess by virtue of men's regard for their holy office. Julius, a pope who was by no means universally approved, succeeded in rousing this hurricane of wars. Cannot Leo, who is scholarly, honourable, and devout, succeed in quieting it?[107]

Just as he believed war had been unleashed by one evil man who sat in Peter's chair, he hoped it might be stilled by one man of good will. In the former case his understanding of the complexity of the diplomatic situation has been found wanting. Here one wonders how well he grasped the fact that peace was possible in 1514 only because each of the contending parties found war no longer in his interest.[108]

Erasmus' most mature reflections on the wars of the League of Cambrai and the Holy League are to be found in the political essays which first appear in the 1515 *Adagia*, published by Johann Froben in Basel: 'Scarabaeus aquilam quaerit,' 'Dulce bellum inexpertis,' 'Aut regem aut fatuum nasci oportet,' 'Spartam nactus es,' 'Tributum a mortuo exigere,' and 'Ut fici oculis incumbunt.'[109] At least four of these tracts can be dated from the summer of 1514 (Erasmus left England in August) or later.[110] In them he traces wars not to the personal vices of individual rulers but to the unchecked and hence capricious power vested in a single frail mortal by the institution of monarchy.

Before proceeding further, it will be useful to establish the limits within which Erasmus' critique of monarchy must be understood. Like other cultivated men of the early sixteenth century – apart from those who might dwell in Switzerland or one of the Italian republics – he accepted the institution of monarchy as part of the established order of things. His occasional references to the ancient doctrine of cosmic hierarchy, according to which it was fitting that kings governed on earth in the image of God's rule of the cosmos, ought not be dismissed as mere rhetoric.[111] Moreover, as one whose mind was largely formed by classical sources, he was deeply suspicious of any dramatic change or *nouatio* in the existing order,[112] and he regarded the *populus* as a 'naturally' tumultuous element in the body politic which had to be held in check by the strong hand of a prince.[113] If his writings were to be searched for some conception of an ideal state, the answer must be not that he dreamed of some leaderless federation of city republics,[114] but that he accepted the thoroughly commonplace notion of mixed government: the best state was one which combined elements of monarchy, aristocracy, and democracy.[115] But, cosmopolitan though Erasmus may have been, his thinking on monarchy was nonetheless conditioned by the traditions of his native country. The notion that *consensus* was the true foundation of royal government had a definite institutional context in the Netherlands,[116] where the Estates stood for a still vigorous tradition of limited monarchy which, as recounted in the last chapter, finds expression in the *Panegyricus*. As a Netherlander, Erasmus was disposed to look not for the overthrow of monarchy, but for its confinement within a framework of consent.

Classical authors were another common source for the idea that monarchy must be limited. For satirists and historians of the Roman imperial era, monarchy may have been a fact of life, but it was far from being the best of all possible worlds. Seneca's *Apocolocyntosis*, a satiric apotheosis of the Emperor Claudius, was published in 1515, for the first time north of the Alps, by Beatus Rhenanus, a scholar working with the Froben press with whom Erasmus developed a close friendship; Seneca's newly rediscovered work furnished the text for the adage 'Aut regem aut fatuum nasci oportet' ('One Ought to be Born either a King or a Fool').[117] The satirist Lucian, on the translation of whose works Erasmus collaborated with Thomas More, made sport of the kings and heroes of the *Iliad*.[118]

But no combination of sources or influences fully accounts for the vehemence of Erasmus' attack on the concentration of power in the hands of one man. In certain cases he credits to classical authors a critique of monarchy which is more his own than theirs.[119] If, as was suggested in the introduction, the ability of monarchs to mobilize their nations' resources for war was during Erasmus' lifetime growing to a new dimension,[120] it may be that traditional reservations about royal power and its uses were intensified in like measure. More, a man of some experience in affairs of state, knew better than Erasmus that 'licence without limit enervates good minds.'[121] In places the political *Adagia* of 1515 echo or correspond with More's *Epigrams*.[122] Men like More or Guillaume Budé, the humanist councillor of Francis I,[123] hoped and at times were able to exert some influence on the actions of their princes. To protect their access to the royal presence they tempered their speech accordingly. More, for example, was willing to indulge in forms of royal flattery Erasmus now thought foolish. Unlike More or Budé, Erasmus never had access to a prince (save perhaps at the time he wrote his *Panegyricus*)[124] and doubtless did not wish it. He was thus in a position to articulate thoughts which his friends may have kept to themselves.

From the latter middle ages on, kings increasingly surrounded themselves with ceremonial magnificence. Erasmus, deeply suspicious of the hold of 'ceremonies' on men's minds,[125] saw in this development a sinister exaltation of the king's might. Among Christians, he believed, the power to govern (*imperium*) ought to mean simply 'the administration of public affairs,' not an 'absolute right' (*dominium*).[126] 'But when you see the sceptre, the insignia, the attendants, when you hear such titles as Most Serene, Most Clement, Unconquered, do you not think you are beholding something more than a man? Do you not worship the prince like some earthly god?'[127] The king was now called not just *rex* but *monarcha*, a term which connoted autocratic rule.[128] Such flattery might unsettle the best of men. But although 'we entrust the tiller of a ship only to an experienced man,' since lives and cargo are at stake, 'we entrust the state, in which thousands of lives are at stake, to just anyone' who happens to succeed by hereditary right.[129]

In hereditary monarchies, the education of princes was thus of paramount importance.[130] Generations of humanists, like their classical models, believed that a mind steeped in counsels of moderation and self-respect might have some hope of withstanding the incessant adulation to which a prince was daily exposed. But for Erasmus the whole tradition of princely education, even when framed in terms of classical models, was corrupted at its root by a dependence on the pagan notion of *gloria* rather than the Christian notion of *utilitas*: 'Even if [young princes] have their leisure interrupted by reading, they are given childish fables, or histories worse than these, from which the youthful spirit, not being provided with any antidote, imbibes an admiration of and a zeal, as the Greeks say, to emulate some pestilent leader, such as Julius Caesar.'[131] The *Iliad*, that most cherished of classics,[132] was no improvement: 'What could be more stupid than to quarrel over a barbarian girl, so that [Agamemnon] took away Achilles' slave girl when he could not keep his own, even at the greatest peril to the host? But then how stupidly Achilles rages when robbed of his love, how childishly he complains to his mother!'[133] Hence courtly education, combined with 'superstitious'[134] ceremonies of the court, helped to persuade the young prince that 'what pleases him is law.'[135]

Supplementing the description of eagles in Pliny's *Natural History* to fit his purposes, Erasmus, in 'Scarabaeus aquilam quaerit' ('The Grub[136] Pursues the Eagle'), made the royal bird an apt symbol for his conception of monarchy. To Erasmus' contemporaries the eagle was in particular the distinctive standard of the Holy Roman Empire. 'Scarabaeus' in fact contains an unmistakable reference to – and may even have been occasioned by – Maximilian's current fiscal demands in the Low Countries. Nature, says Erasmus, has providently kept the number of eagles small by causing the adult birds to hate their young. But 'this characteristic is more easily wished for than seen in Roman eagles, who plunder the people without end and without measure. While their thirst for demanding grows with age, they never bear down more heavily than when a chick has been hatched. Then the people are struck again and again with contributions.'[137] Erasmus' comment about the hatching of young eagles clearly points to the arrangement by which the Estates of Brabant, in return for Maximilian's emancipation of Prince Charles, granted in January 1515 a subsidy of 450,000 florins, of which 100,000 were specially earmarked for the emperor, in consideration, it was said, of expenses incurred during his grandson's tutelage.[138] Friends in the Low Countries would doubtless take Erasmus' meaning.

But the eagle stood also for kingship in general. 'Some birds,' Erasmus says, 'are gentle by nature. Others are wild, but can be tamed by human craft so they become gentle. Only the eagle resists all training, and cannot be gentled by any effort. It is borne precipitously as if by an impulse of nature, and whatever it strongly wishes, that it demands by right.' So in human society, 'at the cry of the eagle, the people quake, the Estates draw together in fear, nobles are obsequious, judges say aye, theologians fall silent, lawyers offer flattery, laws and customs lose their force.'[139] Erasmus did not say all princes were like eagles, since 'I am not speaking about good and pious princes: which, having once been said, I wish the reader to keep in mind.' But elsewhere in the same essay he doubted whether one might find even in antiquity but one or two princes worthy of comparison with Plato's ideal ruler. In recent times, 'I fear not one will be found for whom that vile insult Homer's Achilles flings at Agamemnon is not appropriate: "O king, devourer of the people!"'[140]

No recent monarch could be found, in other words, who had not sacrificed the public interest to his quest for personal glory. Thus there would continue to be conflicts like the War of the Holy League so long as there were 'monarchs,' whether on papal[141] or royal thrones. For wild beasts fight one another 'for food or in defence of their young, whereas our human wars are generally caused by ambition, anger, lust, or some such disease of the mind.'[142] Recognizing that emergency powers were reserved to governments in wartime, Erasmus accused the noble councillors of princes of making every effort to prevent the public from enjoying peace, 'since they know less is allowed them in peacetime, when things are governed by law and consultation, not by weapons and tricks.'[143] Indeed, it was with him a settled article of belief, repeated in several works of this period, that princes feign enmity, 'colluding' with one another to oppress their subjects by war.[144]

At times, as once in a poem directed against Julius II, he let his mind dwell on drastic remedies to monarchical tyranny. 'While the useless prince plays dice, dances, or enjoys his fools' in the safety of his court, 'towns are burnt, fields laid waste, churches destroyed, innocent citizens cut down.' Is there, Erasmus asks, no justice for such crimes? 'O race of Brutus! O bolt of Jove, either blinded or blunted!'[145] Yet Erasmus was no revolutionary. The invocation to Brutus is followed by an important qualification: 'Yet for now [evil princes] are to be tolerated, lest tyranny be replaced by anarchy, an evil almost worse.' Elsewhere he remarked that the inconveniences of doing away with the hereditary character of monarchy might be greater than those of maintaining it.[146]

Precisely because of what he perceived as a flagrant abuse of power by princes, however, he was not wholly without hope for the future. 'Fine cities,' he says in one of the 1515 *Adagia*, 'are built by the people, subverted by princes ... good laws are borne by popular [*plebeiis*] magistrates, violated by princes; the people desire peace, while princes stir up war.' Given this radical conflict of interest, there was a possible 'anchor of public safety: the tyranny of princes may be constrained by honest harmony among towns and townsfolk.' Years later he still believed there would be fewer wars if princes did not take up arms 'without the consent of cities and of the nation [*patria*].'[147] In the same vein *Julius exclusus* finds it quite natural the pope should fear a general council of the church: 'Why not ask of monarchs why they hate Estates and assemblies of notables? It is not because the royal dignity is rather obscured by such a crowd of excellent men?'[148] One ought not to conclude from such passages, as Kurt von Raumer apparently does, that Erasmus believed control of national policy by the third estate would necessarily put an end to war. A man of the sixteenth century could hardly fail to notice that 'the Swiss, who once slew or drove into exile every tyrannous noble, are now a grave threat to the world, and may destroy even themselves unless they are fortified with concord.'[149] But Erasmus' decision in 1514 to migrate from England to the Netherlands, where towns and Estates could still defy their prince, may have involved more than a search for patronage.[150]

To his evaluation of royal power in the 1515 *Adagia* Erasmus brought, among other elements of his background and experience, the political attitudes characteristic of the national or francophile party in the Habsburg Netherlands. The 'landen van herwarts over' were a collection of contiguous but distinct provinces brought together in a single complex by the Valois Dukes of Burgundy during the course of the fifteenth century. Only gradually did the population, especially in the

Dutch- or Flemish-speaking towns, come to accept the unifying tendencies promoted by their French-speaking rulers. Such good will as the ducal government had built up was, however, wasted in the disastrous campaigns of Charles the Rash (d. 1477). Under Maximilian of Habsburg, husband and then widower of Charles's daughter Mary, the local Estates were once again restive under the centralized rule of a foreign prince. To many in the Netherlands, royal power seemed a needless, alien imposition on provinces capable of governing themselves. In France, on the other hand, where the development of monarchy had been far more continuous and deeply rooted, royal power was more commonly viewed in quite a different light. It is thus instructive to compare Erasmus' views on war and monarchy with those of his great contemporary Guillaume Budé, who was just as much a humanist, but even more a Frenchman than Erasmus was a Netherlander.

Born to a family which had been in royal service for three generations, Budé (1468–1540) turned aside from the emoluments of an official career and the pleasures of court life to pursue his beloved *philologia*. Late in the reign of Charles VIII his reputation for learning won him an invitation to court. Under Louis XII, however, he received scant notice, so that, though embittered at the favour shown to Italian scholars by the king's powerful ministers, he had leisure to produce the works which brought him fame. *Adnotationes in XXIV pandectarum libros* (1508) built up from slender Italian beginnings the foundations for a critical, historical understanding of an important segment of Justinian's *Institutes*, thus accomplishing for the study of Roman law what Erasmus' Greek New Testament was to do for biblical theology. *De asse et partibus eius* (1515) unravelled, in a manner still largely accepted by modern scholarship, the entire ancient system of weights, measures, and coinage; it revealed a detailed understanding of ancient society not rivalled by any contemporary, probably not even in Erasmus' *Adagia*.[151]

Given the pleasant humanist custom of cultivating friendship with other members of the 'ordo' of good letters, it was inevitable that two such eminent men should correspond. Erasmus, shortly after publication of his New Testament, gallantly made the first approach, in a letter which is now lost. Budé was delighted, although, as a man who preferred scholarship on a massive scale, he could not refrain from chiding Erasmus for occupying himself with 'things of little weight,' such as his compilations of rhetorical formulae, proverbs, and adages. Mildly piqued, Erasmus defended himself against the charge by referring in particular to the long essays he had prepared for the 1515 *Adagia*: In this

> work of detail, how often do I wander into the fields of the philosophers and theologians and, as if forgetful of the subject at hand, go into things more deeply than might be considered proper. My meaning will be more clear if you read the adages 'Aut regem aut fatuum nasci oportet'; the same for 'Spartam nactus es, hanc orna,' and 'Dulce bellum inexpertis' and 'Sileni Alcibiadis'; now in the adage 'Scarabaeus aquilam quaerit' I plainly give free play to my thoughts.[152]

Budé responded that he too had not restricted himself to learned topics; would that Erasmus took time 'to read some parts' of *De asse* 'with attention,' especially where he answers 'those who attribute everything to Italians, even to the extent of claiming everyone else has been unsuccessful in their attempts at eloquence,' and where 'I have not been afraid to accuse those in power.' In fact, the long digressions of *De asse* to which Budé refers are, as a commentary on how war springs from the egotism of the mighty, just as interesting as the 'adages' to which Erasmus pointed. Thomas More recognized their importance, and, after Budé's prompting, so did Erasmus.[153]

Like Erasmus, and like Thomas More in *Utopia*, Budé did not believe that distant wars fought in Italy for the king's glory contributed to the welfare of the French nation. Writing about the time of Francis I's accession, he spoke of 'Italy loved by us to our perdition,' and sadly took note of preparations for still another campaign: 'So we pay the price now also, so we shall always do, by what seems a necessity of birth for each new reign in France.' Tournai had fallen to Maximilian in 1513, he believed, partly because 'our forces were detained elsewhere,' that is, in Italy.[154] Noting the enormous burden of war taxes – the *taille* had trebled in the space of a few years – during a period when the countryside was plagued alike by bad weather and by the king's foreign mercenaries, he marvelled at the patience of the populace in bearing such ills.[155] Yet he also distinguished between wars which might serve the national interest and those which did not: 'Happy would you be,' he apostrophized France, 'were you content within your borders.' But there had been occasions when limited aggression was proper (he may have been thinking, for example, of Louis XI's annexation of the Duchy of Burgundy, or of campaigns in Brittany under Charles VIII):

> Now if at some time it seemed appropriate for your welfare or reputation to reclaim, with every resource, some dominion pertaining to you by race [*gente*] or kinship, and you were unable to do so save by invoking the judgment of Mars, then it was fitting to display some specimen of your powers beyond the borders: it was fitting, to be sure, though it is most difficult to maintain a proper self-restraint while things go well. But what angry god has so driven you beyond your senses, that you think it so wonderful to dance a war dance at the bidding of priestly [*pastophoris*] choreographers?[156]

He thus raised more a national than a purely moral objection to France's Italian campaigns.

The blame for diverting national policy from its true course could, Budé believed, be fixed on a few individuals. Far from displaying any class consciousness as a man of the *noblesse de robe*, Budé complained that the great noble families of the realm (*proceres*) were, under Louis XII, unjustly excluded from their traditional positions of influence at court;[157] a clue to his attitude may be found in a laudatory reference to the Constable of Bourbon,[158] son-in-law of the Duke of Bourbon who helped guide French policy before Charles VIII became enamoured of adventures in Italy. Conversely, the villains of recent French history were certain 'red-hatted ones,'[159] men whose scandalous cumulation of church benefices enabled them to compete in wealth and splendour with the king himself. The two churchmen most prominent in French affairs during this period were Georges d'Amboise, Cardinal of Rouen (d. 1510), and Guillaume Briçonnet, Cardinal of St Malo (d. 1514). Despite Budé's description of those in power as men of mean birth,[160] both Amboise and Briçonnet came from families which had served the king as long as the Budés. Amboise is clearly the principal target of Budé's wrath. A keen partisan of the duke of Orléans before his elevation to the throne, Amboise was subsequently rewarded with Louis XII's full confidence. Budé laid at his door the fact that Italian humanists were given court appointments while native French scholars like himself were ignored (Budé made fun of Frenchmen who preferred Italian, just as More ridiculed Englishmen who disdained their native tongue to lisp in French).[161] Although a bitter critic of Julius II, the pope whose garments 'are purpled in human blood,'[162] Budé accused Amboise of drawing France into conflict with the pope in pursuit of his own ambition for the tiara; thus it was the Cardinal of Rouen who 'applied to our national treasury this great leech of war.'[163] Briçonnet seems not to be included among those highly placed men whom Budé attacked specifically. But he had been a friend and collaborator of Etienne de Vesc, tutor of Charles VIII and later Seneschal of Beaucaire, who was credited with persuading the king to turn his attention to conquest in Italy.[164] Thus it happened, according to Budé, that momentous decisions arose 'from the convenience of a few, who have learned to draw the edicts and decrees of the prince into their own interest.'[165]

For Budé, the only hope against those who were so powerful with the king lay in the king himself. The French Estates (*comitia*), meeting only rarely, and even then with the approval of the king's chief ministers, 'cannot delay or undo the work of those who pronounce justice and make appointments as it pleases them.'[166] Even the prestigious Parlement of Paris (*senatus*), eulogized by Budé in his 1508 *Adnotationes*, was more interested in its own rights than in those of the public. As for the council (*curia*) charged with advising the king, its members vied with each other to follow the wishes of their more influential peers 'in all matters sacred and profane, in affairs both of war and of peace. Not only do they vote with their feet, as used to be done in the Roman Senate, but they are cleverly obsequious in applause, and in flattery by facial expression.'[167] Commenting toward the end of *De asse* on the death of Louis XII (December 1514), he remarked that the worst feature of the reign just completed was that 'the captain of such a great ship, either by a fatal carelessness or because of ill-advised and excessive trust in others, did not take his place either at the prow or the stern: not even with a great storm coming on did he review how the sailors were performing the duties he had entrusted to them.' Elsewhere, a saying attributed to Louis XI, that truly strong king, brought to mind a similar thought: 'O kings [of France] entirely happy, if only they could sufficiently take cognizance of their own role [*persona*], and if they would desire that, in the high governance of affairs, every truly grave matter be transacted under their own guidance, not in their name only, or at least not without their knowledge.'[168] Budé was careful to point out a few years later, in *De l'institution du prince*, that royal power is not 'absolute,' since it was instituted for the common good, and since God alone is truly sovereign and absolute in His power.[169] But while Erasmus would not allow *maiestas* as a term for Christian rulers, Budé believed that *maiestas* was the necessary source of 'fear and shame.' Since *maiestas* was concentrated in the royal person, the king should show himself frequently to his subjects and take personal charge of state affairs as often as the occasion required.[170] Only thus might France be spared senseless and extravagant foreign military adventures.

Budé and Erasmus, both noting how royal *amour propre* could be fed by self-interested courtiers, are agreed that, in Erasmus' words, 'greed for glory drives us to war.' From the standpoint of a dynamic understanding of power, both humanists might be accused of a moralist's error in supposing that governments can create mighty armies and then refrain from their use. Speaking of what Budé and Erasmus would call *imperium*, Bertrand de Jouvenel writes that 'to the extent that command is a species of egoism, it tends naturally to grow.'[171] Federico Chabod, a historian sensitive to Machiavelli's insight into the meaning of power, points out that the Duchy of Milan, with its great wealth and its strategic location, was the natural focal point in a contest for supremacy between the two greatest European powers, France and the Habsburg-Spanish Empire. Moreover, the struggle was understood in these terms by diplomats, at least in the period when Chabod begins his account of Milanese affairs (1530s).[172]

This interpretation of the Wars of Italy is not, however, so satisfying as it might appear. Struggles for land and influence along the borders of major states were a matter of course in the Middle Ages. But warfare in the generation of Erasmus and Budé had become something that was arguably quite different. Late medieval developments in administration and royal finance permitted the mobilization of larger and better equipped armies.[173] No French king prior to Charles VII (d. 1460) had at his disposal a permanent force of some nine thousand armed men and the assured tax revenue to pay their wages. No king of Aragon prior to Ferdinand the Catholic had the use of a standing army for his ventures in Mediterranean politics.[174] Artillery, employed scarcely at all during the Hundred Years War, was developed to a new level of effectiveness in the Wars of Italy.[175] While Henry V led nine thousand Englishmen against the French at Agincourt in 1415 and Edward IV mustered eleven thousand for his expedition in 1475, Henry VIII crossed the Channel in 1513 with an army of thirty thousand;[176] in 1494 and 1515 French kings marshalled forces of comparable size against Naples and Milan.[177] New military forces – like the Burgundian standing army created by Charles the Rash – made for grander princely dreams. Charles's effort to annex the territories lying between Burgundy and his Netherlands provinces, thus reconstituting the Carolingian 'middle kingdom' between France and Germany, marked an abrupt break with the cautious Burgundian tradition of expansion by diplomacy.[178] In like manner Charles VIII and Louis XII of France mobilized the resources of their kingdom in pursuit of distant objectives having no discernible connection either to national tradition or national interest. Thus even those who would endorse limited wars of national aggrandizement, as Budé appears to do, might reasonably object that the battle for control of Italy was a novel and extravagant extension of the king's power to make war.

Moreover, although diplomats might think of the conflict in strategic terms, especially once it had become an accepted fact of European political life,[179] it seems that kings, apart from exceptional figures like Ferdinand the Catholic, did not make their decisions to go to war in the light of strategic considerations. Charles VIII's biographer believes the king was drawn to Italy because of a long history of French intervention in the south, tracing back to Charles of Anjou, brother of St Louis, who became King of Naples in 1268.[180] But Edward Füeter, author of a manual of diplomatic history for this period, finds that 'no political act of that time was so clearly to be traced to the free choice of ruling personalities, so little conditioned by military or economic necessity.' Just prior to the invasion a Milanese ambassador reported that all leading figures at court, saving only De Vesc and Briçonnet, were opposed to the king's project. But, as another student of French history concludes, 'Charles was young and foolish, greedy for glory, and eager for adventure.'[181] The consensus of historians concerning subsequent princes and later campaigns is no different. Henry VIII invaded France in 1513, according to a recent military historian, who writes with a frankness Erasmus did not permit himself, 'partly because he was by nature a bully, and partly to prove to himself, to his people, and above all to his peers, the heads of state beyond the English Channel, that mastery of the art of war ranked high among his many accomplishments.'[182] Another writer disputes the view that Francis I devised the battle plan for his great victory at Marignano (1515): 'Any policy he knows is concerned with adventure.'[183] Finally, to cite a later campaign that has been studied with great care, Lucien Romier traces the last French invasions of Italy (1550s) to the ambition of the Guise family and their partisans.[184] One might of course argue, particularly from an Hegelian perspective, that the private passions of those who govern are a vehicle for deeper processes which they themselves need not comprehend. But the basic contention of Erasmus and Budé – that nations were being thrown into war by princes (or by those who preyed on their power) in quest of personal glory – is at least plausible, and certainly not naive.

The two humanists differ in their perceptions as to how the misuse of royal power might best be curbed. Just as Netherlanders were accustomed to think of the prince as being restrained by contractual agreements with his Estates, French writers had a long tradition of looking to the king to correct the faults of his ministers.[185] From the vantage point of a later century, one can readily discern trends in contemporary royal policy which belied the expectations of both Budé and Erasmus. Francis I, who came to the throne as Budé wrote *De asse*, took a vigorous hand in matters of state, as Budé might have wished, but displayed equal vigour in leading his armies across the Alps, sometimes to victory (Marignano, 1515) and sometimes to disaster (Pavia, 1525). Conversely, it cannot be said of Burgundian and Habsburg rulers of the Netherlands that they merely drained the nation's resources for foreign wars without making a contribution to national development. Erasmus justly complains of Charles the Rash that, while bitter civil wars between two traditional factions (the Hoeks and the Kabiljauws) flared anew in Holland, 'that good prince, as if all this had nothing to do with him, was off laying siege to a town far away.'[186] But a modern historian points out that during the period from 1477 to 1492, when the Estates of Holland governed with little interference from Maximilian, the same partisan conflict raged more violently than ever.[187] The prince, for all his dynastic schemes, was the only force in the country able to rise above the intense localism of the Estates. Royal power was thus less benign than Budé hoped, but more necessary than Erasmus believed.

Beyond this difference of opinion lies another, deeper and more subtle. Erasmus tended to believe that men were peacefully disposed by nature, and that the habit of violence was a product of one's upbringing.[188] In patriotism he apparently saw only a divisive force; thus he chided Budé for his partiality to France, because it was more worthy of a philosopher 'to hold the whole world as the common fatherland of all.'[189] For this reason he belongs among those thinkers who have viewed political union as rooted less in man's passional nature than in a shared rational agreement (*consensus*) about its ultimate moral purpose. In such a perspective the king had only an executive function; the popular notion that kings were different from ordinary mortals, that *gloria* and *maiestas* were vested in the royal person, served no purpose, save to distract attention from the Christian principle of public *utilitas.* Budé was of course familiar with the idea that royal government rests on a tacit agreement between prince and subjects. But his concept of the public good allowed more room than Erasmus did for what a modern student of Machiavelli has called the necessity of strife.[190] Although long and constant peace is something 'for which all sound minds must pray to God,' it tends nonetheless, Budé believes, to produce laziness and luxurious living.[191] Musing on his fellow countrymen, Budé wondered whether 'our restless spirit is able to bear that we should not be at war somewhere.'[192] Indeed, one might gather from the passage quoted at length above that the welfare of the realm sometimes required just such a 'restless spirit.' But if strife be reckoned among the components of civic well-being, its centrifugal tendencies must somehow be checked by a unitive force of comparable strength. Accordingly, in places where he discusses the cohesion of the political order, Budé dwells not on the compact between king and subjects, but on the peculiar affection which a people feels for its own land, and which in France was concentrated in the person of the king; the king himself is best able to govern France because the *maiestas* of the nation is vested in him.[193] The same royal splendour which for Erasmus detracts from the true purpose of government fulfils it for Budé.

One might see in this difference between Erasmus and Budé the beginning of a long and momentous debate. Montaigne, in his essay 'On Cannibals,' spoke in the spirit of Erasmus when he reported that Brazilian Indians brought to France 'thought it very strange that so many grown men, bearded and strong and armed ... should submit to obey a child' (the young Charles IX).[194] These children of nature were, it seems, able to compose differences among themselves without the use of such artifices as hereditary kingship. Pascal, more sombre in his estimate of men's struggle for preference and of the need to set limits to it, responded in the spirit of Budé: 'The people have very sound opinions, for example ... in having distinguished men by external marks, such as birth or wealth. The world again exults in showing how unreasonable this is; but it is very reasonable. Savages laugh at an infant king.'[195] At this point the discussion merges into one of those questions which the study of history will always raise but never resolve.

THREE

The Stupid and Tyrannical Fables of King Arthur

MARGARET OF AUSTRIA'S APPOINTMENT as Regent of the Netherlands (1506) put an end to a period when government was in the hands of the 'national' party. Yet Habsburg partisans still could not mount a military action against Guelders, a French ally whom their opponents hoped rather to conciliate. The Estates General's persistent refusal to vote funds for war with Guelders forced Margaret to seek alliance with France (the League of Cambrai) and, at the same time, to bring Chièvres, head of the national party, back into government as first chamberlain, which made him Prince Charles's official guardian.[1] After the Anglo-imperial campaign in northern France (1513), Margaret was able, in collaboration with Maximilian and Henry VIII, to appoint three new first chamberlains, thus removing the prince from Chièvres' influence.[2] But thereafter the Estates General declined her request to grant funds for a journey to Austria by Charles. Chièvres then promised Maximilian that if Charles were emancipated from tutelage, the Estates would grant a subsidy. In the ensuing turnover Margaret lost her position as regent.[3] Charles was emancipated in January 1515, the Estates of Brabant and Flanders granted large subsidies,[4] and Chièvres was reappointed first chamberlain, or head of that branch of government service reserved to the nobility. His close collaborator Jean Sauvage was named Chancellor of Burgundy.[5]

As far as circumstances permitted, Chièvres followed a policy of conciliating first France, then England. The Peace of Paris (March 1515) provided for a marriage between Charles and a French princess.[6] Discussions could then begin on the renewal of a commercial treaty (the 'Intercursus malus') which Philip the Fair had signed with England in 1506. English commissioners, including Thomas More, arrived in Brussels in May 1515 to begin several months of negotiations.[7] Francis

I's brilliant victory over the Swiss at Marignano (September 1515), regaining control of Milan, compelled the other powers to consider once again an alignment against France. In October Richard Pace was sent from England to persuade the Swiss to re-enter the war.[8] Swiss Cardinal Matthaeus Schinner, who shared Pace's antipathy to the French, enthusiastically seconded his proposals. Maximilian joined the Swiss force, paid by English gold, that crossed the Alps in March 1516. But since the Swiss wished to attack Milan, while the emperor hoped rather to defend Brescia, the army broke up in disarray.[9] Meanwhile, once the Anglo-Burgundian commercial negotiations were completed (January 1516), Cuthbert Tunstall was sent to Brussels to seek from Chièvres and Sauvage a renewal of the alliance against France. Early in April, however, Charles's 'governors' were busy meeting with French representatives at Noyon.[10] Although the conference at Noyon was prorogued until August – French demands proving unexpectedly rigorous – Chièvres and Sauvage had powerful motives for preserving amity with France. Ferdinand's death in February 1516 left the realms of Aragon and Castile to be claimed by Charles; like his father, Charles could not journey south without protecting his rear by contenting France. Thus by late August a new marriage treaty was arranged: Charles was to wed, when she came of age, Francis' infant daughter, Louise, who was to have as her dowry the French claim to Naples (Treaty of Noyon).[11] With this treaty signed, Chièvres was ready, indeed eager, for negotiations with England.[12]

Maximilian was less troubled by his grandson's succession in the Iberian peninsula than by a combined Franco-Venetian threat to his hard-won conquests in the Veneto. Hence he sent Cardinal Schinner to London in October 1516 with a fresh proposal: if Henry would advance forty thousand crowns to pay for his journey to Brussels, Maximilian would break the Treaty of Noyon, dismiss Chièvres and Sauvage, and then resign his imperial crown in favour of Henry. Tunstall and Pace thought it unwise to join the English crown to the crown imperial, and in any case they doubted Maximilian's sincerity. But Henry preferred the encouraging counsel of Schinner and Margaret of Austria. The Treaty of London (October 1516), for which Wolsey's secretary, Ammonio, drafted the preamble, provided for the defence of Verona, the overthrow of Chièvres and Sauvage, and Henry's succession to Maximilian as emperor.[13] Schinner reached Hagenau in December with the first instalment of English gold. But the fickle Maximilian, having been assured he would be compensated for the loss of Verona, had already sent to Brussels full powers to affix his name to the Treaty of Noyon.[14] Telling Schinner he still intended to break the treaty, the emperor graciously accepted payment for his trip to Brussels.[15] But in March 1517, accompanied by Margaret and Charles, he met Francis I in Cambrai for a conference that had been agreed on the previous December. At Cambrai the three sovereigns confirmed the Treaty of Noyon and, in secret, agreed to a partition among themselves of Venice, Milan, Naples, and Tuscany.[16]

Despite the twisting course of imperial diplomacy, Henry persisted in trusting Maximilian. Not satisfied with Tunstall's reports from the Netherlands, he sent the Earl of Worcester to replace him, with instructions not to take Tunstall into his confidence.[17] Negotiations with Chièvres for an Anglo-Imperial-Netherlandish treaty of amity were not completed until Henry agreed to drop from the draft treaty a clause which seemed to commit Charles's government to support English financial claims against France.[18] Still Henry, if not Charles or Maximilian, hoped to convert the tripartite agreement of May 11 into an alliance against France.[19] For a time he had support from Italy. In return for an English subsidy to help restore his nephew to the Duchy of Urbino, from which he had been expelled by a rival claimant with French support, Pope Leo X adhered in July 1517 to the treaty between Henry, Charles, and Maximilian, here interpreted as being directed against France. But a joint mediation effort by Maximilian and Francis I soon restored Leo's nephew to Urbino, thus ending the pope's interest in an anti-French coalition.[20] Henry had to content his martial ardour by participating in discussions of a crusade against the Turks.[21]

If Henry was frustrated, Chièvres had achieved his goal: the way was now clear for Charles's journey to Spain. Delayed for a time by a new outbreak of war with Guelders, to be discussed in the next chapter, Charles sailed in September, leaving behind a land deprived once more of its 'natural' prince.[22]

Erasmus left England seeking patronage and a publisher for his books. The latter need was met in Basel, where Jerome's *Epistulae* (January 1515) and the new *Adagia* (April 1515) were published by Froben. As to the former need, Erasmus hoped to make suitable connections in his native country,[23] where, as noted in the last chapter, the anti-imperial flavour of 'Scarabaeus aquilam quaerit' may have found understanding readers.[24] In August 1514 friends in Ghent introduced him to Jean Sauvage, 'a man most learned in every kind of literature,' who was then president of the Council of Flanders.[25] By the time Erasmus was next in the Netherlands – after a quick visit to England – his new acquaintance had become Grand Chancellor of Burgundy.[26] Some time during the next few months – perhaps in May, when Sauvage 'held up' Erasmus for three days in Ghent[27] – the chancellor obtained for him an honorific and (when the salary was actually paid) lucrative appointment as councillor to Prince Charles.[28] Erasmus was expected not to give practical advice, but to explain for the benefit of the young prince 'certain as it were sources of all advice.'[29] In other words, Sauvage commissioned him to write a general manual of instruction for Charles, who was then fifteen.[30] Not long after receiving this commission he left once more for Basel, where he was to publish his Greek New Testament.

Institutio principis christiani was written in Basel during the winter; it was ready for the press in March and published in June.[31] Returning from Basel, Erasmus was in Antwerp by early June, when he wrote Sauvage that the book was still in press, though he 'greatly desired' to present the prince with a personal copy.[32] Within a day or so he dined with Sauvage in Brussels, where he waited long enough to greet Tunstall on his arrival (June 3) before travelling south to visit Lord Mountjoy (who was now commander of Hammes castle, near Calais) and the Abbot of St Bertin.[33] Shortly after his return to Antwerp he was greeted by a letter from Sauvage, dated July 8. That Erasmus might live 'a peaceful and pleasant life in honourable leisure,' in the Low Countries, Sauvage was conferring on him a canonry in Courtrai 'forthwith.' Nor would that be all which he might expect 'with sure and certain hope from the generosity of his catholic majesty, my master.'[34] Erasmus, not slow to take a hint, was in Brussels by July 10. It was presumably on this occasion that he inscribed a copy of *Institutio principis* for Charles.[35] There apparently was talk of appointing Erasmus to the archbishopric of Saragossa, since Sauvage's chaplain informed him a week later that the incumbent archbishop 'has not yet passed away; but I hope that when some vacancy occurs my master himself will not forget you.'[36] Erasmus later told friends that he discouraged such efforts on his behalf, since he would not 'exchange [his] leisure for a bishopric no matter how splendid.'[37] But it seems in fact he looked forward to the prospect of a life in dignified leisure as an absentee bishop. In anticipation of promises made by Sauvage he turned down a splendid offer of support in England.[38] In August, while Sauvage wrote on his behalf to the pope,[39] Erasmus went to England in order to clear away the canonical obstacle to his reception of an important benefice posed by the fact that his father was a priest. He then returned to Antwerp to await, with considerable anxiety, the successful outcome of his appeal.[40] When he next visited Sauvage in Brussels, in September or early October, 'the chancellor said to the councillors standing about, "he [Erasmus] does not know yet what an important man he is."' The prince, Sauvage explained, had proposed his name for a Sicilian bishopric.[41] As it turned out the bishopric in question had already been filled. But it was evidently in expectation of some such appointment that Erasmus now moved to Brussels, where he stayed until the following February (1517) and intermittently for several months more, the longest period he is known to have lived in continuous proximity to the court.

His closest associate during this time was an old friend and fellow humanist, Cuthbert Tunstall, Henry VIII's envoy to Brussels. Erasmus found a room in Brussels, 'very cramped, but near the court and, what commends it to me more, close to Tunstall,' with whom he was in 'constant communion.' He even thought of spending the winter in Tunstall's more spacious lodgings if his own funds did not hold out.[42] This close association with Tunstall throws a curious light on Erasmus' position in the world of court politics. Later in the same month (October 1516) that Erasmus moved into his new quarters, Tunstall received instructions in keeping with Cardinal Schinner's negotiations with the king in London: he was to wait in Brussels for the arrival of Maximilian, who, in return for English funds to finance a Swiss expedition against the French in Italy, would dismiss Chièvres and Sauvage, resign his imperial crown to Henry, and join Henry and Charles in a new league against France.[43]

Tunstall remonstrated with both Wolsey and the king about what he thought to be an ill-advised scheme. Eventually, when rebuked by the king for suggesting that Margaret of Austria had been won over to the party of Chièvres,[44] he took upon himself the responsibility of transmitting, through Margaret, the ten thousand florins Maximilian had requested to continue his journey down the Rhine.[45] But both before and after this politic decision he opposed the entire project with considerably more courage and perspicacity than he has been given credit for.[46] Already in July he had written Wolsey that 'the whole expense' of a similar project then being discussed 'would rest on England, whose interest is least in it.'[47] Now he suggested that Henry should rather conserve his funds against the possibility of another Scottish attack on England in support of France, as at Flodden in 1513.[48] To Tunstall's legal mind, 'the crown of England' was 'an empire of itself'; hence Henry should reject the imperial crown, since by accepting it he would seem to make England subject to the Empire.[49] Finally, having apparently for a time won over to his point of view his colleague the Earl of Worcester,[50] he exhorted Wolsey to have the king shut his purse: 'My lord, at the reverence of God, move the king to take good counsel at this time, and refrain his first passions.'[51] Later he learned the king was angered by his 'obstinacy.'[52]

Both Erasmus and Tunstall opposed, each for his own reasons, an Anglo-Burgundian coalition against France. Moreover, Tunstall seems to have resembled Erasmus in his fears about the influence of kingly passion on state policy, and in his particular suspicions of Maximilian.[53] But apart from a possible hint that Erasmus knew Henry was seeking to buy Maximilian's friendship,[54] there is no evidence Tunstall told him anything of his instructions, particularly as regards Chièvres and Sauvage, although the latter knew of Henry's plan almost immediately.[55] In political matters Erasmus was able to temper his natural talkativeness with discretion.[56] But Tunstall was an extremely cautious man.[57] Moreover, by confiding in Erasmus he would have placed him in the cruel dilemma of having to betray either a friend by his speech or a patron by his silence. For these reasons it seems best to assume Tunstall was not so foolish as to reveal to Erasmus the precise nature of his commission.[58] Erasmus represented an atmosphere of intellectual excitement in which a cultivated diplomat like Tunstall could breathe more freely; during Tunstall's stay in Brussels his learned correspondence with the French humanist Budé, encouraged by Erasmus, showed how national antipathies might be submerged in the common pursuit of scholarship.[59] This was a dream of learned men of the age, and Erasmus was its symbol. Thus he lived, a cherished and untroubled innocent, amid swirls of court intrigue.

Whatever Erasmus may or may not have known about the devious side of contemporary diplomacy, it is clear that, as at the time of the *Panegyricus*, his own pacifist inclinations coincided with the interests of his patrons (in this case Sauvage) among the 'national' or 'francophile' party at court. *Institutio principis*, for example, aimed a shaft at those who might still claim for the emperor some supranational prerogative: 'Even Caesar, I think, would prefer to yield his right rather than seek to attain that ancient *monarchia* which the literature of the jurists confers upon him.'[60] More germane to contemporary issues was a new commission he received from Sauvage some time during the winter and spring he lived at court. 'A great effort was being made,' he recalled several years later,

> to arrange at Cambrai [March 1517] a meeting of the highest princes of the earth, Maximilian, Francis I, Henry VIII[61] and our Charles, that there they might make peace among themselves with, as the saying goes, adamantine chains. This affair was principally managed by the excellent Guillaume de Chièvres and by the Grand Chancellor Jean Sauvage, a man born for the service of the state. Certain men, who found no profit in tranquillity, were opposed to this plan, and so, like Philoxenus (he it was who said the sweetest meats are those which are not meat, the tastiest fish those that are not fish) wanted a peace which was not peace, and a war which was not war. Therefore I wrote *Querela pacis* by order of Sauvage.[62]

The identity of those who found 'no profit in tranquillity' is open to question. Leo X, who knew that a partition of Italy was being planned, sought to prevent the Cambrai meeting. But the *Querela pacis* praises Leo as a peacemaker, as Erasmus had consistently done since the pope helped to arrange peace between France and England in 1514.[63] Henry VIII also had an interest in preventing an accommodation between France and the Habsburgs. There may be, in fact, a reference to English policy – a policy which Tunstall had opposed – in the dedicatory letter of *Querela pacis*, to Philip of Burgundy, Bishop of Utrecht:

> Recently we have seen how certain people, more burdensome to their friends than their enemies, left nothing undone lest there be at some time an end to wars; while others, who heartily wish well to the state and the prince, were barely able to extract peace with France, something always to be desired, but indeed necessary at this time.[64]

As for Maximilian, only the king of England's new ambassador, Worcester, refused to believe that he was now willing to make peace with France.[65] Moreover, Erasmus, in a letter dated February 26, full of hope for the new learning and the new age, was willing to believe that the emperor had determined to devote his last years to the arts of peace,[66] a thought that may have been suggested to him in a poem by the Viennese humanist Caspar Ursinus Velius.[67] Several months later Erasmus even wrote cryptically to More of some important project on behalf of the emperor which was to be entrusted to him,[68] possibly having to do with the education of Charles's younger brother, Prince Ferdinand.[69] Nonetheless it is clear that Erasmus in *Querela pacis* still looked for opposition to a peaceful settlement with France from Maximilian or his Netherlands partisans. While Francis I is described as eager for peace, Maximilian is merely said 'not to abhor' the prospect.[70] Elsewhere, implying that Flanders itself was a part of Gaul, Erasmus employed an argument in vogue among the francophile party at court: certain 'spirits eager for war,' in their search for an excuse, 'divide Gaul itself, and separate by words what is not separated by seas, by mountains, nor by the true names of regions; from Gauls they make Germans, lest friendship be formed by partaking of a common name.'[71] Netherlands readers would find an allusion to the emperor's Guelders campaigns in Peace's apostrophe to princes: 'You wish to reconquer some part of your dominion? What has that to do with the welfare of your people?'[72] The clearest indication of the political situation Erasmus envisioned when he wrote *Querela pacis* is provided by a letter of March 10 to Richard Bartholinus, secretary to Maximilian's pro-French[73] councillor Matthaeus Lang:

> O happy Germany [for Erasmus, *Germania* included the Netherlands],[74] if she might finally rest from wars! This I hope will soon come to pass by the wisdom of the princes, though some are still ensnared by the ignoble crowd who pile up torches for taking up war against the French. O impious thoughts! Shall the Christian world conspire against the purest and most flourishing part of the Christian realm? For only France is not infected with heretics or Bohemian schismatics, nor by Jews or half-Jewish Marranos, nor affected by the nearness of Turks.

Continuing with a eulogy of France as the flower of Christendom, which is repeated point for point in *Querela pacis*, he concludes with an argument that was clearly directed against Maximilian's party in the Netherlands: 'Those to whom a blind hatred of the French promises a sure and quick victory, does it not occur to them for how many years we have struggled with Guelders without success? For the outcome in Friesland is not yet certain.'[75] In its political context, then, *Querela pacis* is, like the *Panegyricus* of 1504, a tract on behalf of that party in the Netherlands which favoured both peace with France and a peaceful solution of the conflict with Guelders.

Indeed, Erasmus' enthusiasm for the diplomatic projects of Chièvres and Sauvage is in one respect a bit surprising. In *Institutio principis* he had a healthy scepticism of the notion that treaties were drawn up with the objective of creating a stable peace. Too often, he wrote, 'more quarrels arise than are settled' from the detailed clauses of diplomatic agreements; thus in drawing up of treaties 'the presence of many secretaries is a sign of bad faith.' Pushing the argument a step further, he even suggested that 'good and wise princes' could better do without treaties altogether (as More's Utopians did) and trust in each other's good faith.[76] But he was apparently quite sanguine about the Cambrai conference. 'They say,' he reported to Ammonio in late December of 1516, 'that there will shortly be a meeting at Cambrai of the highest princes, Maximilian, the King of the French, and our Charles. There they will discuss a peace never to be broken.'[77] Some time after the meeting at Cambrai, Peter Gilles, Erasmus' Antwerp host, saluted Sauvage as the man by whose labour 'after the long and calamitous tumult of war, peace has come to the world.'[78] A letter to Duke George of Saxony, dated from Antwerp (that is, Gilles' house) in June 1517, may describe the kind of settlement which Erasmus felt had taken place at Cambrai:

> I would judge it most helpful to the peace of the Christian world, if by fixed treaties according to public usage the boundaries of the jurisdiction of each prince be prescribed, which being once determined cannot be extended or contracted by marriages or other agreements, and which will invalidate the right of ancient titles, such as one usually alleges in the event of war in the place of rightful claims.[79]

Erasmus might not have been shocked to discover, if he did not know, that the parties at Cambrai were to forge 'adamantine chains' of peace by partitioning northern Italy; he had no love for Venice and believed Italians would be served better by a plurality of foreign masters than by a single dominant power.[80] The dream of creating a lasting equilibrium among major states by satisfying the interests of each was not unknown to Renaissance thinkers and statesmen. Diplomatic historians, however, will not view the Cambrai conference as any more consequential than earlier or later efforts to content various powers by dividing the spoils of Italy. Probably it was the sheer novelty of proximity to great events which inspired in Erasmus an exalted view of the proceedings at Cambrai.

But although he may have been unduly enthusiastic about the diplomatic achievements of Sauvage and Chièvres, he was also willing, as he had not been in the *Panegyricus*, to venture opinions that were not likely to please his patrons. Part of the arrangement by which

Chièvres and Sauvage came to power was Charles's journey to visit his grandfather in Austria, financed by a grant from the Estates; but *Institutio principis* urges princes to reduce their fiscal demands by curtailing such needless expenses as 'war and long travels.'[81] The goal of Chièvres' diplomacy was to permit Charles to take possession of the Spanish kingdoms bequeathed by his mother's parents; but Erasmus suggests that, in an ideal world, princes would eschew such dynastic unions and marry within their borders,[82] so that one born and raised in 'Syria' would not suddenly become king in 'Italy.'[83] Commercial negotiations with England, guided by a man close to Chièvres, were stalled for some months in 1516 by Burgundian insistence on the collection of tolls at Antwerp;[84] *Institutio principis* remarks that border tolls, which formerly served a useful purpose in paying for the protection of trade, 'have become completely transformed into a tyrannical institution by the vicious practice of public officers.'[85] Subsidies granted by the Estates, like that which in effect purchased Charles's emancipation in 1515, were traditionally funded, at least in Holland, by the levying of excise taxes (*accijnsen*) on grain, beer, and other basic consumption items; yet *Institutio principis* argues that 'the good prince will burden as little as possible those things in common use among the lower orders of society [*infimae plebis*], such as grain, bread, beer, wine, cloth and the like, without which human life is not possible. But these are now burdened most heavily, and in more than one way: first by most heavy exactions, called *accijnsen* [*asisias*] in the common tongue.'[86] Since the coming of the Habsburgs, Netherlands governments had relied for defence on mercenary soldiers, whose quartering on the local population was the subject of bitter complaint. *Institutio principis* broaches this politically delicate subject with unaccustomed frankness: must it be, Erasmus asks, that when the prince approaches a city, his subjects hide their daughters and their precious goods? Someone will say, on the prince's behalf, '"I cannot stay the hands of all my men; what is in me I do." Make them understand that you vehemently wish it and from the heart, may I perish if they will not observe restraint: you will finally convince the people that these things are done without your will, if you will not permit them to be done with impunity.'[87] Even Erasmus' critique of Maximilian, especially in an earlier writing like 'Scarabaeus aquilam quaerit,' was probably more vehement than Sauvage or Chièvres might have found useful; Charles's 'governors' attained their position, after all, by agreement with the emperor, and they continued in need of his goodwill, even when he seemed to be plotting their overthrow.

Erasmus later felt he had been 'rather free' on the subjects of war and taxes in the *Institutio principis* and other writings, just as he felt that in the 1515 *Adagia* he went into things 'more deeply than might be proper.'[88] In fact, criticisms of government policy written in Latin were probably not taken as seriously as scholars might like to think. But it is worth noting that when Sebastian Franck some years later (in 1531) published in his vernacular world-chronicle a description of the imperial eagle as a bloodthirsty bird – a translation of Erasmus' 'Scarabaeus' – he was expelled from the city of Strasbourg as a dangerous radical.[89]

More profound than Erasmus' discontent with specific policies of the government of Chièvres and Sauvage was his rejection of the chivralric ethos which for generations had pervaded the Burgundian court. Humanist beliefs about the morally formative power of education made the manual for princes an ideal means for articulating the conceptions of government that More and Erasmus shared. But Erasmus must have known that Prince Charles's education had not thus far been guided by humanist principles. Charles's tutor was Adrian of Utrecht, the future Pope Adrian VI, who, as Dean of Louvain in 1504, had offered Erasmus a professorship of rhetoric at the university. Although Adrian was a professor of theology, whom Erasmus mistrusted,[90] he had instructed his royal pupil in some of the classical works which Erasmus himself would recommend, such as Plutarch's *Moralia.*[91] But the real influence in Charles's life after 1509 had been Guillaume de Croy, Lord of Chièvres, scion of a family long prominent in the chivalric culture of the Burgundian court. One contemporary reports that Chièvres actively discouraged Charles from studying Greek or Latin. Instead, he began taking Charles on hunts at the age of ten, to the great pleasure of the prince's grandfather, Maximilian.[92] In leisure time, Charles read in the literature traditionally popular at court, chivalric romances of the Arthurian cycle, often mingled with tales of the heroes of Greek legend and antiquity, such as Achilles and Alexander the Great. It was entirely characteristic of the Burgundian blend of chivalric and epic themes that the French ambassador, speaking before a chapter of the Order of the Golden Fleece in October 1516, addressed Charles as a descendant of the Trojans.[93]

Charles's upbringing was typical for a French or Burgundian prince of the late middle ages. Sixteenth-century humanists called upon to supervise a prince's education or write a treatise on the subject had a variety of strategies to choose from in adjusting the existing tradition to their own conceptions about the nature and value of classical learning. They might capitalize on the avid interest in classical heroes which is characteristic of late medieval romance and restate the chivalric ethos in a form at once more classical and more attuned to a notion of the common good. Cicero's argument that true glory lay in the esteem won by distinguished public service, rather than in a selfish lust for conquest,[94] provided a natural bridge from the values of Froissart to those of Livy or Thucydides. Alternatively humanists might treat the culture of chivalry as unredeemedly baneful and attempt to restructure princely education around austere principles of Christian duty, conceding no more to the prince's vanity than was commonly done in the medieval 'Mirror of Princes' literature. These two approaches roughly correspond to Budé's *De l'institution du prince* (1519) and Erasmus' *Institutio principis christiani* (1516).

For the Greeks and Romans, Budé notes early in his work, honour and renown constituted the sovereign good. This pagan understanding of life was, to be sure, supplanted by the revelation in Christ of man's spiritual destiny. Nonetheless 'we have nothing so highly regarded and recommended in all the powers of the soul (as far as temporal things are concerned) as honour in this life, and a good and honourable renown after death.'[95] Flattered by Strabo's comments about the ancient Gauls, Budé allowed himself to believe that a thirst for glory was especially keen among the French. His fondest hope was that French noblemen, who hitherto 'had sought glory in breeding rather than in learning,' might embellish their native distinction with the study of letters and so imitate Homer's Achilles, who put away his sword at the command of Athena, goddess of wisdom.[96] For the chief path to glory as the ancients understood it was *prudence civile*, a sagacity in human affairs, which could grow by learning as well as by experience. Learning of this kind was concrete and practical rather than abstract and speculative; it was mediated especially through *histoire*, the record of great deeds in the past.[97] Thus Budé praises the king for his reputed skill in recounting *histoires anciennes*.[98] Without denigrating the literature of chivalry, whose element of fantasy he seems elsewhere to appreciate,[99] he makes clear that his *histoires* will be drawn from ancient sources. Some of his topics are biblical, as when the proberb 'Sow in the morning and in the evening' is made to yield a moral appropriate for a young prince. But his material is primarily classical, since *De l'institution du prince* is loosely structured around Plutarch's *Apophthegms*.[100]

Alexander the Great, a subject of much interest in medieval romance, is treated at great length. Were the King of Macedon not 'eager for a noble glory above all other kings, he would not have been moved to undertake his great enterprises and conquests.'[101] The praise of Alexander is, however, hedged in several ways. The conqueror's violent temper must be counted a vice, since cruelty and revenge are pursuits of a pusillanimous and not a magnanimous man. Emphasizing again that praise is man's greatest temporal good, Budé then describes how Philip of Macedon, Alexander's father, cared more for his reputation than for his conquests.[102] Earlier, in an aside that must have puzzled Francis I, he remarked that previous French kings had gained no honour 'from the useless undertakings they made in foreign countries, to their own confusion.' True glory, he suggests, comes to the prince from good government, not from the hazard of battle.[103] Finally, in a passage meant to be climactic, he argues that the glory of Pompey the Great (as portrayed in Lucan), unspotted by cruelty or excess of ambition, outshines that of Alexander.[104]

Thus was the Christian prince to be led by degrees to an understanding of his duties. But Budé was not able fully to harmonize the classical and biblical elements of his exhortation. The fact that the classical ethic was founded on self-esteem, so contrary to the monastic tradition of humility, did not cause him a problem, for, like many earlier humanists, he preferred a Christianity that could be active in the public forum and doubted the sincerity of many who professed their contempt for the world.[105] But he could not integrate ancient notions about conquest with the Christian doctrine of limited war. He praises the great adventures of Alexander, yet notes that Christian princes 'cannot laudably desire war, or undertake it for pleasure, save against infidels, or those unjustly occupying our borders.'[106] In one place he says that the path which leads a prince to temporal glory leads also to eternal salvation. Elsewhere he concedes that the practical sagacity (*prudence civile*) which brings success in human affairs – it teaches a prince, for example, when to break his treaties – is often opposed to 'equity,' as taught both in Aristotle and in the Gospel, and that prelates or princes can be damned eternally for following the 'civil prudence' of their predecessors.[107] This tension in Budé's thought is not resolved until *De transitu hellenismi ad christianismum* (1534), his last work, where he ends by condemning the *prudentia* which courtiers have acquired by, among other things, a study of the classics.[108]

Erasmus agreed with other humanist educators that virtue might be stimulated by *ambitio*, the desire for praise.[109] In the *Panegyricus*, he seemed willing, like Budé, to indulge the prince's thirst for *gloria* in the hope of persuading him that wise governance brought a more lasting *gloria* than military conquest.[110] Not so in 1516: 'What is all this that men call reputation [*gloria*], except a perfectly empty name left over from paganism? Not a few things of the kind have survived entrenched among Christians, when for instance they use "immortality" for leaving a name to posterity.' Such relics of pagan ideals were especially pernicious in the context of princely education. 'Remember always,' counsels the *Institutio principis*, 'that *dominium, imperium*, kingdom, and *maiestas* are the words of pagans, not Christians. For Christian empire is nothing but administration, beneficence, and custody.'[111] The flattery of the royal ego implied in such terms inspired in the prince a sense not of his duty to the commonwealth but of his arbitrary power. Yet Erasmus well knew that Prince Charles had had a typical chivalric upbringing. Indeed, in what seems a rather daring allusion to Chièvres' tutelage, he explains how it is that princes nowadays are taught little except how to ride a horse: not only are princes exposed to constant flattery, but 'the very guardian and tutor of the prince's boyhood is out for himself, concerned not that he render the prince better, but that he himself become wealthier.'[112] Prince Charles had been raised on much the same tales of glory and conquest which had inflamed the imagination of his great-grandfather, Charles the Rash.[113] Many wars could be traced to inflated conceptions of princely honour, which in turn, it seemed, had kinship with chivalric ideals. Hence the concern of *Institutio principis* was not to build on what Charles had been taught but to undo it.

Normally Erasmus would enthusiastically endorse the common view that *exempla* were the most important ingredient of persuasive discourse: 'Now it is surely common knowledge that, as far as prose style is concerned, its resources and its pleasures alike consist of epigrams, metaphors, figures, paradigms, examples, similes, images, and such turns of speech.' But the concrete record of ancient or fictive princes had been only too persuasive on impressionable young minds: 'Examples of famous men vehemently inflame noble spirits, but it is far more important what opinions are imbibed.' Consequently Erasmus built his manual for the prince not around the deeds of famous princes – the normal humanist procedure – but around the proverbs contained in Isocrates' *Nicocles*.[114] Budé's use of *histoires* may be linked with a belief that political wisdom is gained from experience, even if vicarious. Yet Erasmus found the *prudentia* gained from experience dangerous to the commonwealth: the prince who plunged into war in the ardour of youth might still be fighting twenty years later. Hence, again, his preference for inculcating into the young prince's mind abstract moral precepts.[115] If stories are to be read, tutors of princes must be careful to give a moral meaning to striking or violent episodes: 'Let [the prince] learn that the battles and butcheries of the Hebrews, and their barbarity towards their enemies, are to be read allegorically; otherwise it would be most disastrous to read them.'[116] Even classical historians, whom Erasmus elsewhere preferred to the Old Testament narratives because 'they at least have a moral,' must not be read without suitable instruction: 'Sallust and Livy say much that is excellent, and learned besides, but they do not approve everything they relate, and some things they approve are not to be approved by a Christian prince. When you hear Achilles, Xerxes, Cyrus, Darius, Julius, do not be carried off by the prestige of a great name. Rather you hear of great and furious thieves: for so they are sometimes called by Seneca.' Best of all would be to exercise a careful choice among authors, 'for it matters a great deal what books a boy first reads and imbibes.' Evil speech worked its way into the mind, but evil reading no less. 'Those silent letters flow into customs and feelings, especially for a personality prone to some vice.' As he had indicated in the 1515 *Adagia*, Erasmus did not think the *Iliad* suitable reading for princes. But other kinds of literature on the heroic theme were still worse:

> A boy by nature ferocious and violent will with little difficulty be moved to tyranny if he should read, without being provided an antidote, of Achilles, or Alexander the Great, or Xerxes, or Julius. But today we find many delighted with Arthur and Lancelot, tales not only tyrannical, but wholly unlearned, stupid, and silly, so that it would be better to pass the hours with comedies or fables of the poets rather than with such ravings.[117]

Unlike Budé, Erasmus had little familiarity with the aristocracy. His personal background was clerical, and he had intellectual roots in the 'Epicurean' tradition of humanism tracing back to Lorenzo Valla. Conscientious churchmen had never fully endorsed the ethos of chivalry, with its violent and erotic overtones; Valla had attacked the whole conception of honour as a motive for human conduct. Thus while Budé demonstrated that classical Latin was supple enough to sing the praises of the kingly sport of hunting, More and Erasmus considered this favourite aristocratic pastime barbarous and brutalizing.[118]

Budé was familiar with the commonplace humanist notion – to be found even in literature produced for court circles in fifteenth-century Burgundy – that true nobility was a matter more of virtue than of birth.[119] But he saw in the aristocracy of birth a pillar of the French nation and, potentially, of French culture: if only the nobility would embrace the new learning, France could surpass proud Italy in intellectual glory.[120] Erasmus saw not what nobles might become, but what to his mind they had always been, a useless class of men living on the labour of others,[121] enervated by luxury,[122] whose imagination was fed on foolish fantasies, such as heraldry,[123] the ritual of the Knights of the Golden Fleece, or belief in the 'Trojan' ancestry of the ruling house.[124] If the nobility, he says, are such as we often see today, 'grown soft by leisure, effeminate by pleasures, ignorant of all good arts, merely good eaters and strenuous dice-throwers, lest I say anything more obscene, what reason is there, I pray, why this class of men should be preferred to cobblers or peasants?'[125]

But perhaps the deepest level of the contrasting attitudes of Erasmus and Budé towards the quest for glory lies in the respective orientation of each man's religious thought. For Budé the fundamental theological problem was to validate, as against a pagan notion of *fortuna*, the sovereignty of God as ruler of human history, even in its least details; God claimed the glory of being acknowledged as Lord, just as princes might do in the sinful human realm.[126] To Erasmus theology meant the art of making Christ's example efficacious in the lives of believers. For him the *gloria* of Christ lay in His mildness and humanity rather than in His divine power.[127] The king who surrounded himself in godlike majesty was, for Erasmus, imitating a pagan and not the Christian God.[128]

Erasmus did not deny, as some have thought, that the king possessed legitimate *imperium* in the sense of war-making power; he accepted the argument, which he describes as conventional among theologians, that *potentia*, along with *sapientia* and *bonitas*, was a fundamental attribute of true kingship.[129] But the theoretical issue – whether princes might justly wage war – was for him much less important than his conviction that, as recounted in the last chapter, contemporary wars among European Christians were in practice fought because of 'private hatred or youthful ambition' or 'the wrath of princes,' all of them 'more trivial reasons' than those which led the ancient pagans into war.[130] In these circumstances, Erasmus argued, God is a God of vengeance not for those who may provoke a prince's *amour propre*, but for the prince himself, should he waste the lives of his subjects in a war undertaken to appease some private passion.[131] His solution to the problem with which Budé wrestled – the relation between *imperium* and Christian morality – was simple and drastic: the prince who would be a Christian must reject the models offered by pagan writers.[132] As Otto Herding rightly maintains, the originality of *Institutio principis* consists in its advocacy of a specifically Christian or evangelical kingship. Though generally opposed to a strict literal interpretation of Christ's commands in the Gospel, Erasmus took Matt. 20:25–6 rigorously, extracting from it a political message:

> 'The Princes of the Gentiles,' He says, exercise dominion over them. 'But it shall not be so among you' ... What is the meaning of this phrase, 'it shall not be so among you,' unless that the same thing is not proper for Christians, among whom the principate is administration, not imperial power, and kingly authority is service, not tyranny.[133]

New Testament passages enjoining obedience to rulers were construed by Erasmus to apply to pagan princes only, 'since at that time there were not yet any Christian princes.' Thus 'render unto Caesar what is Caesar's' says nothing about what Christians owe their princes. Rather, Jesus told His disciples, 'among you let no one owe another anything, save that you love one another.' Although St Paul elsewhere instructed slaves to be subject to their masters, Erasmus found in *Philemon* a passage suitable to his argument: if pagan laws admit that slavery is contrary to nature, 'think how ill it befits a Christian to usurp *dominum* over Christians, whom the laws do not wish to be slaves, and whom Christ has redeemed from all bondage. Indeed Paul calls Onesimus, born a slave, brother to his former master Philemon.'[134] Erasmus contends that he 'who exercises *imperium* in a Christian manner' will not lose his state, but will possess it 'differently,' indeed more splendidly: 'Those whom you oppress with servitude are not your subjects, for *consensus* makes a prince.'[135] But he does recognize that he is asking the Christian prince, like other believers, to 'take up his cross.' He must, for example, bear injury rather than be avenged at great public loss. Even more: 'If you are not able to maintain your kingdom except by the violation of justice, except by a great shedding of human blood, except by a mighty destruction of religion: resign it rather, and yield to the force of circumstance.'[136]

Perhaps no passage in Erasmus' political writings has drawn more comment. To Ferdinand Geldner the injunction to resign means that

Erasmus has lost touch with political reality, since the consequences of such an ethic would be chaos. Otto Herding finds in it proof that *Institutio principis*, though based on a work of Isocrates, takes seriously, in a new and radical way, the doctrine of the cross.[137] Both views are correct. Rejecting the entire *cultus* of late medieval court life, with its high and pugnacious notions of honour, its military saints and splendid fêtes, Erasmus condemned the only form of princely government which then existed. Instead, he would have the prince fix his gaze on the gentle, long-suffering image of Christ found in contemporary Netherlandish painters.[138] Erasmus could not sustain this view consistently, nor did he try. He recognized, as will be seen in the next chapter, that the prince needed more than love and good example to deal with enemies like the Duke of Guelders. In the course of time he conceded more and more to princely authority, admitting in later writings that coercive force was necessary to punish evildoers both at home and abroad.[139] But for a time, notably in the period 1515–17, he dreamed of a better world. Ultimately it is not for historians to decide whether one who presents to his contemporaries an ethical ideal impossible of fulfilment is engaged in prophecy or folly, or perhaps, as Erasmus might say, a folly to be praised. One can only observe, as Hans Hillerbrand has, that Erasmus' thought at this point approaches the political ethic of the original Anabaptist community in Zürich.[140]

Since Erasmus now had enemies among the theologians, he sympathized, as he had not in 1504, with the anti-clerical feelings of lay courtiers. The attempt of certain Louvain theologians to influence the prince against him was 'crushed, partly by the favour of the nobles, who particularly hate all theologians, and partly by the favour of learned men, notably Bishop [Caraffa] of Thieti.'[141] Sauvage was probably not offended by Erasmus' criticisms of churchmen, for he 'especially liked' *Julius exclusus*, which in his circle was thought to be 'Erasmian.'[142] But court life included also a constant strife among 'factions,' 'Spaniards, Marranos, Chièvrists, Frenchmen, Caesarists, Neapolitans, Sicilians.'[143] Erasmus referred in particular to the rival groups of Aragonese and Castilian nobles who had frequented the court in Brussels for some years. 'Spanish greeters' wore him out; he apparently read a sinister intent into their unaccustomed ceremony.[144] On one occasion Alvar Gomez, a Spanish nobleman, pressed Erasmus to write some complementary verses for his *History of the Order of the Golden Fleece*. Perhaps because of Gomez' connection with Luigi

Marliani, Charles's influential physician, Erasmus acceded to the request; but he avenged himself upon 'Spanish greeters' by affecting to praise the author's 'magniloquence' and 'grandiloquence,' terms that would have one meaning for Gomez and another for Erasmus himself.[145] Even apart from their affectations of grandeur, courtiers offended Erasmus by their skill at manipulating the arts of friendship in the service of rivalry or enmity:

> [At Court] I see mild greetings, friendly embraces, joyful compotations, and all the other marks of humanity. But, for shame! even the shadow of true fellowship is not to be seen in all of this. Everything is contrived and deceiving, everything is ruined by open factions, by secret quarrels and rivalries.[146]

Worse still, Erasmus, contrary to his expectations, had to pay court to Sauvage:

> Although I told him not to expect any obsequiousness of me, and he approved my words, he afterwards requested of me not [only] that I camp at his door every day to dine or sup with him, but I even had to wait oftentimes hungry until midnight, and then, in bitter cold winter, go home at night, which at that time was not safe because of the Spaniards.[147]

Thus in February 1517, when Tunstall left Brussels to follow Maximilian, Erasmus moved to Antwerp, returning to Brussels only sporadically over the next several months.[148]

In the summer of 1517 Erasmus 'entirely separated' himself from court. In July, while Charles with his chief advisers waited for a favourable wind at Middleburg, Erasmus, at Sauvage's suggestion, went to Louvain, there to await from Spain further word on what the chancellor had promised him.[149] The immediate occasion for his departure from court was probably the appointment of Jean Briselot, suffragan Bishop of Cambrai, as confessor to Charles.[150] Briselot's predecessor, Michael of Pavia, had befriended Erasmus on his visits to court some twenty years earlier.[151] One of the candidates to succeed him was the Flemish humanist-theologian Josse Clichetove, who, like Michael of Pavia, had been professor of theology in the College of Navarre in Paris. According to Erasmus, Clichetove had been rejected by the 'courtiers' because 'he was too lean, and had only ten hairs on his head.' Clichetove was Erasmus' friend.[152] But Briselot, Erasmus told

More, 'not only barks loudly against me in court, there is not even a drinking fest at which he does not declaim against Erasmus, being particularly offended by my *Praise of Folly*, since he cannot bear to see [Saints] George and Christopher attacked.'[153] Erasmus was suspicious of the influence a royal confessor could exercise over a prince.[154] But he probably found most ominous about Briselot the fact that 'this portent has great influence with the Lord of Chièvres, by whose nod [*nutu*] all things are done here,' and by whose favour he had apparently secured his appointment.[155] Like other observers, Erasmus here attributed to Chièvres a virtually absolute power in all decisions taken by Charles's government in the Netherlands.[156] If Chièvres heeded Briselot, it was not unreasonable to think that the favour which Erasmus had enjoyed among 'noble men'[157] at court would be of short duration.

Erasmus knew that Chièvres, by arranging peace treaties on several occasions, had kept the Netherlands out of war with France.[158] But the passage just cited indicates a dislike of the first chamberlain. The metaphor of ruling 'by nod' has for Erasmus the connotation of tyrannical and arbitrary power; he notes in one of the political adages of 1515 that ancient poets, in keeping with their tendency to portray kings as stupid, 'attribute wisdom to Apollo and Pallas, while to Jove, the monarch of gods and men, they leave only the three-pronged thunderbolt and that arrogant nod by which he causes all Olympus to tremble.'[159] Erasmus disliked the 'Chièvrists' as much as other court factions;[160] he perhaps feared that Chièvres' numerous Croy relations would be preferred to him in ecclesiastical appointments.[161] But one suspects that Erasmus' dislike of Chièvres had a broader basis in his rejection of the aristocratic or chivalric culture which was typified by the Croy family, and which Chièvres had passed on to Prince Charles. As one who believed that character was formed by education, Erasmus hoped that, if statesmen were raised up from boyhood on 'good letters,' the principles of civility and harmony would carry over from their habitual reading into their statecraft.[162] Conversely, he perhaps found a grim satisfaction in the fact that the Anglo-French war of 1512–14 was zealously promoted, on both sides of the channel, by certain friars whose scholastic education had made them hostile to 'good letters.'[163] Traditional aristocratic education, in Erasmus' viewpoint, trained youth to be arrogant and pugnacious.[164] Andreas von Walther has noticed a prejudice against Chièvres among humanist chroniclers and historians.[165] Erasmus probably did not know of pleas on behalf of peace in courtly literature,[166] nor of Commines' sober warnings against the terrible hazard of battle.[167] He did not reckon with the possibility that 'men of the long robe' might counsel war while experienced noblemen advised against it, as had happened in 1505.[168] Thus he was apparently unable to cope with the fact that the chief architect of European peace in this period – for it was Chièvres and not Sauvage who took the leading role in diplomacy – was a man steeped in the 'stupid and tyrannical' tradition of chivalry.

In the summer of 1517, just as Erasmus 'entirely separated' himself from court, mercenary forces loyal to the Duke of Guelders invaded Holland. Erasmus' deep suspicion of those who governed in Charles's name does much to explain the sinister interpretation he put upon this latest phase of the Guelders-Habsburg conflict, which must be discussed in the next chapter.

FOUR

The Mystery of Our War with Guelders

MARGARET OF AUSTRIA, named Regent of the Netherlands in 1506, inherited from her brother's regime a serious military situation complicated by a grave political problem. Although Philip had occupied large portions of the Duke of Guelders' lands during his 1505 campaign, his urgent need to depart for Spain permitted his enemy to escape with a truce. Instead of accompanying Philip on his journey, as provided for in the truce, Duke Charles began instead, with French help, to reverse the tide of war. As Philip weighed anchor, mercenary captains from Guelders conducted successful raids into Holland and Brabant. One of them, called Cutwind by contemporaries, seized and garrisoned the strategic castle of Poederoy, lying astride what was then the main channel of the Maas between 's Hertogenbosch (northern Brabant) and Dordrecht (south Holland); from this position he was able to block vital river traffic at will and ravage the surrounding countryside. Troops in French pay, led by Robert de la Marck, a military adventurer aligned with France, first aided the duke in recapturing his own territory, then carried the campaign to Brabant.[1] Thus, despite what had appeared to be the strength of Philip's position in 1505, Margaret was placed immediately on the defensive.

Moreover, unlike her Burgundian grandfather, Duke Charles the Rash, she had at her disposition very little in the way of a standing military force. Charles the Rash had organized twelve *compagnies d'ordonnance* modelled on the permanent military units created by Charles VII in France in the 1440s. In Burgundy each *compagnie* comprised 100 *lances*, each made up of a man-at-arms, three mounted archers, three foot-soldiers, and a page. In reduced form the *compagnies* survived for at least a short period the political debacle consequent upon Charles the Rash's defeat and death. But Baron Guillaume, historian of the Burgundian *compagnies*, finds no subsequent record of their existence until 1505, when four *compagnies* of fifty lances each, comprising now only a man-at-arms, two mounted archers, and a page, were called to arms for Philip's campaign against Guelders. The *compagnies* at this time were normally commanded by provincial governors, such as the Grand Bailli of Namur or the Stadhouder of Holland, or their deputies.[2] But such companies, dependable as they might be, were of little use against the thousands of men Robert de la Marck was able to lead against the Low Countries on behalf of the Duke of Guelders.

Margaret's father, Maximilian, had won his victories in the Netherlands with armies of *landsknechte* recruited in Germany, fighting under German princes like Albert of Saxony. Margaret in turn depended mainly on German princes like Rudolf of Anhalt, Duke Erich of Brunswick, and Count Felix of Werdenberg, who had served as commanders on her father's Italian campaigns. Rudolf of Anhalt, Maximilian's most trusted commander, brought to the Netherlands a force of 2,500 German *landsknechte*, divided into three 'bands,' one of which he entrusted to his friend and loyal supporter Floris of Ijselstein. In June 1507 Anhalt prevented the juncture of a force from Guelders with the French army led north by Robert de la Marck. But in September la Marck returned against Brabant with a force of ten thousand men. While the town of Diest was successfully defended by its lord, Count Henry of Nassau, Tienen was overwhelmed and brutally sacked before the French army drifted away of its own accord in October. Anhalt's inactivity during the campaign – Margaret had instructed him to preserve his forces intact – was a subject for comment and doubtless strengthened the common feeling that mercenaries were useless.[3] It is at this point that Margaret's military difficulties were compounded by the political problems which beset early Habsburg rulers of the Netherlands.

In the Netherlands, as elsewhere in western Europe in the late middle ages, the problem posed by mercenary armies, whether recruited on a temporary or permanent basis, was an important part of what may be termed the twilight of political independence for towns and Estates. In most areas the authority of princes gained slowly and steadily at the expense of traditional urban and provincial liberties.[4] Two Florentine writers, Bruni and Machiavelli, proposed reviving the urban militia as a means of maintaining urban or regional independence. Military historians point out, however, that improvements in tactics and weapons since the fourteenth century favoured the emergence and development of professional rather than citizen armies. The headlong flight of Machiavelli's militiamen before the Spanish *tercios* in 1512, which sealed the doom of the second Florentine republic, seems an apt illustration of the superiority of trained, professional troops.[5] The lesson of such episodes was clear. Towns which hoped to be secure from attack had best purchase the protection of a mercenary army, either by hiring such forces themselves as need be, or by contributing to the support of forces maintained by the prince.

But mercenary armies were notorious for causing as much trouble to their friends as to their enemies. Even when mercenary companies were organized and paid on a regular basis, and hence less tempted to attack their employers, citizens might still wonder whether protection was worth its price. In the 1440s townsmen in many parts of France resisted the new *compagnies d'ordonnance*, not merely because of the taxes necessary to support them, but also because of the brutality of the soldiers now to be quartered permanently on the local population. A single example may suffice. In 1453 an archer was quartered on Yonnet Carracht, citizen of the small town of Ytrac. Upon arrival, the archer threatened to seduce Carrachat's wife; he then robbed a local church, and after dinner was slain trying to eject Carrachat from his own house. Paul Solon, a student of Charles VII's military reforms, concludes that Carrachat was fortunate to escape with a royal pardon; towns which expelled or killed members of the royal *compagnies* were often fined heavily. In time the *compagnies d'ordonnance* developed a certain loyalty to the king, and complaints about the brutality of garrison troops grew less numerous. The Estates General of Tours in 1484 still found it appropriate to compare soldiers absent from their garrison to animals escaped from captivity. But in the end French towns acquiesced in the transformation; they accepted a measure of security in return for a diminution of their independence. By 1480 Louis XI found it difficult, in the more secure parts of the kingdom, even to induce towns to maintain their own fortifications.[6]

The experience of towns in the Netherlands was in many ways similar. In 1482 Haarlem expelled a company of foreign mercenaries in Maximilian's pay who had been plundering the local countryside; subsequently the city had to pay the heavy fine of twelve thousand gulden for this offence against the archduke's dignity.[7] The 'Groote Gaard' which fought for Albert of Saxony in Frisia, like the 'Black Band' which fought for his son, earned a special reputation for brutality.[8] Josse de Weert, an Antwerp chronicler, records that on 29 June 1516 'there were in Antwerp around 500 men-at-arms from Namur who did much damage in the city and in Berchem, for they overpowered and held captive the men, carried off the women, and refused to pay the inns where they were quartered; wherefore three were slain in Berchem, and many taken prisoner in Antwerp; but they were released the next day, which angered the commons.'[9] Like their counterparts in France, the Burgundian *compagnies* or other government mercenary forces could be used to suppress internal opposition. According to Hadrianus Barlandus, a humanist historian acquainted with Erasmus, Engelbrecht of Nassau put down a rebellion in Louvain in 1481 with his 'armed soldiery.'[10] In 1515 Floris of Ijselstein forced the submission of several towns in Frisia by threatening not to pay the Black Band, which was then in his employ.[11] In the spring of 1518 Henry of Nassau, conducting operations against a mercenary band released by Guelders, was invited by the city government of 's Hertogenbosch to intervene in its dispute with the canons of St John's church; the men of Nassau's *compagnie d'ordonnance* obligingly evicted the canons from their houses.[12] In France Thomas Basin, a critic of Charles VII's military reforms, feared that no subject or combination of subjects would now be able to resist the king's will. In the same vein, a noble of Maximilian's party told an English observer in 1516 that the council would not support the emperor's financial requests because they feared that 'prosperity might enable him to rule these countries at will.'[13]

But Maximilian and Margaret did not govern in the Netherlands as Louis XI or Francis I governed in France. The 'Great Privilege' which Mary of Burgundy was compelled to grant her recalcitrant Estates in 1477, effectively dismantling the work of two generations of princely centralization,[14] has no parallel in the contemporary history of England, France, or Spain. Maximilian had in addition the special handicap of being a foreigner who was, with good reason, suspected of subordinating national to dynastic interest. Thus the whole question of military policy took on a peculiar complexion, first because Netherlands towns jealously preserved the tradition of a civic militia, and second because the government exhibited a special reluctance to employ native troops.

In the 1480s and 1490s, some 150 years after the eclipse of the civic militia in Italy, militiamen of the Flemish and Dutch towns were able to fight Maximilian's *landsknechte* on relatively even terms. In Holland during the same period, the final phase of the conflict between Hoeks and Kabiljauws, quite unlike the English Wars of the Roses or the French quarrel between Armagnacs and Burgundians, was still being fought partly between popular forces on both sides.[15] In places, as at Ghent according to the peace treaty of 1493, the civic militia was abolished in the wake of Maximilian's victory.[16] But the common requirement of watch duty still kept able-bodied men at least minimally practised in the use of arms. According to Louvain's watch ordinance for 1521, for example, each evening one of the two companies of watch from each of the city's five quarters was to come 'with banner and drum' to the city hall and from there fan out to appointed places of watch.[17] In time of need local governments still relied on a general military levy. During the invasion of 1517 the Council of Holland ordered every fourth man from every village and town to join the Stadhouder's forces at Sparendam;[18] a similar order was apparently issued during the campaign to retake Poederoy castle in 1508.[19] Finally, in the special case of Holland, it should be noted that the seafaring population was accustomed to provide for its own defence. During a conflict with Lübeck in 1511, Gouda alone fitted out and manned eight ships of war.[20]

Netherlands towns had also developed what might be called a military reserve. The guilds of 'shooters' (*schutters*), which had sprung up in a wide arc from northern France to southern Germany during the fourteenth century, were especially common in the Low Countries. Formed originally of bowmen, the guilds grew in numbers and equipment to accommodate changes in weaponry. Guilds of this type initially spread outwards from Flanders and Artois and, in the sixteenth century, were still disproportionately concentrated in the Low Countries.[21] In 1489, a few years before the militia in Ghent was to be formally abolished, a guild of *arquebusiers* was formed with Maximilian's approval, for the protection both of the city and of the prince. Guild members held monthly target practice – grants of immunity from the claims of injured passersby protected them from the consequences of poor markmanship – and enjoyed an honoured place in the ceremonial life of the city.[22] Unlike the old town militia, *schutters'* guilds normally recruited their members only from the patriciate, those who could afford to equip themselves with the necessary armour and weapons. But not all *schutters* were necessarily patricians. In 1481, the Hoek government of Leiden called six thousand men to arms and chose one thousand to be trained as *schutters*. By 1522, Amsterdam had four such guilds, two armed with firearms and two with halberds and lances; it is difficult to believe that, in a city of some twelve to fifteen thousand inhabitants, the patriciate alone could furnish eight hundred to one thousand able-bodied men. The *schutters'* guild, in short, was a fighting force, and not just an ornamental feature of the city's social hierarchy and ceremonial life.[23]

The fact that citizen forces of various kinds were maintained in peacetime or called to arms in emergencies need not of course mean that they were effective against mercenary armies. Erasmus' friends Willem Hermans and Reyner Snoy, both of whom wrote on the Poederoy campaign, took a dim view of mass mobilization: 'So, the peasant will fight for you,' says Hermans. 'He has indeed a banner, but he is ignorant of orders, and lacks leaders; what, after all, can you expect from an undisciplined multitude?'[24] In fact, it does appear that neither town militiamen nor *schutters'* guilds had scored many significant victories since the 1480s.[25] But for political purposes, public opinion concerning citizen armies is perhaps more important than their actual effectiveness. The Habsburg government, which consistently encouraged the formation of new *schutters'* guilds, evidently did not regard such forces as negligible.[26] Moreover, citizen armies professionally led and leavened by a mercenary contingent could perform quite well. Poederoy castle was eventually retaken by the town militia of 's Hertogenbosch, strengthened by a contingent of Rudolf of Anhalt's *landsknechte* and led by Anhalt himself.[27] The Estates of the Netherlands were thus wrong to believe (as they often did) that mercenary forces were useless; but they had reason to puzzle over the government's neglect of military resources which the peculiar political and military development of the Netherlands had placed within its grasp.

The special character of Habsburg military policy in the Netherlands is made evident by the government's persistent preference not merely for mercenary armies, but for foreign mercenary armies. As late as 1518 the government was still interested in recruiting a band of German *landsknechte* for the defence of Holland and Brabant.[28] Margaret of Austria requested an English force to defend the Netherlands against Guelders as early as 1507, and Prince Charles was still seeking English money for defence against Guelders as late as 1517. In 151[illegible] Maximilian was vague about Henry VIII's request for permission to recruit troops in the Netherlands for the projected campaign against France; he apparently wanted Henry to supply the men as well as the money.[29] The employment of foreign troops was in the sixteenth century regarded as insurance against desertion. But while the Habsburgs employed Walloon soldiers (as in the *compagnies d'ordonnance*), men from the Flemish and Dutch provinces were not so employed.[30] The basis for this apparent unwillingness to employ Dutch-speaking troops is to be sought not in a putative military incapacity of Netherlands levies[31] but in memories of the violent rebellions against Maximilian in the 1480s and 1490s, when the 'Princes of the Blood' were joined in opposition by the militiamen or locally hired mercenaries of many towns in Flanders, Brabant, and Holland. Chièvres, like the Bergens and the Nassaus and others with whom he differed on many issues, had risen to prominence as a partisan of Maximilian during this troubled period. Men of his generation might well prefer to accept the risks inherent in a weak military posture rather than summon the strength of once-rebellious towns.

This latent conflict over military policy was one of the reasons why Margaret had great difficulty extracting money from the Estates to conduct the war against Guelders. At Mechelen in July 1507, the Estates General were asked to approve funding a mercenary army by a general levy of one gulden per hearth (including noble and clerical hearths, exempt from normal taxation) in all of the 'landen van herwarts over.' After going home to deliberate, the deputies returned in January 1508 and, commenting that mercenary armies were unnecessary, recommended (for approval by the provincial Estates, according to a quota system) a smaller grant of 200,000 gulden.[32] In February the Estates of Brabant, meeting to discuss approving their share of the 200,000 gulden recommended by the Estates General, requested Rudolf of Anhalt to appear in person in order to quiet rumours that he was being held captive by his troops. Anhalt appeared as requested, but as he did so his *landsknechte*, complaining of arrears in pay, made good on their threats to carry out raids into the Brabant countryside. The provincial Estates, understandably, refused to grant any money. The Estates General, reconvened in March, altogether rejected a further request for funds.

Given Margaret's decision to conduct the war with foreign mercenaries and the Estates' refusal to pay for them, the government's financial position worsened steadily. Duncker calculates that Margaret's war expenditures for the period 1506–9 amounted to over ,122,000 gulden, and that she was already 300,000 gulden in debt by July 1508. Accordingly, Anhalt was ordered to dismiss a third of his men in October 1507, and then in March 1508 to disband the entire force. To keep the war effort alive, Anhalt was ordered to 's Hertogenbosch, where the force beseiging Poederoy – made up largely of militiamen from 's Hertogenbosch and south Holland – had been discouraged by its conspicuous lack of success. Anhalt negotiated an agreement with 's Hertogenbosch (later joined by the cities of Holland) according to which he promised to conquer Poederoy in return for a payment of 26,000 gulden. Leading the town militiamen and a force of *landsknechte* he had recalled to service, Anhalt soon broke down Poederoy's defences and occupied the castle, making the Maas safe for commerce.[33]

The participation of militiamen from north Brabant ('s Hertogenbosch) and south Holland (Dordrecht, Gouda) in this campaign points up an important and rather neglected feature of the Guelders wars. While most regions in the Netherlands regarded the struggle with Guelders as a purely dynastic issue, of no national interest, the region lying just across the western frontier of Guelders (north Brabant and south Holland) was, for obvious reasons, conspicuous in its support of the war. To obtain cash for the war, 's Hertogenbosch in 1505 adopted the unusual expedient of selling villages in its *meierij* to wealthy buyers. In May 1508 the city raised a force of 2,250 German mercenaries, to be sent with its own militia against Poederoy. Between 1508 and 1514 Dordrecht mortgaged its future by selling rents to raise cash for the war. In 1511 alone the city raised 35,250 gulden, a sum six or seven times greater than Dordrecht's share of the annual subsidy granted to the prince by the entire province of Holland.[34] It might seem, then, that Anhalt's success at Poederoy could have pointed a way for Margaret's government to continue the war. If the Estates persisted in refusing to support the war with Guelders, she might at least have cast her lot with the towns and nobility of a region known for its reliability during the long struggle.

But this region's support for the war was not an unambiguous asset. The province of Holland was still divided by ancient rivalries. At the most obvious level, south Holland (Dordrecht, supported on many issues by Gouda) was pitted against the cities of north Holland (Leiden, Haarlem, Amsterdam), supported by Delft, Dordrecht's traditional competitor. Dordrecht still claimed the staple rights resisted by other cities for over a century. Moreover, taking advantage of a privilege granted Holland in the wake of the Great Privilege of 1477, Dordrecht and Gouda refused to be bound by decisions of a majority of the six 'great cities' represented in the provincial Estates. Thus the north Holland towns, feuding with Dordrecht and remote from the conflict, reneged on a promise to support the attack against Poederoy. According to Willem Hermans, who like Erasmus had been a monk of the cloister of Steyn near Gouda, Delft, Leiden, Amsterdam, and Haarlem began to 'complain about the war, and refuse their contribution, first because they did not give their assent to the siege [of Poederoy], and then because it was not going well.' So it befell Holland 'as in the fables: the frog and the mouse were having a fight; the crow, watching from on high, snatched up both warriors and tore them to pieces.' Only in the spring of 1508, when an enemy force seized two fortified towns on the approaches to Amsterdam, did Holland for a time unite.[35]

A deeper level of division within the province is suggested by the fear of Mercurino Gattinara, Margaret's trusted councillor, that Holland might rise in support of the Duke of Guelders.[36] It must be remembered that the war party in Holland – Counts John of Egmond and Frederick of Ijselstein and his son, Floris, and the patrician governments of Dordrecht and Gouda – was made up of the same Kabiljauw leaders (or their descendants) who sided with Maximilian in the 1480s in order to gain a definitive victory over their Hoek adversaries in the last and bloodiest phase of Holland's long factional wars.[37] Conversely, the lesser nobles of Guelders, the mainstay of Duke Charles's aggressive policy, had traditional ties with the Hoek families of Holland and Utrecht.[38] Although the last war which might be regarded as a struggle between Hoeks and Kabiljauws in Holland ended in 1492,[39] both parties in the Guelders-Habsburg conflict expected to find secret partisans in each other's cities. In 1500 Dordrecht executed several burghers for an alleged plot to betray the city to Guelders; in 1507 Anhalt counted on the clandestine support of a pro-Burgundian party in Nijmegen.[40] The ancient feud between the Kabiljauw Egmonds and the Hoek nobles of Utrecht flared up again in 1511 when an invading force from Utrecht laid siege to the town of Ijselstein.[41] Thomas Spinelly's report that the Hollanders would raise troops for Henry of Brunswick, but not for Floris of Ijselstein, may be malicious gossip, or it may reflect fears in Holland that Ijselstein, whose uncle was head of the Kabiljauw party in the 1480s, wished to pursue the war for his own reasons.[42] Although the party war-cries might no longer be heard, contemporaries still wondered, even as late as the 1520s, whether 'remnants of this pestilence' might not still be felt.[43] Factions often remain alive in the calculations of statesmen long after they have ceased in reality to be of much importance. Thus it seems likely that Margaret and her councillors, like Gattinara, would have preferred not to lean too heavily on the heirs of those Kabiljauw nobles and patricians who had supported Maximilian for their own reasons.

If Gattinara feared an anti-government rising in Holland, Margaret herself feared a general rebellion in the Netherlands.[44] She was perhaps especially anxious about the southern provinces, including

Flanders, which were loath to be drawn into a war with France for the sake of what was for them a remote and inconsequential struggle in the north. The war could be carried on only by finding an army which would not have to be paid by the Estates, or by neutralizing French support of Guelders. In August 1507 Margaret asked the King of England for troops to be used against France's ally, the Duke of Guelders.[45] When Henry VII refused, she took up the task, ultimately successful, of persuading her father to enter a coalition with France against Venice (the League of Cambrai).[46] Once Maximilian had made peace with France, however, Margaret had difficulty inducing him to pursue the war against Guelders. The emperor proposed a peaceful settlement of the conflict by means of a marriage between the Duke of Guelders and Isabella of Austria, Prince Charles's younger sister. In 1510 Margaret sent Floris Oem van Wijngarden, a member of the Council of Holland and scion of a prominent Kabiljauw family in Dordrecht, on a secret mission to Maximilian to argue against the marriage (Oem van Wijngarden was later accused of falsely claiming authorization for his mission from the Estates of Holland).[47] But her real hope of continuing the war lay in the bellicose young prince who had succeeded to the English throne in 1509. Bolstered by appropriate promises from Henry VIII, Margaret found ways to delay and then break off negotiations with Guelders in 1511; members of her council who favoured a peaceful settlement – Count Henry of Nassau and Philip of Burgundy, Admiral of the Netherlands – resigned in protest. In September an English expeditionary force under Richard Ponynge, together with local troops raised by Floris of Ijselstein, encircled the city of Venlo in upper Guelders. But Venlo was well defended; contrary to the wishes of both commanders, the siege was broken off in October. Margaret's precious English army went home with nothing accomplished.[48]

Charles of Guelders now took the offensive, seizing Woudrichem, a town on the Maas between 's Hertogenbosch and Dordrecht. Three hundred militiamen from 's Hertogenbosch were captured by a Guelders raiding force early in 1512, and merchants from several Brabançon cities were taken and held to ransom on their way home from the Frankfurt fair a few months later. Once again, however, there was little support for the war outside the area directly affected. Dordrecht and Gouda continued to raise large sums, and Gouda accepted Ijselstein as its captain, as 's Hertogenbosch had done in 1508 with Anhalt. But Ijselstein complained that Delft and Amsterdam were failing to keep their promises of financial aid.[49] In the Estates General only Brabant responded to appeals from the regent. In February 1512 Margaret requested the Estates General, if they wished the war to be prosecuted, to support six thousand foot and twelve hundred horse; she asked also for a 'donative' of 200,000 gulden for Maximilian. In April the representatives of Brabant agreed to provide their share of the cost of the troops requested and of a donative of 150,000 gulden; the other provinces offered smaller sums for Maximilian and none whatever for the war.[50]

Two views of the matter were possible. Hadrianus Barlandus wrote several years later that Maximilian 'extracted a mighty sum from the people [at the 1512 Estates General] on the pretext of the Guelders war,' but then 'sent nothing more than sterile letters of consolation' to the afflicted town of 's Hertogenbosch. A chronicler of 's Hertogenbosch records, however, that Maximilian did at least send Henry of Brunswick, who led a successful raid into Guelderland before returning again to Germany.[51] Erasmus' old friend Cornelius Aurelius (Goudanus), a monk of Hemsdonk near Schoonhoven (some ten miles from Gouda), felt that 'only Guelders' detracted from the glory of Holland; he traced Holland's misfortunes in war to the 'great sluggishness' of the provincial Estates.[52] Whether one blamed Maximilian for pretending that a state of war existed or the Estates for not recognizing that it did, it was clear to all that Margaret's government could not prevent recurrent and destructive raids from Guelderland. 'Even now the prince is in the Low Countries,' Tunstall wrote in 1516, 'and the Duke of Guelders takes his subjects prisoners.'[53]

Chièvres, Margaret's successor, had to deal with an expansion of the war into Friesland. For over a century the Counts of Holland had vainly sought to assert their claim to overlordship of Frisia. In the 1490s Maximilian had pawned this ancient claim to his military commander, Duke Albert of Saxony. In 1514 Albert's son George sought to make good the claim he had inherited. It was under Duke George and his Stadhouder for Friesland, Floris of Ijselstein, that the Black Band, perhaps the most feared of all mercenary companies in the Netherlands wars, first made its appearance. Opponents of Habsburg/Saxon expansion in Friesland offered lordship over their lands to the Duke of Guelders, who proved eager to extend his authority in the region. In 1515 Duke George abandoned the struggle, offering to allow the Habsburg government to redeem Holland's claim to Frisia for 100,000 gulden. Chièvres quickly accepted. The Black Band, released by the Duke of Saxony in May or June, entered the service of his enemy long enough to capture for Guelders the Frisian town of Kuinre, a port which faced north Holland across a narrow neck of the Zuider Zee. Soon, however, they marched off under Robert de la Marck to form a part of the large force the French king, Francis I, was mobilizing for his Italian expedition.[54]

Meanwhile, Floris of Ijselstein, who now served the Habsburg government as Stadhouder in occupied Frisia, urgently requested troops for an expedition against positions held for Guelders. But Chièvres trusted that his cultivation of France would bring peace with Guelders, France's ally; he was doubtless especially reluctant to offend Francis I after the latter's great victory at Marignano in September 1515. Thus he instructed Ijselstein to conduct operations in Frisia as best he could, but refused to furnish troops. The Stadhouder managed to recruit for the Habsburgs in January 1516 a company of the Black Band which had remained behind in Frisia in the service of Guelders, but he was unable to make much headway. In February 1516 he left Friesland, intending to accompany Prince Charles on his journey to Spain. By this time, Chièvres, together with Habsburg partisans in Friesland, realized that France would not or could not exert pressure on Guelders not to continue the war.[55] In June 1516 a substantial attack force was launched against Frisia from Holland; its leader was the new Stadhouder of Holland, Count Henry of Nassau, who had just been appointed, replacing Ijselstein and his uncle. Why Chièvres should replace Ijselstein at the very moment when he adopted Ijselstein's Frisian policy is not clear. Ijselstein's Kabiljauw background may have been considered a liability, and Nassau probably received preferment because he was no longer reckoned among the opposition to Chièvres at court.[56]

The campaign of June 1516 was preceded by what appears to have been an improvement of the government's financial position after Prince Charles was declared of age. In the early months of 1515, the Estates of Flanders[57] and Brabant[58] approved three-year annual grants of 200,000 and 150,000 gulden respectively. Holland, which had voted 100,000 gulden for each of four years in 1513,[59] renewed the grant in the spring of 1516, while at the same time the Estates of Artois approved its largest grant ever, 42,000 florins for each of four years.[60] News of the death of Ferdinand the Catholic in February 1516 was the occasion for further special grants to finance Charles's voyage to his new realms. The Estates General voted a sum of 400,000 gulden to be paid over three years, a grant which became effective as the Estates of Brabant and Holland and the other provinces each accepted its allotted quota of the total sum.[61] Finally, in the fall of 1516, special requests were made for funds to revive the *compagnies d'ordonnance*, which had had to be disbanded in 1513 for lack of money. The Estates General, asked to endorse a grant of 100,000 gulden from each of the 'landen van herwarts over,' approved instead the sum of 50,000,[62] a grant quickly ratified by the Estates of Flanders (November 1516).[63] These grants would amount to a total pledge of at least 450,000 gulden in 1515, and, assuming that all provinces approved the grant for Charles's Spanish voyage, some 670,000 gulden in 1516. Measured against the government's accumulated debts – in 1515 a total of 600,000 gulden was allegedly owed to the families of Bergen, Ijselstein, and Nassau alone[64] – these sums are perhaps not large. But the flow of cash nonetheless gave Chièvres options which were lacking to the Duchess of Savoy; her one offensive against Guelders was made possible only because the King of England kindly furnished her with an army.

Nassau's force sailed across the Zuider Zee in June 1516. But the Duke of Guelders' return from Italy – he had fought with Francis I at Marignano – soon placed Holland and its Stadhouder on the defensive. Troops loyal to Guelders crossed into south Holland in August and occupied the town of Nieuwport not far from Gouda. Since the Duke of Guelders disclaimed responsibility for the raid, Nassau, upon retaking Nieuwport, ordered captured leaders of the raiding party to be hanged publicly in The Hague as 'highwaymen.' Greater danger loomed in the north. In October Groot Pier, a Frisian pirate who preyed on Holland shipping in the Zuider Zee, occupied the port of Worichum in Frisia, giving Guelders another base of operations across the narrow strait from north Holland.[65] North Holland, often hostile to the Guelders war in the past, now evinced a different spirit. Nassau, taking note that in the Amsterdam region many 'are disobedient about coming to watch duty in the places where they are instructed, and that many are set upon bringing fire and war against the Lord Charles [of Guelders], and that ships are being fitted out to protect the Zuider Zee and to resist the undertakings of Lord Charles,' appointed a general captain for the district to bring order into its defences.[66]

Early in 1517 the main force of the Black Band reappeared in the Netherlands. Returning from Italy after Marignano, the company, still commanded by Robert de la Marck, fought for the Duke of Lorraine, a French ally, against a Rhenish noble loyal to Maximilian, Gangolf von Geroldseck (May 1516).[67] Subsequently, perhaps in view of the forthcoming peace negotiations at Cambrai, the company was dismissed from French service. In February of 1517 they seem to have sent emissaries to serve notice of their availability to prospective employers.[68] On March 22 Tunstall and Worcester wrote to Henry VIII about the '3,000 Almains' whom they described as having been dismissed from the service of Charles of Castile in Frisia. Matthaeus Schinner, Cardinal of Sion, was anxious to engage the company's services, presumably as part of his plan to revive the Anglo-Imperial coalition against France.[69] Meanwhile, in 'mid-Lent,' not long after the meeting of sovereigns at Cambrai, a letter from Francis I to the Duke of Guelders was intercepted and brought before the council, presided over by Chièvres. According to the text as given by the chronicler Macquereau, Francis urged his ally to attack Brabant as soon as Charles should depart for Spain. Toward this end Francis sent a sum of money, which was also intercepted. Apparently in view of the recently concluded peace agreement, Chièvres determined that, although defensive measures were to be taken, there must be no public acknowledgment of the hostile initiative from France.[70] It may have been French promises of financial aid which permitted the Duke of Guelders to engage the Black Band for his service. By late April it was known that the main body of the company, now estimated at 5,500, was bound for Guelders.[71] The company's passage through the Netherlands in March has left a number of traces. On March 22 the Bailli of Lille was instructed to take action against armed men travelling the roads without authorization.[72] On March 27 the Estates of Brabant consented to a subsidy but stipulated in return that the king (of Castille) must 'keep the land unharmed from people of war' and 'keep the highways safe, so that merchants can travel freely and safely everywhere.'[73]

To build a defence against the expected attack, the government renewed its requests of the provincial Estates. On February 23 the Estates of Brabant were asked to renew for three years more the annual subsidy of 150,000 gulden first granted in 1515 and to approve the special grant of 50,000 for the 'maintenance of the king's horses' (that is, the *compagnies d'ordonnance*) which had been endorsed by the Estates General the previous fall. Brabant agreed on March 27 to both requests, with the stipulations mentioned above. As to Holland, the evidence is fragmentary and possibly contradictory. Chancellor Jerome Vander Noot assured the Estates of Brabant on February 23 that the other 'landen van herwarts over' – by name, Holland, Zeeland, Artois, and Namur – had already consented to support the king's cavalry.[74] But on February 21 the Vroedschap or town council of

Gouda instructed the burgermaster to 'resist the contribution of 50,000 philippus gulden requested by his Royal Majesty of all the landen van herwarts over, since we have not consented to it'; if necessary, they say, one must go to prison in The Hague rather than accept the new levy.[75] The two statements might be reconciled by assuming that Gouda was asserting its claim, as Dordrecht had done in the past, not to be bound by an affirmative vote of the other cities represented in the Estates. But it might also be that other cities voted as Gouda did.[76]

Whether or not the Estates of Holland consented to support the *compagnies d'ordonnance*, Nassau made new dispositions in the spring of 1517 for the defence of the province. A part of the Black Band led by a captain named Recalf Dachstein, preferring apparently to remain Burgundian, offered its services to the city of 's Hertogenbosch. The city seems to have rejected Dachstein's offer. But Nassau, hearing of his presence, ordered Dachstein to enlist as many 'banners' (*vaendelen*) of *knechten* as he could in the 's Hertogenbosch region, and to join his forces at Alphen, between Leiden and Gouda. Correctly sensing that the coast of north Holland lay most exposed to danger, Nassau concentrated his 'banners' in the coastal cities, particularly in Medemblik and Enkhuizen, directly across the Zuider Zee channel from Frisian ports held for Guelders.[77]

Despite his precautions, disaster struck precisely where it was expected. On June 25 the main force of the Black Band, ferried across the channel by Groot Pier, attacked and occupied Medemblik, even though the city was defended by one 'banner.' Next the invaders marched south to Hoorn, where – as Floris of Ijselstein and town militiamen watched from the walls – they turned east against Alkmaar, which they also took by storm. Ijselstein followed after with a contingent from Hoorn, blocking their retreat, while the Council of Holland issued a call-to-arms for every fourth able-bodied man in every town and village. Nassau gathered a large militia force, bolstered by fifteen hundred *knechten*, at Sparendam near Haarlem. But the Black Band, marching south from Alkmaar, managed to bypass Nassau and turn off on the dam or dike-road leading to Amsterdam. Before reaching Amsterdam they again moved south, to the small town of Asperen, which, having taken by storm at a considerable loss to their own forces, they brutally sacked and burned (July 9). Nassau eventually retook Asperen (August 5) and pursued the Black Band across the frontier into Guelders, ravaging as he went.[78] A truce signed in September brought an end to this phase of the war, if not to the Black Band. Dismissed from service by the Duke of Guelders, they conducted free-booting operations in the lower Rhine valley until, in the spring of 1518, they were surrounded at an abbey near Venlo by forces jointly commanded by the Count of Nassau, the Duke of Cleves, and the Archbishop of Cologne. At the same time, as a result of negotiations in a town nearby, Robert de la Marck, the band's erstwhile commander, agreed to exchange his traditional French allegiance for a Burgundian alliance. The men of the Black Band, compelled to lay down their arms, were allowed to depart freely.[79]

As the invading army passed just to the north of Hoorn, according to the seventeenth-century historian Theodorus Velius,

> the burgers of Hoorn were in arms on the wall, and the lord Floris of Ijselstein (who had just entered the city) stood with the lord of Wassenaer and a few other nobles on the north bulwark, and seeing the foe march past, said to the by-standers, 'so it was not said,' which some burgers hearing, interpreted the words incorrectly, as if the noble lords had known something of this attack in advance.

One may presume Velius is also recording contemporary fears or suspicions when he remarks that the Black Band's ability to manoeuvre past Nassau's forces at Sparendam was due to 'cowardice, bad leadership, or disloyal service on the part of some in particular.'[80] In Amsterdam men seem to have been just as fearful of a force that came ostensibly to relieve the city as they were of the Black Band. On July 2 news came that the band had overpowered a fortress at Hart on the Haarlem road manned by a half a company of Amsterdam *schutters*. The same day a force which the Estates of Holland had dispatched to Friesland a few weeks earlier returned to assist in the defence of Amsterdam. Its commander at first refused a request from the city to set out along the Haarlem road to strengthen the garrison at Hart. When news came that the fortress had fallen, meaning that the road to Amsterdam lay open before the enemy, the commander of the relief force requested permission to march his men through the city so as to come out on the Haarlem road, between the city and the Black Band, as quickly as possible. The burgermaster and the city council, who had previously declined to admit the relief force to the city, now granted permission reluctantly; but the citizen military companies who had been manning the gate opposite the relief force's camp rejected the council's orders and continued to bar the gate. According to a contemporary Amsterdam chronicler, their stubbornness saved the city from destruction:

> Without doubt, it would have happened, for (as some of the *knechten* [of the relief force] thereafter admitted) had they come into the city, they would at once have cried out, 'Guelders! Guelders!' and they would have given the Guelders forces [the Black Band], who were turning away [from Amsterdam], a signal to come back.

Fears similar to those expressed by the chronicler were apparently current in the city, for five days later the city authorities issued an order forbidding citizens to 'speak ill of the lords.'[81]

Leonardo Bruni remarks in his history of Florence that men believe more readily that they have been betrayed than they have been defeated.[82] In the Netherlands, Hadrianus Barlandus seems to have been suspicious of Anhalt's failure to protect the town of Tienen in 1507.[83] Suspicions of this kind, normal in the event of a serious military setback, were probably strengthened during the campaign of 1517 by the obscure and tangled history of the Black Band itself. As great numbers of mercenary soldiers straggled or marched through Netherlands provinces in March, their destination was known to Chièvres and the council, but not to the public, since Chièvres chose for reasons of diplomacy to maintain an official silence about French efforts to renew the war.[84] Once it became known that these mercenaries belonged to the Black Band, many would recall that the band had first appeared in Friesland a few years earlier under the Habsburg (Saxon) banner. Moreover, Habsburg forces in Holland in 1517 included at least two contingents of *knechten* formerly counted among the Black Band, one recruited by Ijselstein in January 1516, and another, under Recalf Dachstein, which chose in March 1517 to fight for the Habsburgs. Dachstein became one of Nassau's principal commanders; another was Caspar von Ulm, a councillor of Duke George of Saxony, who had dealt on his behalf with the Black Band in Frisia.[85] Contemporaries might thus be excused for raising questions as to whether these former units of the Black Band could still be operating in concert with the main force; in the Netherlands, as elsewhere, mercenary companies had been known to conduct operations on their own behalf rather than in the interest of their current employer.

There were thus two distinct if related grounds for popular mistrust of the Habsburg government's military policy. It could not protect its subjects, and it persisted in entrusting the nation's defence to a military force – the foreign mercenary band – which, even when successful, was feared and hated among the general population. Events moved in a vicious circle. Since the government feared rebellion by its Dutch- or Flemish-speaking subjects, it sought continually to recruit mercenaries from outside the region; since the Estates would not pay for foreign armies, the nation lay exposed to attack from Guelders or France. The circle may have been broken by the loyalty of *knechten* from Brabant and popular levies from Holland during the 1517 campaign. In 1521 the Council of Holland proposed an ordinance which reflects a new set of military and political assumptions. The province would be divided into five captaincies. In each city or village, local officials would choose one man in thirty – men experienced in war or otherwise deemed suitable – and have them fitted out with military gear. Those selected should hold themselves ready for summons by the commander of the captaincy in which they lived. They would be paid an annual salary, supplemented by active duty wages on a scale slightly higher than Nassau's *knechten* were paid in 1517. Whatever the reasons for the promulgation of this proposal may have been, it offered, in effect, a belated response to a problem which had brought government and Estates to an impasse. Henceforth Hollanders would no longer suffer the presence of foreign mercenaries, while the government would be assured a reliable and readily available force of *knechten*. The proposal was, however, rejected as too costly by the Estates of Holland.[86] Had such a system existed in 1517 it probably would not have prevented the destruction of Alkmaar or Asperen. But it might have dampened somewhat the ensuing suspicions about the government, none of which were more extraordinary than those articulated by Erasmus.

Both in his attitude toward mercenary soldiers and in his general conception of the Guelders war, Erasmus reflected attitudes common in the Netherlands Estates. His strong feelings about mercenaries probably owed less to the anti-mercenary tradition in Italian humanist historical writing than to living memory in the Netherlands of atrocities committed by bands like Albert of Saxony's Groote Gaard.[87] *Querela pacis* described mercenaries as 'the vile excrement of criminality,' holding 'human life less dear than a small bit of profit.'[88] The same treatise alludes to a class of military adventurers, common among the aristocracy of border regions (like Robert de la Marck), who made a living as mercenary commanders: when princes seek to stir up war, 'this office is performed for them by certain criminal types who have no employment during times of peace.' Horror of bloodshed was one element of what might be called primitive religious consciousness which Erasmus himself still felt. Though he might attack 'Judaism' or 'the superstition of ceremonies' as it affected Christian piety, he could accept the Old Testament verse describing David as 'polluted' by the blood of gentile enemies, even though the Lord God had commanded the king to make war. Hence he could not comprehend how those who hired mercenaries to kill fellow-believers in Christ 'are counted as Christians, and dare, polluted with human blood, to approach the holy temples and the holy altars.'[89] One modern scholar believes Erasmus exaggerated in characterizing mercenary soldiers as robbers and murderers. But the dreary record of crimes committed by professional troops quartered on civilian populations suggests he was not far wrong.[90] In June 1514 he told the papal legate that Leo x should seek not a peace but a truce between France and England: 'There ought not be mention of peace ... For peace cannot be sealed all at once; and while the kings treat of conditions, the soldiers, at the odour of peace, will contrive worse things than they do in war. But the bands of soldiers can be restrained at once through a truce.'[91] Coming from a cloistered scholar, this was shrewd advice.

Erasmus' one actual encounter with a mercenary band came in May 1516. Travelling overland from Basel to Antwerp, his party found at the southern border of Lorraine 'bands of soldiery everywhere, and the country people in many places moving from the country into the towns.' He then turned aside to follow the Rhine, but never felt out of danger, even after joining a party of eighty mounted men at Cologne. Rumour was that the intruders 'were ready to attack Lorraine, but it was uncertain who sent them.' Erasmus had an explanation of his own: 'I suspect they were men discharged by the emperor and looking for someone to pay them wages instead of him.' In May of 1516 two opposing mercenary forces were conducting operations in Lorraine. One was the Black Band, led by Robert de la Marck, fighting for the Duke of Lorraine, a staunch ally of Francis I. The other was a company led against Lorraine by the Rhenish lord Gangolf von Geroldseck and his ally Franz von Sickingen. The two German nobles had private reasons for pressing their attack, but the Lord of Geroldseck was also an ally of the emperor, having recently been restored to his family lands by Maximilian. The Black Band had served the Habsburgs in Frisia before entering French service, and in May 1516 Maximilian was negotiating for the use of Geroldseck's *landsknechte* for a projected Italian campaign.[92] Thus whichever force had crossed Erasmus' path, he might have picked up information about it that would permit him to make a legitimate connection with Maximilian. But he may also have been predisposed to make such a connection, with or without information to support it. For a Netherlander of his generation, mercenary armies had been the traditional mainstay of Habsburg power.

Given his outlook on mercenaries, Erasmus was able in the *Querela pacis* to urge upon rulers the view that a bit of territory lost was not the worst thing that could happen: 'How much more you degrade your majesty by making offerings of gold to barbaric legions, the lowest excrement of criminality, who are never to be satisfied!' In most cases the cause of war was not worth the risk of putting oneself in the hands of such men: 'You wish to reclaim this or that part of your territory, what has that to do with the business of the people? You wish vengeance on him who broke faith with your daughter, what has that to do with the state?'[93] The latter statement clearly refers to Maximilian's perennial *casus belli* against the French – the capture in 1491 of his intended bride, the Duchess Anne of Brittany, and her enforced marriage to Charles VIII. In 1498 Louis XII, engaged to Maximilian's daughter, Margaret (later regent in the Netherlands), repudiated his fiancée in order to marry the same Anne of Brittany, his predecessor's widow.[94] Thus in the previous sentence – about reclaiming a portion of territory – Erasmus was probably thinking of Maximilian's perennial claim to the Duchy of Guelders, which he had ruled from 1477 to 1493. Erasmus hence shared the opinion, dominant in the Estates General, that the Guelders war was a purely dynastic affair, of no concern to the national welfare.

His views on the war are more explicit in letters from the same period (1517) to Thomas More and Cuthbert Tunstall, many of them written from the house of his Antwerp friend Peter Gilles. With two exceptions, these letters, together with others to be discussed in this chapter, were never published by Erasmus; they were first published by P.S. Allen from manuscript copies in the letter-book he found in Deventer. Taken together, the letters represent the kind of indiscretion in writing about political matters which Erasmus had been warned about by Jerome Busleiden. He had at least the prudence to restrict his written comments about Maximilian and the war in Guelders to a narrow circle of intimate and like-minded friends.

More's friendship with Erasmus is well known and often discussed.

As pointed out in the last chapter, both men shared a healthy suspicion of the uses to which kings might put their power, especially in questions of war and taxation. Tunstall, though an obscure figure in comparison with More, was probably more important for Erasmus' political views at this time. Tunstall's English commission, directing him to remain with Charles and his court, kept him in the Netherlands until September 1517. During the spring and early summer, living mostly in Gilles' house in Antwerp, Erasmus kept in close touch with his English friend. In May, when Erasmus passed through Ghent as Charles held court there, Tunstall helped him in collating Greek manuscripts for a second edition of his New Testament.[95] The two men apparently continued to correspond after Erasmus moved to Louvain in July, though no letters from Tunstall have survived from this period. In the fall of 1516, as has been argued previously, Tunstall most probably did not communicate to Erasmus Henry's plan to depose Chièvres and Sauvage. But in the spring and summer of 1517 there will be hints of a convergence between Erasmus' letters to More and Tunstall's dispatches to Wolsey.

Erasmus had a large circle of acquaintance among learned men and public functionaries in the great commercial centre of Antwerp. Peter Gilles, who was the town clerk, came from a respected local family; his father had several times been burgomaster.[96] The town advocate or Pensionaris, Jacobus de Voecht (Tutor), had given lodging to Erasmus in Orléans in 1501 in the house he kept for his two noble pupils, one of whom was the young Henry of Nassau.[97] Erasmus was friendly also with Cornelius Grapheus, one of the town secretaries,[98] Nicholas of 's Hertogenbosch ('Buscodensis'), headmaster of the town Latin school,[99] a commercial agent named Jan Crull,[100] a 'senator' of the city,[101] and Gilles' friend Gaspar van Halmal, Sheriff of Antwerp.[102] One can imagine that political issues would be a subject for lively discussion among such men. Unfortunately, however, the few writings produced during this period by Antwerp humanists – Gilles, Tutor, Buscodensis, Grapheus – yield almost no clue as to political questions they may have discussed.[103] The one exception is Gilles' commentary on the triumphal arches (or 'spectacles') designed by Grapheus which Antwerp raised to welcome Charles v as emperor in 1520. In the fifth 'spectacle,' as explained by Gilles, the goddess Astrea, returning to earth to celebrate the new Golden Age to be inaugurated by Charles v, crushes underfoot 'tyranny, the most horrid monster of all, especially to be hated by princes.' In the second spectacle 'Homeric Jove' is seated between Justice and Power (*kratos*). At

Jove's command an eagle bestows upon the emperor a sceptre, while Justice invests him with a sword and Power with a golden diadem. As Gilles interpets the 'mythology' of the spectacle, 'the fact that Power bestows the crown means that crowns – that is, cities, whose figure is defined by walls and turrets – are not to be oppressed by power, but rather are to be guarded by laws, so that they may acknowledge the power of the prince and feel his humanity and mildness.' Lest such comments about royal power seem mere convention, it must be kept in mind that warnings against tyranny, however mild or veiled, were simply not a feature of contemporary royal triumphal entries. Moreover, the unusual iconography Gilles employs – the classical motif of the 'walled crown' had not previously been used outside Italy – suggests he was going out of his way to make a point.[104] One may conclude that Gilles, at least in 1520, had a view of urban liberties and royal tyranny that was congenial to his friends Erasmus and More. Erasmus' comments to More about Maximilian's governance of the Netherlands thus might reflect, in part, conversations with Gilles and other Antwerp friends.

On 1 March 1517, writing from Gilles' house, Erasmus reported to More on local political developments:

> A mighty sum is demanded of the people and right away. The demand has been accepted by the nobles and the prelates, that is by those who alone are to pay nothing. Now the cities are consulting. The emperor [*autokrator*] otherwise *unarmed* is now here with a magnificently armed band, and the fields everywhere are filled with flocks of soldiers, and whence they come or in whose name is uncertain. Oh wretched land, gnawed by so many vultures! oh happy land, were there harmony [*concordia*] of the towns among themselves![105]

The record of subsidies recently granted by the Estates of Brabant provides background for Erasmus' complaint about the government's fiscal demands. In 1515 the Estates granted a subsidy of 150,000 gulden for each of the following three years, on condition that no further subsidy be requested during that period. In addition to its being incorporated in the Estates' act of consent to the subsidy, this stipulation was also inserted in the *joyeuse entrée*, the province's charter of liberties. Nonetheless, in the following year, the Estates agreed to grant Charles Brabant's share of the 400,000 gulden requested of all the 'landen van herwarts over' to pay for his journey to Spain.[106]

Charles's departure for his new realms was delayed, however, while Chièvres first negotiated a treaty with France, and then persuaded Maximilian to give his consent. Now in 1517, just as the princes were to meet at Cambrai, the Estates of Brabant were convened in Brussels on February 23 and requested to renew the grant of 1515 for a further three years. One of the reasons given for the request was to defray 'the costs that he [Charles] had had for fitting out ships for his journey to Spain, which were now in vain, since he had delayed his journey at the request of the Estates.'[107] It must have been widely appreciated that Chièvres' decision to postpone the king's journey was in reality based on diplomatic considerations rather than requests from the Estates; thus the Estates were being asked to pay a second time for their 'natural prince' to depart for another country. It was a clear test of whether, as Erasmus believed, 'the tyranny of princes might be constrained by honest harmony [*concordia*] among towns and townsfolk.' Erasmus' letter to More falls within the period when the four major cities of Brabant – Antwerp, Louvain, Brussels, and 's Hertogenbosch – were deliberating on their response to the request. On March 27 the Estates convened again and, doubtless to the disappointment of men like Erasmus, agreed to renew the subsidy for three more years.[108]

The references in this letter to troop movements are less clear, but perhaps more important for an understanding of Erasmus' view of the political situation. His description of the emperor (*autokrator*) as normally 'unarmed' (*anoplos*) would make sense to an English friend, who might recall that Maximilan brought to the Tournai campaign his reputed skill as a commander but no troops. The 'magnificently armed band' Erasmus mentions must be the company of two hundred men-at-arms who rode with Cardinal Schinner as he accompanied Maximilian to Brussels.[109] More interesting is his statement that 'the fields everywhere are full of soldiers.' Dated references to the movement of Black Band units through the Netherlands are three or more weeks later than Erasmus' letter to More. But it is reasonable to presume that these later statements describe something that had been going on for a time. For instance, the instructions to the Bailli of Lille (dated March 22) to proceed against armed men travelling the highways without licence would have been issued only after the government had had time to receive and process local complaints.[110] Erasmus' statement about fields full of soldiers thus appears to be an early indication – perhaps the earliest – that troops of the Black Band were moving north.

The language of the letter suggests, if it does not say, that Erasmus associated these troop movements with Maximilian's presence in the

Netherlands. Maximilian's armed band and the mysterious soldiers in the field are linked by an *and*. The description of these unidentified bands ('Whence they come, or in whose name, is uncertain') is reminiscent of the letter to John Fisher, ten months earlier, describing mercenaries in Lorraine, whom Erasmus suspected to have been 'dismissed by Caesar' to seek another paymaster.[111] Finally, both the emperor himself and the soldiers in the field are included among the 'vultures' gnawing at the land, as if Erasmus thought they might be acting in concert. On March 22 Tunstall and his colleagues, reporting to Wolsey that England was being invited to bid for the Black Band's services, spoke of the mercenaries as if they had just recently been dismissed by the Habsburg government in Frisia.[112] If Tunstall were in possession of this (mis-)information some weeks earlier, he could have provided added reason for Erasmus to connect these soldiers in the fields with Maximilian.

His next letter to More was dated from Gilles' house May 30; it and his March 1 letter to More are the only letters to be discussed in this chapter ever published by Erasmus himself. It gives information about the emperor's stay in the Netherlands not otherwise known from published sources: 'Our Charles,' he says, 'held council in Ghent, to which Caesar was not admitted.' Erasmus had just returned from Ghent, where he spent considerable time with Tunstall, then in attendance on Charles and the court; his account of a quarrel between Maximilian and the council, presided over by Chièvres, is thus likely to have come from good sources. But it seems the quarrel was more apparent than real: 'They say [Caesar] is going away [from the Netherlands] dissatisfied. Good gods! When has an angry man ever been more fortunate? Peace was about to be made with Guelders, indeed on terms most favourable to Caesar; but he blocked the negotiations, lest there be no war left to us anywhere.'[113] These negotiations have left no trace in published records, but Erasmus' account would at least be consistent with his own view, at the time *Querela pacis* was composed, that Maximilian or his party still opposed peace with France.[114] (Philip of Burgundy, mentioned in this letter as the new Bishop of Utrecht and known as an advocate of peace with Guelders, was soon to be the dedicand of *Querela pacis*.)[115] For some months Tunstall had been arguing in his dispatches that there was far more agreement between Chièvres and Maximilian than Henry VIII or Cardinal Schinner wished to believe. One might, then, trace to Tunstall Erasmus' belief that Charles's councillors, whatever their differences with Maximilian might be, had yielded to his designs in regard to Guelders. Cardinal

Schinner, with whom Erasmus dined in Antwerp on May 29, found the emperor's designs decidedly sinister: 'The Germans,' he told his guest, 'are working to make all kings subordinate to the emperor.'[116] Erasmus passed the Swiss prelate's remark on to More without comment; he himself, as is clear from the rest of the letter, still regarded Maximilian as the principal threat to the peace and liberty of the Netherlands.

On August 23, writing from Louvain to Beatus Rhenanus, Erasmus set down a brief account of the Black Band's recent invasion of north Holland. In April of the following year he described to More and Tunstall how the Black Band had been surrounded at Venlo and its members released by order of the princes who commanded the allied army. Still later, in a letter of August 1519 to Luther's friend George Spalatin, he commented on the lingering significance of the sack of Asperen for inhabitants of the Habsburg Low Countries. Each of these letters is remarkable for its frankness. Rhenanus, Erasmus' close friend in Basel, had introduced him to Seneca's satirical attack on the tyranny of the Emperor Claudius.[117] Spalatin was not well known to Erasmus, but the theme of their correspondence in 1518–19 was Luther's importance as a symbol of resistance to what Erasmus perceived as the tyranny of pope and kings. Thus Rhenanus and Spalatin, like More and Tunstall, seemed to be men who would appreciate Erasmus' private opinions about the tyranny of modern times.

The letter to Rhenanus is remarkable also for its wealth of detail about events in Holland. Here more than anywhere in his correspondence, one has the impression that Erasmus' friends were keeping him abreast of political developments. Unfortunately, barring the discovery of extant letters to Erasmus which were overlooked by P.S. Allen, one can only conjecture about his sources. His oldest friends still resided in south Holland, where Erasmus spent his boyhood and youth: Cornelius Aurelius, at this time a monk of Hemsdonck near Schoonhoven, and Reyner Snoy, town physician of Gouda (Willem Hermans had died a few years before).[118] The writings of these men make it clear that they supported the aggressive posture toward Guelders which was generally favoured in south Holland. Aurelius, for example, praised Henry of Nassau for his victories, lauded the recapture of Nieuwpoort (near Schoonhoven) in 1516, and blamed 'the sluggishness of the Estates' for the enemy's successes.[119] Not surprisingly, Aurelius received the laurel crown from Maximilian during the emperor's sojourn in Holland in 1508; like Hermans, he was in correspondence with Floris of Ijselstein. More interesting is the fact that Snoy's *De rebus Batavicis*, written some time after 1519, agrees with Erasmus in the important and also incorrect assertion that Holland was denuded of troops at the time of the Guelders invasion.[120] Unfortunately, there is no evidence that Snoy or Aurelius corresponded with Erasmus at this time. Nicholas Everardi, President of the Council of Holland, had known Erasmus since their days of common service with the Bishop of Cambrai. But he and Erasmus seem not to have kept in touch during this period.[121] Alard of Amsterdam,[122] who taught at the Latin School of Alkmaar before coming to Louvain in 1515, was perhaps Erasmus' most likely conduit of news and opinion from Holland. An enthusiastic member of Erasmus' circle in Louvain, he was in touch both with Erasmus' friends in south Holland[123] and with prominent men in the areas directly affected by the Black Band campaign. As late as September 1516 he still corresponded with his former superior in Alkmaar, the famous schoolmaster Johann Murmellius, whose house and goods were destroyed in the Black Band attack.[124] In his native Amsterdam he discussed learned matters with, among others, the wealthy merchant Pompeius Occo, who represented Fugger interests in the city.[125] More important, he was evidently in north Holland during the spring and summer of 1517, since he was ordained priest in Amsterdam in April of that year, and his presence in Louvain cannot be established again until November 1518. Some time during his absence Alard forwarded to Erasmus a manuscript translation from the Greek by Rudolph Agricola, presumably borrowed from Pompeius Occo's collection of Agricola's papers.[126] That Alard sent along with the manuscript a letter recounting recent events in Holland is at least an interesting possibility.

In order to assess Erasmus' interpretation of the Guelders war, some judgment must be made as to the reliability of his factual information. Especially since it cannot be determined who his sources were, it is necessary to test against other sources (as far as possible) the accuracy of his main assertions about what happened during the campaign. The discussion will thus proceed in stages. Relevant portions of the letters to Rhenanus and the others will first be quoted in full; an estimate will next be made as to how reliable these letters are with regard to the events they describe; finally, it will then be possible to assess Erasmus' broad interpretation of the Guelders war.

After discussing the situation at Froben's press, in response to Rhenanus' letter of July 7, Erasmus turned, as he had before in letters to Rhenanus, to politics: 'The situation at court is such that good men prefer to be absent; lest I say anything of others, to speak against whom is not so much impious as unsafe.' There follows a highly critical portrait of Jean Briselot, the prince's new confessor, whom Erasmus elsewhere described as appointed through the influence of Chièvres, 'by whose nod all things are done.' (It should be remembered that Sauvage, Erasmus' patron and Chièvres' normal collaborator, had already departed for Spain in June.) 'There is,' the letter continues,

> a swarm of men they call the Black Band, who have taken and destroyed Alkmaar, a flourishing town in Holland. Great wrath was vented on the women and children, because they had defended themselves fiercely. Had they had but six hundred *knechten* [*milites*] in the citadel, they would have been safe. Yet these men [the Black Band] were fighting for us a little while ago against the Frisians. Since it was feared these things would happen, emissaries were sent for that reason to ask protection from the prince [Charles had been at Middelburg in Zeeland since June]. They were not admitted, nor were they given permission to defend themselves with their own wealth and their own weapons; indeed they were forbidden, under threat of capital punishment, lest having been despoiled by Guelders, they should invade Guelders in turn. After this atrocious slaughter, the major cities, now fearing for themselves, went to the prince [again]. They did receive grudging [*vix*] permission to defend themselves at their own expense, but on condition that they in turn furnish the prince with a new travel allowance [*viaticum*]; for the old travél allowance was used up, since they had already paid what was to be due over three years. Because the Hollanders were complaining [*gravabantur*] about this, this tempest was loosed upon them by design. There is no one who does not perceive the trick; but it is not easy to remedy it nor safe to speak. Recently some were thrown into prison for saying that, if all those around the prince loved him as I do, they would not treat his towns in such a way. They were fortunate to be released, after three weeks, upon the request of Lady Margaret. The suspicion is that these events are part of a scheme to prevent the prince from departing; that he may fear that the cities, in his absence, will not tolerate this foolishness any longer ... They say the Black Band is blockaded in a swamp. I think they will continue to be blockaded until what the prince asks will be counted out to him.[127]

Erasmus followed subsequent events of the campaign with interest. A few days after the letter to Rhenanus he reported to Tunstall that 'three *milites* of that company which displayed a more-than-Turkish cruelty in the sack of Asperen' had been hanged 'from the same tree.' A bystander who waved greetings to them was seized and confessed to having been a member of the company. 'Would that the whole Band could be burned to cinders, so that they could truly be called Black.'[128] The following spring, some three weeks after the Black Band had been surrounded and captured at Venlo, he wrote to More in disgust at the 'clemency' which these 'most depraved bandits' had been allowed. When they were tightly surrounded,

> so that not a one could escape, the Duke of Cleves, the Duke of Julich, the Duke [*sic*] of Nassau brought it about that they were let go unharmed; and unless a trumpet had sounded by chance – it is not known by whom – not even one of them would have perished. For in the confusion more than a thousand were cut down. Only the Archbishop of Cologne, who prefaced his remark by saying he was a priest, said that if it were his decision, he would treat them so they could never again accomplish anything similar [to the sack of Asperen or Alkmaar]. The people understand this but are forced to bear it.[129]

To Tunstall he explained his meaning more clearly:

> The slaughter was halted, the survivors were given permission to lay down their arms and depart; nor was it to be allowed to peasants or townsmen to seize them anywhere they could and kill them. See how well the state is served! Those criminals will be grateful to one or another of the princes for their safety; but the fact that some of their number are missing they will avenge on the heads of the people.[130]

The whole affair was still in Erasmus' mind as he wrote Spalatin a year later that joy in the Netherlands over Charles v's election as emperor was diminished by anxiety concerning a mercenary army encamped on the borders.

> The example of Asperen, wasted and destroyed two years ago, still frightens many; we regret already the clemency with which the mercenary army was dismissed unharmed. Nor are there

> lacking those who suspect this army is maintained by the counsel of the princes, to be ready to put down the people if they complain at what is being commanded of them; and things are commanded which are scarcely to be borne. But in these matters let the fates find a way; I feel pity for the wretched common folk, and shame at a more-than-Turkish tyranny. In the end I see everything being gathered into a few hands, with a gradual extinction of the remnants of ancient democracy [*democratia*].[131]

Apart from the sack of Alkmaar, these letters recount six distinct sequences of events. 1) At an unspecified date, representatives of one or more towns went to the prince to seek armed protection (*praesidium*) from the government – presumably in the form of hired *knechten* or *milites* – and permission to 'defend themselves with their own wealth and weapons.' Both requests were denied, and the town(s) in question were enjoined against attacking Guelders. 2) Hollanders were complaining about a subsidy which Erasmus says was understood as a further 'travel allowance' (*viaticum*) for Charles's journey to Spain. The term 'were complaining' (*gravabantur*) is vague, but something less than full approval of the subsidy is meant, for Erasmus speaks subsequently of money not yet 'counted out' to the prince as he had requested. 3) Erasmus' claim that Alkmaar could have been defended by six hundred *milites*, combined with his statement that towns were denied the help they requested, amounts to an implied assertion that the government took little or no action to protect its endangered cities. 4) After the sack of Alkmaar, representatives of the [six] cities represented in the Estates of Holland received from the prince permission to 'defend themselves with their own wealth,' but only on condition that the subsidy previously requested be paid in full. 5) Apparently subsequent to the sack of Alkmaar, some citizens who publicly complained that 'those about the prince' mistreated his cities were imprisoned for their remarks, until released by the intervention of Margaret of Austria. 6) After a partial massacre of the Black Band at Venlo, the survivors were released unharmed and under safekeeping, at the insistence of Henry of Nassau and the Dukes of Cleve and Julich. Each of these assertions must be discussed in turn.

1) Printed sources offer no information about such a delegation of town representatives, nor about its reception. There is, however, scattered evidence of sentiment in Holland and north Brabant, in late 1516 and early 1517, for carrying the war to Guelders. One of the

reasons why Henry of Nassau appointed a captain-general for the Amsterdam region in September 1516 was to restrain local citizens who wanted 'to make fire and war against the Lord Charles [of Guelders].'[132] In February or March 1517, Recalf Dachstein, the Black Band commander who wished to remain Burgundian, thought the town of 's Hertogenbosch might be in the market for his services.[133] The military situation during this period – the seizure of Nieuwpoort by Guelders (August 1516), Groot Pier's threat to Dutch shipping on the Zuyder Zee – could readily have roused a warlike mood throughout Holland. But it was also a period of extreme delicacy in Chièvres' long effort to draw Maximilian into a firm peace with the King of France. Especially after the emperor had arrived in the Netherlands to seal the peace, it would not do to have Dutch towns attacking a French ally, the Duke of Guelders. Any town delegation that showed up at court requesting aid against Guelders would surely be told in the firmest terms not to take aggressive action. Erasmus' account, at least in this one detail, is thus quite plausible.

2) Erasmus' account of the government's fiscal demands in Holland can in several respects be checked against other sources. In April of 1516 the Estates General recommended a grant of 400,000 gulden for the prince's voyage to Spain, payable over three years. A resolution of the Gouda Vroedschap or city council (May 1516) makes it clear that Holland, through its Estates, had consented to pay its quota of the 400,000 gulden. It seems further that, although the grant was to be paid over a three-year period, it was collected and spent within a year. Both a later Gouda Vroedschap resolution[134] and the correspondence of the Stadhouder, Henry of Nassau, indicate that the government was able, in Holland as in Brabant, to collect subsidy payments in advance of the due date.[135] The practice was being resisted in Holland in June 1517,[136] and it is not evident from these sources that the government was able to collect such advance payments as much as a year or more in advance. But in February 1517 Jerome van der Noot, Chancellor of Brabant, informed the Estates of that province that money collected for Charles's journey to Spain had already been spent, partly to outfit ships that did not sail and partly for other expenses. What representatives to the Estates were told on this occasion was probably known to Erasmus as well, for it was this session of the Estates that he described to More in his letter of March 1.[137]

His account would hence appear, thus far at least, to be based on the best information available. It seems, however, that he was not quite correct in claiming that Holland was requested to provide the prince with a new *viaticum*. In Brabant, Chancellor Vander Noot asked the Estates not for a new travel subsidy as such, but for a three-year renewal of the normal triennial subsidy, which had last been granted in 1515. Part of this money would be used, to be sure, to defray the prince's travel costs; but the subsidy itself was not described or understood as a *viaticum*.[138] Holland, which granted a four-year subsidy in 1516,[139] would not have been asked at this time to renew its normal subsidy. As far as can be gathered from published materials, the only special request made of Holland at this time was for fifty thousand gulden, the sum which the Estates General in September 1516 had recommended that each province pay in order to re-establish the prince's mounted *compagnies d'ordonnance*.[140] Whether this grant was approved by the Estates of Holland is not known. Since it was commonly understood that funds voted for other purposes must be diverted to local defence in case of war,[141] what the Royal Council (in a letter of June 2) describes as a sum of six thousand gulden raised by 'some of the cities of Holland for the affairs of the king and the defence of the land' may refer to a small portion of the requested fifty thousand gulden which was actually collected.[142] But a Gouda Vroedschap resolution for February 21 instructs that city's deputies to the Estates to refuse the grant of fifty thousand gulden, even at the cost of going to prison in The Hague; if the Estates did approve the grant, Gouda and possibly other cities resisted.[143] There is thus a basis for Erasmus' contention that Hollanders 'complained' about a subsidy, though the subsidy in question was not what he thought it to be.

3) When Erasmus speaks of *milites*, one may presume he refers to *knechten* or hired foot-soldiers rather than to the mounted men-at-arms of the royal *compagnies d'ordonnance*, since there were only six hundred of the latter, or four companies, for the entire Habsburg Netherlands.[144] Both the *Divisie Chroniek* and a letter of the council to Holland (June 2) indicate that the Stadhouder had raised a force of fifteen hundred *knechten*, divided into eight 'banners' (*vaendelen*); the council's letter speaks also of a force of one thousand commanded by Simon de Ferrette. The disposition of Ferette's troops is not known. But the *Divisie Chroniek* relates that, apart from one 'banner' stationed at Schagen, inland from Medemblik, Nassau positioned his forces in the coastal towns which faced the Frisian ports held for Guelders across the Zuyder Zee. One 'banner' (ca. two hundred men?) was placed in Medemblik, which proved in fact to be the point at which the Black Band chose to invade Holland.[145] If some two hundred *knechten* were unable to hold Medemblik against the invading force,

one wonders about Erasmus' claim that six hundred *milites* could have defended Alkmaar. More important, it seems he was wholly ignorant of Nassau's extensive and sensible defensive preparations; either his sources were themselves uninformed about military policy or Erasmus ignored what they had to say. Reyner Snoy's contention that Holland was 'denuded of troops' at this time shows that Erasmus was at least not alone in his error.

4) There is no record in published sources of a delegation from the major towns of Holland to the prince – Charles had been at Middleburg in Zeeland since June, awaiting a favourable wind for his voyage – after the sack of Alkmaar. But a Gouda Vroedschap resolution for July 8 indicates that the President of the Council of Holland (Erasmus' friend Nicholas Everardi) had asked town representatives gathered in Leiden for a special additional grant to meet the costs of war; Gouda instructed its representatives to refuse.[146] A week or so earlier, after the Black Band had passed by Hoorn en route to Alkmaar, the city council, concerned lest the enemy return, ordered a double ring of stakes to be placed about the town walls; the work was finished in three days. Velius reports that the men of Hoorn 'placed here and there many Burgundian crosses on the defensive works ... to show their loyalty.' Thus it appears that one town was a bit nervous about undertaking defensive works on its own authority.[147] Both details are at least consistent with Erasmus' contention that the central government requested added funds of the Dutch towns in return for permission to see to their own defences.

5) Three Dutch burgers were allegedly imprisoned for political remarks and released at the request of Margaret of Austria. On a prior occasion Margaret did intervene in the way Erasmus describes; in 1511 she pardoned a number of citizens of The Hague whom Floris of Ijselstein, as acting Stadhouder, had imprisoned for electing town officials without his permission.[148] In the wake of the Black Band's invasion there was apparently malicious gossip about the government, since the town council of Amsterdam felt obliged (July 7) to declare it 'forbidden to speak ill of the lords.'[149] The town secretary of Dordrecht was threatened with prison in 1515 because his city refused to recognize a new scheme of assessment for the provincial subsidy, and the Gouda Vroedschap anticipated that its representatives might be imprisoned for their refusal to approve a special grant in 1517.[150] One can only conclude that Erasmus' report of arrests for speaking against the prince's councillors is plausible.

6) Erasmus' account of a partial massacre of the Black Band, halted

by order of the princes, is confirmed in detail by several chroniclers.[151] Moreover, at least as regards the Habsburg government of the Netherlands, there is some support also for his intimation that the princes wished to keep the men of the Black Band safe for possible future employment. For while the band was beseiged at Venlo, government officials were successfully completing negotiations in a nearby town to secure the allegiance of the company's erstwhile leader, Robert de la Marck.[152] Erasmus may not have known of these negotiations, but the princes' reasons for wishing the mercenaries not to be harmed must have been obvious to many, especially to those who, like Erasmus, were inclined to place a sinister construction on events.

In sum, the value of Erasmus' factual account of the Guelders war is limited primarily by what it leaves out. Like Reyner Snoy, he knows nothing of Nassau's defensive preparations, nor of the delicate diplomatic situation – which should have been known to Erasmus, since he was writing *Querela pacis* for the meeting at Cambrai – which would have caused the government to discourage any military action by Dutch towns. Because of these omissions, and because of the identification of the contested subsidy as a 'new travel allowance,' one must conclude that his perception of political events is flawed by a bias against the Habsburg government. But his narrative leaves nonetheless a positive impression. In every case where what he does say can be checked against other sources, except as regards his mislabelling of the subsidy requested in Holland, his account is corroborated. The details of his account which cannot be checked in this manner are at least consistent with scattered indications in other sources. It seems, then, that his information must have come one way or another from reasonably knowledgeable men, and that chances are good that he is a reliable source for events known only from his letters.

This favourable assessment of Erasmus' general knowledge of conditions in Holland renders all the more intriguing the fantastic interpretation he gives to the events described. He clearly regarded the Black Band's invasion as a 'tempest loosed by design' (to Rhenanus) by the Habsburg government, in order to punish Hollanders for their recalcitrance in the matter of the subsidy. To his mind, 'those about the prince' were concerned less with Guelders than with the threat of resistance from Charles's subjects in Holland; 'they' sought to prevent Charles's departure for Spain, fearing the towns would grow still more restive in his absence (to Rhenanus). This strange, conspiratorial view of government in the Netherlands becomes less surprising if one recalls a number of the features of Erasmus' political opinions which have been discussed. In writings of 1514–15 he spoke in a general way of 'collusion' between princes, making war on each other so as to enjoy enhanced power in respect to their subjects, as an actual occurrence.[153] If one accepts the interpretation offered here of his letter of 1 March 1517 to More, he believed even at that time, as the soldiers of the Black Band filtered north through the Netherlands, that these mercenaries had some connection with Maximilian. He believed too that Maximilian had some mysterious reason for not wishing to accept a settlement of the Guelders conflict favourable to his own claims (to More, May 30). Maximilian had departed for Germany in May. But, after his own patron, Sauvage, had left for Spain in June, Erasmus was equally suspicious of those who governed in the emperor's absence. He looked upon Chièvres as a man who was steeped in the 'tyrannical' mentality of chivalric romance, and whose creatures, like the royal confessor Briselot, steadily gained influence at court. Other 'princes' – men like Nassau and Ijselstein – were doubtless not much higher in his esteem. This perception of events might make any man suspicious. But it should also be pointed out that Erasmus was prone to detect 'conspiracies' against him by those he took to be his enemies.[154] One might, then, choose to treat his utterly mistrustful reading of the government's role in the Guelders war as merely a political expression of that mild paranoia which often accompanies the scholarly temperament.

Erasmus insists, however, that his interpretation of events is not a personal view, but a matter of common knowledge among informed people. Now that the government has unleashed the Black Band against its own cities in Holland, he tells Rhenanus, 'there is no one who does not perceive the trick.' As to the 'clemency' with which captured Black Band members are treated by Nassau and other princes, 'the people understand this but are forced to bear it' (to More). Thus, according to Erasmus, knowledgeable men in Holland were of the opinion that Charles's council (or perhaps 'the princes') induced hostile forces to attack his own cities in order to cow the populace into submission. If there were no evidence as to current political opinion in Holland apart from these letters, such a contention might be rejected out of hand. But it has already been pointed out that he was not alone in thinking Holland had been left defenceless by the government. Moreover, there is some evidence of the currency in Holland of suspicions about the Habsburg government which are but slightly less extravagant than those of Erasmus. The men of Hoorn, according to

Velius, were quite prepared to believe that Floris of Ijselstein and other lords had prior knowledge of the invasion. According to the anonymous Amsterdam chronicler, burgers of that city were convinced that a relief force marching under government auspices intended to betray Amsterdam to the Black Band; after this episode the town council had to prohibit citizens from speaking ill of 'the lords.'[155] In view of long-standing political tensions in the Habsburg Netherlands (described earlier in this chapter), and of the anguished state of mind normal for a population threatened by invasion, it is not surprising that suspicions of this kind should come to the surface. It remains unknown how widespread such feelings may have been, or whether they persisted after the immediate military crisis. Here again, in a different way, the value of Erasmus' letters as an historical source is vindicated. When he speaks of government 'tricks,' he is not merely giving rein to the inclinations of his own suspicious mind; rather, he gives voice to misgivings, perhaps also to a frustrated political will, felt by some at least of his countrymen.[156]

Erasmus' letters, when tested against other accounts available for this period, have thus proven to be a source for which some value may be claimed. Charles v's politic rule, falling between the unpopular Maximilian and the harsh policies of Philip II, is generally thought to have reconciled the Netherlands population to the Habsburg dynasty. Erasmus' letters suggest that a deep suspicion of the government may have continued into the early years of Charles's reign. Moreover, in connection with a possible focus for resistance to government demands, he refers not to the Estates General, which have claimed the interest of historians, but to the provincial Estates of Brabant and Holland, which were actually more important at this time, and for which a much more abundant documentation has survived. Struck by certain passages in the 1515 *Adagia*, such as the invocation to Brutus in 'Ut fici oculis incumbunt,'[157] E.T. Kuiper wondered whether Erasmus might have been a source for Protestant monarchomachs of the later sixteenth century, both French and Dutch. Against Kuiper, Ferdinand Geldner points out that the passage in question is immediately qualified: 'Yet for now [evil princes] must be tolerated, lest tyranny be replaced by anarchy, an evil almost worse.' Geldner himself did not notice, however, that the entire passage was first added for the 1520 edition.[158] At least at the outset of Charles's reign, some of Erasmus' countrymen may have been more restive under Habsburg rule than has commonly been thought. It is a question which one hopes will merit the attention of Netherlands historians.

The fact that Erasmus' view was shared by some or many others does not make it any more plausible as an interpretation of the Guelders war. In the end, the Rotterdam humanist, as a political observer, was unable to extricate himself from the fundamental internal contradictions which characterized urban and provincial resistance to Habsburg centralization in the Netherlands. He faults the central government for not providing the means to defend its cities; yet it seems that the subsidy which Hollanders (at least the men of Gouda) 'complained' about was a request for funds to establish a permanent defence force, the *compagnies d'ordonnance*. In the letter to Rhenanus he attacks the government also for not allowing the towns of Holland to prosecute the war as they wished. But in earlier writings he appears to regard the war with Guelders as provoked solely by Maximilian's dynastic ambition, and hence not a matter of national concern.[159] These two points of view roughly correspond with the two different political milieux with which Erasmus had been associated. Willem Hermans and Cornelius Aurelius, friends from the south Holland monastic milieu where he spent his youth, stoutly supported Ijselstein and Nassau in their military ventures and called on Holland to unite against the enemy. Erasmus initially came to court in the train of Henry of Bergen, a member of a powerful family which, like the Nassaus and the Egmonds (Ijselstein), had fought for Maximilian in the civil wars of the 1480s; he had become an important person at court when he was able to boast to Hermans of his personal acquaintance with Floris of Ijselstein. But as early as the *Panegyricus* of 1504 he was, probably for reasons of conviction as well as of patronage, converted to the party of opposition to Maximilian, led by nobles like Chièvres, and by men of the robe like Francis Busleiden and Jean Sauvage; in keeping with sentiment in most Netherlands provinces, especially in the south, this party saw no national interest at stake in the conflict with Guelders. J.E.A.L. Struick, a recent student of the Guelders wars, believes Chièvres was wrong first not to recognize that national security demanded incorporating Guelders into the Burgundian sphere of influence, and second to believe that Guelders was controlled by France and hence could be neutralized by diplomacy.[160] As a client of Sauvage (and hence in a way of Chièvres), Erasmus seems to have shared the overly simple view of the Guelders conflict held by his patrons. As a private citizen, he sympathized with the aspirations of the towns represented in the Estates, towns which, to be sure, were still capable, within limits, of asserting an effective political will. But his dream that towns might stand together against Habsburg 'tyranny' was rendered idle by the jealousies and rivalries which prevented towns from sustained co-operation even on a provincial level. Those who supported both the war against Guelders and Habsburg rule in the Netherlands had perhaps the most consistent view of the national interest. For while subjection to the Habsburgs drew the Netherlands into unwanted foreign complications, the dynasty, at least in the person of Margaret of Austria, was the only force in the country which consistently took a broad view of national concerns. But in 1517, although he now appreciated the seriousness of the threat from Guelders, Erasmus could not draw from it the conclusion that the dynasty deserved the support of its subjects. He had already made up his mind, firmly, that the emperor had sinister designs in the Netherlands, and that Chièvres, steeped in the tyrannous traditions of an otiose aristocracy, was not to be trusted. He was, perhaps, too clever to see things in a sober and unimaginative way.

FIVE

Pope and Princes Play a Comedy

FROM THE BATTLE OF MARIGNANO in 1515 to 1521, Europe was filled with talk of peace and preparations for war. Worried by Turkish successes in the east, Leo x took up the old strategy of turning Europe's warlike energies to a better purpose. In Bologna in December 1515 the victorious Francis I promised the pope to go on crusade; accordingly, for 1516, and again the following year, the king received permission to levy a crusade tithe on the French clergy. News of the conference at Cambrai in March, where a partition of Italy was planned, made the task of peace more urgent. But by now the pope had other worries. Unlike Julius II, who never sought church lands for his relatives, Leo had found a pretext to deprive Francesco Maria della Rovere of the Duchy of Urbino in March 1516, so as to install his nephew, Lorenzo de'Medici. But Francesco Maria recaptured most of his territory in January 1517. In April a plot by several cardinals to poison the pope was uncovered. Pastor finds 'no doubt whatever' as to the existence of the plot, but many contemporaries thought otherwise, especially since the popular Cardinal Raffaele Riario, against whom the Medici had a family grievance, stood among the accused. Meanwhile the war in Urbino dragged on, at enormous expense to the pope, until Lorenzo was restored by Franco-Spanish mediation in September. Freed of domestic problems, but much diminished in moral stature, Leo now turned his attention to the crusade.[1]

On November 6 envoys from the major powers of Europe met with a commission of cardinals presided over by the pope himself. By November 12 a memorandum detailing plans for the crusade was ready for dispatch. Leo counted on a favourable reply from France, since he now endorsed French proposals for a marriage between his nephew, Lorenzo, and one of the king's Bourbon cousins. But while the marriage was quickly agreed to, the crusade proved a more difficult subject. Maximilian responded with a set of counterproposals intended chiefly to highlight his own role as commander-in-chief. Spain promised little, Venice nothing at all. Determined to try once more, Leo appointed four cardinals as legates *de latere* to Spain, France, England, and the Empire. After some delay, the legates, including Cardinals Campeggio for England and Cajetan for Germany, set out in April 1518.[2]

Modern historians admit both the reality of the Turkish peril and Leo's earnestness in resolving to meet it.[3] But the cry of 'crusade' had by now a hollow ring. As early as January 1517, a French agent in English pay was confident that 'the crusade is a fiction.' A few months later King Henry told the Venetian ambassador there could never be a crusade so long as Europe's princes (meaning the French) continued to practise their wonted treachery. After considerable delay in responding to the November 12 memorandum, Wolsey replied that no concerted action was possible at present, because 'they on whom the pope most relies [the French] are preparing a numerous army, and seeking for new causes of dissension.' Maximilian's counterproposals evoked even less enthusiasm. As Pace wrote Wolsey on March 24, the king 'did right well laugh at the device of the Emperor enempst the expedition to be made the first year against the Turk with other men's money.'[4]

There was indeed room for Wolsey's suspicion. New warships built in Normandy would serve no purpose in a crusade, but they could convey England's enemy, the Duke of Albany, into Scotland. For the Genoese galleys France sought to engage, Naples might be a more attractive goal than the far-off dominions of the Turk. In Switzerland the Anglo-Imperial alliance grew difficult to maintain, since Leo X seconded French diplomacy by undermining the position of Cardinal Schinner. In February 1518 Schinner reported to Margaret of Savoy that Francis I was asking a league with the Swiss 'for the security of his kingdom during his absence' on crusade. Should the Diet not want a formal alliance, the king wished to hire fifteen thousand men 'against the Turks and his other enemies.' If French proposals are accurately represented here, Schinner's blunt comment is understandable: 'Whither they tend is easily seen. If the rest sleep, at last on their head the beam will fall.' But it must be said that France was not the only nation whose purposes admitted of various interpretations. Writing to Pace in April 1518, Budé felt Francis I was inclined to peace, but wondered whether England was not attempting merely to gain time to secure her exposed position at Tournay.[5]

In such a climate of mutual suspicion, the pope's legates had an impossible task. Campeggio was told that English law prohibited the exercise of legatine authority by a foreign cardinal. The king might waive the prohibition, but only if the Cardinal of York were to share in the office of legate *de latere*. Campeggio was thus kept waiting in Calais until the necessary permission arrived in late July. At the Diet of Augsburg Cajetan met a humiliating rebuff. To allay fears about how crusade contributions might actually be spent, Cajetan proposed to entrust the collection and custody of the tithe to a committee appointed by the Diet. But in late August the Estates of Germany, enflamed by long-standing national grievances against the Roman Curia, refused to grant a crusade tithe under any conditions.[6]

Meanwhile the Cardinal of York matured his own plans for a concert among the nations. Some scholars believe that Wolsey genuinely sought to promote peace, others that his real aim was to bring the pope and the Catholic king into a league against France.[7] Whatever his aims, there can be no doubt of his success in making himself, and not the pope, the arbiter among nations. Skilfully offering an English alliance to each in turn, Wolsey induced Francis, Charles, and Maximilian to conclude a 'treaty of universal peace' signed in London in October 1518.[8] In vain did Leo protest that 'universal peace' was more difficult to achieve than the five-years' truce envisioned in papal proposals, and that chances for a crusade would accordingly be diminished (on this point the Venetian ambassador to London concurred).[9]

As Wolsey strove to bring Habsburg and Valois closer together, the two dynasties struggled against each other over the imperial succession. From early 1518, Spanish gold vied with French largesse to bind the allegiance of wavering Electors either to Francis I or to Charles of Spain. When Maximilian died in January 1519, the bargaining for votes intensified. To complicate matters, the pope supported Francis I's candidacy, while in May Henry VIII sent Richard Pace to Frankfurt with secret instructions to promote his own candidacy.[10] For some days after the Electors convened no majority could be found. According to some reports (including one by Erasmus), anti-Habsburg forces made a last-minute effort to throw the election to Frederick the Wise, Elector of Saxony, who, on June 27, was offered the crown and refused; other sources (whose credibility is sharply disputed) maintain that Frederick was actually 'elected' but abdicated soon after.[11] In any event, on June 28 the Catholic king was duly elected and proclaimed as Charles v, King of the Romans.

By tradition the King of the Romans must be crowned in Aachen. The fact that Charles's route thither lay through the English channel provided Wolsey with another opportunity to interpose his diplomacy between Valois and Habsburg. He arranged for personal meetings between his own sovereign and the two continental monarchs, but with precedence given the Catholic king. After Charles had conferred with Henry at Sandwich, Henry, with a retinue of 3,997 persons, set sail for a rendezvous with Francis I on the border of Calais and Picardy. The Field of the Cloth of Gold, more important for its pageantry than for any diplomatic results, lasted from June 4 to June 24. Henry then visited once more with Charles at Gravelines and Calais (July 5–14) before the emperor set forth for his coronation at Aachen, followed by a meeting of German princes in Cologne, and, finally, his historic encounter with Martin Luther at the Diet of Worms.[12]

The concurrent Revolt of the Comuneros in Castile, promising (as it seemed) to occupy Charles's attention for some time, encouraged Francis I to support military probes against Spanish Navarre and the southern Low Countries. Unexpected Habsburg victories in both areas prompted the two parties to accept still another offer of mediation by Wolsey in the summer of 1521. But Leo x had now concluded an offensive alliance with Charles, and when Wolsey came to Calais in August to mediate, he was armed with secret instructions for an alliance with Charles against France. A treaty to this effect was signed in late November, just as news came that Hispano-papal forces had defeated the French in Milan. As Karl Brandi has said, the war which Chièvres spent his life trying to avoid had now begun.[13]

Now at the height of his fame, Erasmus was favoured more than ever by Europe's great men. For example, he was present for meetings between Charles and Henry at Calais (July 1520), and between Charles and Wolsey at Bruges (August 1521), both as a councillor to the emperor and at the invitation of his English friends.[14] His extant correspondence, however, reveals little of what he may have thought about Wolsey's carefully orchestrated diplomacy. In some published letters, mostly written while seeking an invitation from England, he does compliment the cardinal (or the king) for converting the truce proposed by Pope Leo into a 'perpetual peace.'[15] But his true opinion of Henry's all-powerful minister is probably better indicated in a guarded comment to John Fisher, which clearly refers to church reforms decreed by Wolsey in his new capacity as legate *de latere*: 'As to what is being done there about reform of the clergy, as they call it, I fear those responsible will zealously imitate the example of physicians, who first empty the body they undertake to cure.'[16] Moreover, if he commented less often on political events during these years, prudence was not the only reason, for he was increasingly preoccupied with the defence of his program for religious and moral renewal. Successive editions of his Greek New Testament brought the active hostility of conservative theologians in many quarters, who were not slow to charge that Erasmus, by tampering with interpretations long hallowed, opened the way for the heresies of Martin Luther. His life's work threatened, the great humanist gave way to fantasies of a 'conspiracy' against him by those he called 'mendicant tyrants.'[17] Hence when he viewed this or that court, he was less interested in questions of war or peace than in whether the prince was (like Charles v) under the sway of the enemies of *bona literae*,[18] or whether he had strength enough to still their voices – as Henry VIII did, thanks to More and Pace.[19]

While not as rich in political comment as the years he spent at court, this last period of Erasmus' stay in the Netherlands does display, as it were, a *terminus ad quem* for the evolution of his political opinions. Both on international affairs and on events in the Netherlands, the last chapter in the history of Erasmus' political opinions is a first chapter in the story of his view of the Reformation.

Just as he believed certain Lowlands 'princes' had plotted against the liberties of Holland in the Guelders war, Erasmus saw pope and princes conspiring together under the false banner of a crusade. Like his reports on the Black Band campaign, his reports on the proposed crusade are found in letters not meant for publication and directed to the same circle of intimate friends: More, Colet, Fisher, and Warham in England, and Beatus Rhenanus in Basel. A further link between the two sets of letters is that Rhenanus himself – to whom Erasmus addressed the most circumstantial account of the Guelders war – seems to have been a source for the news 'from Switzerland' which Erasmus passes on to English friends.[20] Finally, in two of the letters, Erasmus makes reference to what may have been unattached mercenary bands ('thieves,' 'robbers')[21] immediately before or after his remarks on the crusade.

On 22 February 1518 he wrote to John Sixtin, a Netherlander long resident in Britain, that 'pope and prince are acting a new comedy, pretending war against the Turk when something much different is in the works.'[22] Two weeks later, in letters to Warham, Fisher, More, and Colet, all dated March 5, he spells out the accusation in greater detail, based on 'what they write from Switzerland.' With his usual sensitivity to personality, Erasmus approached each of his friends in a different way. To Colet, the zealous church reformer, he wrote that the shamelessness of the papacy was displayed also in 'these incessant indulgences.'[23] The studious and devout Fisher was told that 'the tricks of princes, the impudence of the Roman Curia' made Erasmus wish to 'withdraw from this most wicked world.'[24] To More, who loved practical jokes, he quoted a papal pronouncement (invented by Erasmus himself) on the proper penitential spirit for a time of crusade: till this terrible war is brought to a happy conclusion, 'husbands and wives may sleep in the same room, but not in the same bed.' The point of the joke seems to be that Dame Alice would now find a pious excuse for doing as she wished.[25] In each case, however, the basic message was a variant on his comment to Warham: 'Concerning the war against the Turks, it is not pleasing to write about what appears to be so. Unless I am deceived, one thing is being done, another pretended. From Switzerland they write that the project is aimed at driving the Spaniards from Naples. For Lorenzo, the pope's nephew, seeks to occupy Campania, having taken to wife the daughter of the King of Navarre. These details do not altogether escape the Swiss, crude though they be.' (In fact, although Lorenzo was indeed about to contract a French marriage, Erasmus' informants were a year behind the times as to the identity of his bride).[26] Hence things were come 'to the summit of tyranny,' so much so that the unabashed tyranny of the Turks themselves might be preferable. 'For the pope and the princes,' as he wrote Rhenanus, 'are treating the people not like men, but like milch cows.'[27] It was in the context of these reflections on papal 'tyranny' that a hitherto obscure Saxon monk first came to Erasmus' attention. Along with the crusade memorandum of November 18, he sent More a copy of the *Conclusions* (as Luther's 95 Theses were called) *concerning Papal Pardons*, to which his comment to Colet on indulgences seems also to allude.[28]

As noted earlier, many observers were sceptical about the 1517–18 crusade project. But in English documents of the period the papal Curia is treated far more gently than by Erasmus: Francis I is the villain, Leo must be persuaded to withdraw his trust in him.[29] Erasmus' views about the 'shamelessness' of the Curia were perhaps closer to those of Cardinal Schinner, who might have been one of his informants 'from

Switzerland.' Since the Cardinal of Sion knew that Leo x was actively working against him in order to satisfy the French,[30] he may have seen the pope more as an active collaborator in French schemes than as their dupe. But Erasmus says nothing about France in particular. Save for comments about the 'tricks' of princes in general, he reserves his indignation for the curia. It may be that the Urbino war embittered him towards a pope whose peace-making intentions he had once trusted,[31] or that charges against Cardinal Riario – an old friend and patron[32] – convinced him of Leo's duplicity. Whatever his reasons, Erasmus speaks with uncommon sharpness. At one time he vilified Julius II. Later he denounced Maximilian I in terms which would have surprised his francophile patrons. Now, where men like Pace or Schinner might have seen in papal politics the usual double game (if Lorenzo's marriage did not bind Francis I to the crusade, it would still advance the Medici family), Erasmus saw a sink of iniquity.

At a time when even Luther still spoke of the papacy with respect, only the private letters of young German humanists – men like Wilhelm Nesen and Michael Hummelberger – speak about the Roman Curia with a bitterness which matches or excels that of Erasmus.[33] A trip to Basel (May–September 1518) for the second edition of his New Testament permitted Erasmus to renew acquaintances in Germany. As had happened before, he found the boldness of his German friends contagious.[34] En route back to Louvain he stayed five days with Count Herman von Neuenahr, a humanist official of the Archbishop of Cologne and a staunch defender of the humanist and Hebrew scholar Johann Reuchlin in his battle against the Dominicans of Cologne and their allies. (At Spires a mutual friend, Herman von dem Busche, told Erasmus how the Inquisitor of Cologne had been ejected by his fellow Dominicans after their convent was threatened by one of the count's noble kinfolk; the story was not true, but Erasmus happily relayed it to friends in Basel.)[35] It was probably from Neuenahr, who had been at Augsburg, that Erasmus learned how the Diet rejected Cajetan's proposals.[36] Neuenahr also told him that Charles would be returning from Castile, a bit of good news Erasmus could not quite believe.[37] The news from Augsburg, however, he readily conveyed to the same English friends he had written to about the crusade a few months earlier. To his mind there was still a conspiracy – indeed he now wondered whether the Turks might be colluding with the pope and the princes – but at least Germany was able to resist the effort to 'make men into gods, and turn the priesthood into tyranny.'[38]

In October he was visited at Louvain by Helius Eobanus Hessus, who brought letters from Luther's friends in Erfurt, one containing a coin stamped with the image of Luther's prince, Elector Frederick the Wise. Erasmus sent back letters politely complimentary to Luther, if a bit distant – for he already feared that Luther would serve the enemies of *bonae literae* only too well – but expressing also his belief that (in Greek) *'the monarchy of the Roman High Priest* (as that see now is) is the plague of Christendom.'[39] The following spring Justus Jonas came from Wittenberg, bringing some recent works by Luther which made Erasmus think of him as a 'mighty trumpet of Gospel truth.' Now more than ever he was convinced that Luther must be defended. Jonas also brought a letter from the Elector of Saxony. Frederick impressed Erasmus by saying that he protected Luther not for the sake of the man, but for the sake of the principle that no one should be condemned without a fair and proper hearing.[40] It happened that Erard de la Marck, Bishop of Liège, with whom Erasmus had previously discussed Luther, was then in Brussels for a conference with Margaret of Savoy, possibly concerning the strategy to be followed in the forthcoming electoral meeting at Frankfurt; passing through Louvain, he asked Erasmus for a copy of Frederick's letter, together with the coin in his image, both of which were duly sent on to him.[41]

Like others in the Netherlands and in Germany, Erasmus welcomed the election of Charles v as King of the Romans. In a letter meant for public consumption he described it as a victory of merit over French gold.[42] Charles's cause was warmly promoted in orations by Neuenahr and another Cologne humanist, who borrowed some of their arguments from Erasmus.[43] But Erasmus himself was especially interested in the part Frederick the Wise had played at Frankfurt. Writing to the Elector's secretary, George Spalatin – the same letter cited in the last chapter, in which Erasmus recalls the fate of Asperen and laments that the 'remnants of democracy' are passing away – he praised Frederick's restraint: 'He in my opinion refused the empire with greater praise than others sought it.' This description of Frederick was conveyed to him, he said, by Richard Pace, who evidently passed through Louvain on his way back to England. (En route to Frankfurt, Pace had been furnished with letters of recommendation by Erasmus.[44] Pace later told the Venetian ambassadors to England and France that Frederick was actually elected; it may be that he kept the full story from Erasmus, or, more likely, that his story grew in the telling.[45]) Six weeks later Erasmus passed on to John Fisher some further evidence of Frederick's rectitude which he had gleaned from conversation with Erard de la Marck:

> With magnanimity he refused the imperial crown offered by all, and this the day before the election of Charles – to whom the title emperor would never have come were it not so desired by Frederick, who shone forth more brightly in refusing the honour than he would have by accepting it. For when asked whom he thought should be chosen, he said he thought no one but Charles equal to the burden of so great an office. Offered thirty thousand gulden by our people because of this splendid reply, he steadfastly refused. Urged to permit at least ten thousand to be distributed among his servants, he replied: 'Let them take if they will; but let no one remain tomorrow who has taken a single gulden today.'[46]

Erasmus (or Erard) exaggerated the Saxon Elector's probity, for Frederick did make a profit, even if he was almost the only Elector whose vote was not for sale.[47] But the stories he heard from Pace and de la Marck can only have increased his respect for Luther's protector.

Meanwhile, Luther's own cause gained steadily in Germany, even as proceedings were begun against him in Rome. When the bull of excommunication was promulgated against him in the summer of 1520, Erasmus feared the worst: for Luther's enemies, having destroyed the Saxon reformer by charges of heresy, would next take aim at Erasmus and his program for the reform of Christian piety. Not lacking in courage, he attempted to prevent the condemnation of Luther by publishing an anonymous tract which asserted that *Exsurge, Domine!* was not a genuine papal bull. In his capacity as councillor to Charles v, he followed the imperial train first to Aachen, then to the meeting of princes in Cologne, where he showed his tract to Erard de la Marck and others he believed sympathetic, and had a personal interview with Frederick the Wise, in which he urged the Elector to persevere in his defence of Luther. But the great conflict was not to be put off by stratagems. In May of 1521, when Luther confronted the emperor at Worms, Erasmus retired to semi-seclusion in the small town of Anderlecht outside Brussels, away from the growing storm of controversy. In November of the same year, fearing that Charles might add his own voice to those who wished him to write against Luther, Erasmus migrated to Basel in order to maintain his independence.[48]

The subsequent history of Erasmus' relations with Luther is well known and need not be repeated here.[49] The point to be stressed is that a line of continuity runs between his interpretation of the Guelders war and his initial willingness to defend Luther as a sturdy foe of Roman tyranny. Convinced of the treachery of the great nobles of his own country, he formed a like interpretation of papal crusade politics, and shared it with the same few trusted friends. If Christendom were indeed threatened by a tyrannical conspiracy of such proportions, one had to rejoice that in Germany, at least, Luther and the German princes – the Estates at Augsburg, the Elector who protected Luther – were strong enough to stand against it. No one can or should minimize the profound religious convictions which governed Erasmus' changing views of Luther.[50] But one important strand in this complex skein of thought traces back to his political opinions. If, as was suggested in the introduction, Erasmus in the 1520s turned his attention away from politics to the growing religious controversy, it may also be said that the structure or form of his earlier political opinions left important traces in his understanding of the religious conflict.

As the religious conflict grew in scope, Erasmus' interest in politics in the Low Countries narrowed down to the question of who supported or opposed church reform. On one side were those who treated as heresy the criticism of any particle of church tradition. Erasmus would sometimes describe the court figures who gave ear to such men as misled by a 'superstitious' attachment to the external practices of religion. But the defenders of tradition themselves were nothing but 'hypocrites' or 'mendicant tyrants' who attacked new ideas only in order to protect forms of piety lucrative to themselves.[51] Moreover, enemies of reform tended to see the new learning as the real source of Luther's heresies. Many a preacher who attacked Luther had earlier denounced *The Praise of Folly* or the 1516 New Testament.[52] Hence Erasmus inferred, as he was wont to do, that the mendicants were mounting a 'conspiracy' against him and his vision of biblical learning; Luther's downfall would be but the first stage in a plan whose ultimate aim was to destroy *bonae literae*.[53] This view of the orthodox party's strategy, improbable or not, gained plausibility from the fact that two Antwerp humanist friends of Erasmus (Cornelius Grapheus and Nicholas Buscodensis) were among the first four persons arrested by the Territorial Inquisition established by Charles v in April 1522.[54]

To counteract this campaign against *bonae literae* and against himself, Erasmus looked for men at court who felt much as he did about the 'mendicant tyrants.' Like so many contemporary observers, he believed the 'tumults' of the Reformation were due less to Luther's teaching than to widespread popular hatred of clerical privileges and exactions. 'The greater part of the people in Holland, Zeeland, and

Flanders know of Luther's teaching,' he wrote from Basel during the Peasants' Revolt in 1525, 'and they are carried along by a more than mortal hatred of the monks.'[55] To those he believed might listen, he urged modifications of church law – by secular authority if need be – so as to diminish the privileged position of the clergy and thereby remove the real cause of the schism.[56] During the 1520s many government officials in the Low Countries did in fact attempt to strengthen secular control of church practice and church property,[57] hoping perhaps to forestall popular uprisings against the clergy like that in 's Hertogenbosch in 1524.[58] At the same time local magistrates – notably in Amsterdam – stubbornly resisted Charles v's edicts for the persecution of heretics.[59] The burgermasters of Amsterdam and other public officials have sometimes been called 'Erasmian'[60] in outlook, but, without prejudging the question of how widely his books may have been read, it seems more prudent to reverse the emphasis by saying that the great humanist articulated with particular clarity a point of view fairly common in ruling circles. In any case Erasmus took little notice of government measures aimed at church wealth.[61] His objective was to protect both his own reputation and the new biblical theology which he promoted. With his great faith in the power of education, he doubtless believed that the best remedy for superstition and 'clerical tyranny' was the gradual spread of 'learned piety' (*docta pietas*).

It will be recalled from chapter 3 that Erasmus left court when the Franciscan Jean Briselot was appointed Charles's confessor through the influence of Chièvres.[62] Briselot's attacks on Erasmus were abetted by other friars and preachers who frequented the court, notably the Carmelite Nicholas Baechem of Egmond (Egmondanus), named inquisitor by Charles in 1520, and James Latomus, professor of theology at Louvain,[63] and also by two papal legates accredited to the court, Jerome Aleander and Marino Carocciolo.[64] *The Praise of Folly's* satiric treatment of saints beloved of courtiers enabled Briselot to poison the minds (so Erasmus thought) of John and Anthony of Bergen, brothers of his earliest patron.[65] Briselot and others were successful too with the powerful Antoine de Lalaing, Count of Hoogstraaten, who also had a wife reputed to be 'superstitious' in the traditional manner. Erasmus' friends later regretted his inability to appeal to Hoogstraaten, as well they might, since he became Margaret of Austria's most influential councillor.[66] Erard de la Marck befriended Erasmus for a time, as was seen earlier. But when he returned from the Diet of Worms with a cardinal's hat and took a leading role among those who favoured stern repression of heresy, Erasmus began to regard him as an enemy.[67]

Francis van der Hulst, the lay jurist named head of the Territorial Inquisition in 1522, with Egmondanus among his collaborators, was known to Erasmus as a bitter foe of *bonae literae*.[68] He was convinced that the new inquisitors took advantage of their office to carry on a personal vendetta against the new learning; Grapheus, for example, owed his imprisonment to the fact that he once called Egmondanus a fool.[69] The new tribunal roused much opposition in Holland, where each town claimed for its citizens the right to refuse summons to any court outside its walls. As a gesture of conciliation, Margaret of Austria recognized in Holland the *jus de non evocando*, the right of citizens not to be 'evoked' before any but a local court. She also made Hulst's decisions subject to review by Josse Lauweryns, president of the Grand Council of Mechelen.[70] Although he wrote Lauweryns that he 'rejoiced from the heart' at this appointment, Erasmus in fact had no confidence in the president, since he too was 'more than mortally hostile to good letters,' even to the point of refusing to read Budé and other exponents of the new humanistic jurisprudence.[71] Meanwhile Hulst chafed under his new restrictions. He first secured a papal letter of appointment as inquisitor, then by its authority caused in February 1523 the arrest of three men in Holland and their transfer to Vilvoorde castle (near Brussels) for interrogation and trial.[72] One of those arrested was the humanist lawyer Cornelius Hoen, apparently a close friend of Erasmus. Hoen is believed to be the author of a sacramentarian tract on the Eucharist which greatly influenced the Swiss reformer Ulrich Zwingli. But to Erasmus he was simply one more learned man 'who was heretical because he disagreed with Egmondanus.'[73] Since the internments at Vilvoorde violated the *jus de non evocando*, Hulst united Holland against him; when in the ensuing legal battle Hulst was found to have fabricated evidence, he was dismissed (December 1523). As Erasmus observed, he was saved from execution only by the intervention of two powerful allies, John of Bergen and Erard de la Marck.[74]

Although Erasmus is known to have intervened in Rome for a friend accused of heresy,[75] there is no indication he ever did so in Brussels. Apart from protecting the nascent Collegium Trilingue at Louvain,[76] he merely sought to recover his pension as councillor to Charles (it had not been paid since Sauvage's death) and to procure an order imposing silence on his critics. For some time his efforts to find a patron met with temporary success at best, since those he contacted were not fully reassured by such assurances of his orthodoxy as Erasmus was willing to give.[77] His first bit of luck came in June 1521, when Cardinal Schinner proposed a paraphrase of the four Gospels.[78] Postponed till he was settled in Basel, the project soon gave him an entrée to Charles V. In January 1522 the Spanish humanist Juan Luis Vives sent a long account of the machinations of Erasmus' enemies at court, urging him to write to friends among the courtiers, especially George Halewin. Erasmus responded by sending Halwein a copy of the just-completed *Paraphrase of Matthew*, dedicated to Charles V; Halewin showed the book to Charles's new confessor, the Franciscan Jean Glapion, who brought it to the emperor in chapel with his personal commendation.[79] This news, together with a favourable report by Vives on Mercurino Gattinara and some of Charles's Spanish advisers, led Erasmus to believe that by going to Brussels he might not only collect his pension but also find a sympathetic audience for his views on ending the schism. But an attack of the stone interrupted his journey at Schlettstadt and caused his return to Basel, where he received word of the arrest of Graphaeus and Buscodensis.[80] This triumph for his enemies did not destroy his hopes about Charles V, however, for word from England (where Charles visited Henry VIII en route to Spain) had confirmed reports from the Low Countries that the emperor was highly pleased by the *Paraphrase of Matthew*.[81] Although he had nothing tangible to show for it, he could still boast to a friend in August 1522, 'I have Caesar as my protector.'[82]

A few months later he had further encouraging news from Brussels. The young theologian Herman Lethmatius wrote that his employer, Jean Carondolet, Archbishop of Palermo and an influential member of the council, greatly admired Erasmus and would welcome the dedication of a book. Erasmus in reply urged Lethmatius to defend *bonae literae* against the unprincipled attacks of Hulst and Egmondanus, and announced that the forthcoming *Opera* of Hilary of Poitiers had been dedicated to Carondolet. In a long preface whose application to present circumstances the archbishop could no doubt infer, Erasmus praised St Hilary for, among other things, his resistance to efforts by the Arian Emperor Constantius to impose on Christian subjects by force of persecution the creed of his choice.[83] In return, Carondolet raised with Margaret of Austria the matter of Erasmus' pension; Charles V sent a letter to the same effect some months later. Margaret decided, however, to insist on his returning to Brabant as a condition for collecting it. He could not accept, as he explained to a friend, because 'Egmondanus reigns there ... and has Hulst for a colleague.'[84] By this time

Hulst had been dismissed from office, but his successor, Nicholas Coppin, was in Erasmus' view still another determined foe of *bonae literae*.[85]

Two years later Erasmus was still urging Carondolet and others to see about his pension and still seeking a letter from someone with sufficient authority to silence his critics.[86] The pension never was paid. But early in 1526 'certain friends' did at last obtain 'a severe and threatening prohibition from the emperor against certain knaves in Louvain.' Those affected, however, including James Latomus and Nicholas Coppin, threatened to resign from office as inquisitors 'if their authority were to be infringed upon by such prohibitions.' As Erasmus tells the story in writing Gattinara for yet another *interdictum*, 'The Archbishop of Palermo [Carondolet] took my part, but Josse [Lauweryns], President of the Council of Mechelen, took the other part, a man who has always seemed to me good and learned after his fashion, but, as you know, a professed enemy of letters. What more? Through his agency, the emperor's edict was given an official interpretation which enabled those men to dare still more.' Finally, Gattinara himself wrote to the University of Louvain in February 1527: 'When first I heard that some of you, in contempt of the imperial edict sent you in this regard, are daily conspiring to defame the name of Erasmus, I did not wish to advise the emperor of the matter, knowing he would take it ill that you had thus evaded his commands. Instead, I prefer advising you in a friendly manner not to permit anything further of the kind, to the shame of the emperor, the university, and yourselves.'[87] Gattinara's friendly advice did not really silence Erasmus' critics, but it may well have prevented a formal examination of his works for their theological correctness, such as occurred in Spain later the same year. It was the best Erasmus could hope for.

During this period in Basel, Erasmus kept fairly well informed about events in his 'patria.' Judging from what has survived, many of the now lost letters from close friends in Brussels or Louvain must have given detailed accounts of court politics. The few observations he makes on personal alliances – such as that Hulst was saved by his connections with John of Bergen and Erard de la Marck – are taken seriously by De Hoop Scheffer, the only scholar to have studied the religious policy of the Netherlands government during this period.[88] It must be noted, however, that he was once again misled by his predilection for connecting politics with culture. Just as he thought men raised in the traditional chivalric manner would be proponents of war, he assumed that proponents of *bonae literae* would be enemies of the inquisition and vice versa. In fact, humanists and friends of Erasmus could be found (in Amsterdam, for example)[89] among those who decried the laxity of local magistrates in allowing heretics to go unpunished. More striking is the case of Josse Lauweryns, the president of Mechelen. In 1527, when Amsterdam came under attack by the Council of Holland for not enforcing the 'placards' against heresy, the town secretary and one of the burgermasters came to Mechelen to seek support for the city's position. Carondolet referred them to Lauweryns, who told them exactly what they wished to hear on the points that were in dispute: that citizens need not be prosecuted for their actions against the clergy or their beliefs, but only for violating the emperor's edicts; and that the edicts need not be enforced according to the letter if the circumstances of the accused (such as pregnancy) indicated otherwise.[90] If one cannot infer from this incident that the president of Mechelen favoured the spread of heretical ideas, one should not infer from the episode recounted by Erasmus (as he does) that Lauweryns acted from hatred of *bonae literae* in permitting Latomus and Coppin to evade the imperial command of silence. The common denominator in both cases seems to be a tendency to construe imperial edicts broadly, in keeping perhaps with the vigorous tradition of local autonomy among His Majesty's Netherlands subjects. In general, what Erasmus sees as a struggle between two forms of religious culture is better described as a conflict between time-honoured local privilege and the central government's effort to impose religious uniformity.

Conclusion

MERE COLLATION OF THE POLITICAL VIEWS scattered throughout Erasmus' works is sufficient to dispel a number of misconceptions. For one who has been called 'apolitical'[1] he was surprisingly well informed; even if friends in high places did not make him privy to their darkest secrets, there are occasional hints that he knew more than was safe to say.[2] Far from conceiving of the state strictly as a welfare institution, not endowed with powers of defence, or entrusting the public weal solely to the good will of the prince,[3] he hoped the Estates might check the 'tyranny' of princes (as the Diet of Augsburg in 1518), and blamed the government for not doing enough to ward off invasion from Guelders. Often described simply as a cosmopolitan intellectual, out of touch with the rising national sentiment of his age,[4] he was for a time aligned with the 'national' party in the Netherlands, and he clung stubbornly to the idea that each *patria* ought to be governed by a 'natural' prince of its own. (If any man of this era was truly cosmopolitan, it was Mercurino Gattinara, the Savoyard architect of Charles V's supranational empire, who admired Erasmus but, like many of his critics, did not understand him.)[5]

Perhaps more pervasive, certainly more difficult to refute, is the view that Erasmus the moralist was of necessity blind to the dynamic nature of power, and hence failed to grasp the mainspring of relations between states.[6] The principle which allegedly eluded him may be formulated in different (though not exclusive) ways, depending on whether one is speaking of a prince or of a 'state' in some more abstract sense. According to Machiavelli's *Prince*, a high-minded ruler will naturally desire to increase his dominions, and, if he be successful, will always be praised; Jouvenel echoes Machiavelli in his maxim that 'command' tends naturally to expand because it is a species of egotism.[7] Alternatively, to follow Jacqueline de Romilly's lucid exposition of Thucydides, one may assert that power expands because powerful states are led, even against their will, to intervene beyond their borders.[8] This view too can be found in sixteenth-century sources, when diplomats begin to understand the Wars of Italy as a struggle for hegemony in Europe. But, as noted in chapter 2, the force of such arguments was not apparent until later stages of the conflict.[9] If it is clear that the Wars of Italy or the Habsburg-Valois wars can have no simple explanation,[10] it is also clear that the campaigns which Erasmus and Budé had specifically in view – Louis XII's attack on Milan or Henry VIII's invasion of France – are given more dignity than they deserve if one applies to them the concept of strategic necessity.

Machiavelli's account of power in *The Prince* (as distinct from *The Discourses*) is in fact not far removed from Erasmus' description of monarchical power. Differences in principle between Erasmus and Machiavelli are in part a matter of national perspective.[11] For Italian thinkers, to whom the 'barbarian' invasions were almost as little subject to control as natural disasters, there was little point in asking whether Charles VIII or Louis XII had crossed the Alps on a mere whim or from 'reason of state.' Conversely, 'natural' subjects of these same princes had every reason to inquire into the necessity of campaigns which might cause nearly as much hardship at home as they did abroad. But there is a further difference which can only be explained in the light of Erasmus' Christian ethics. If his objections to contemporary warfare were based solely on the principle of the well-being of the *patria*, he would have granted, as Budé did, that the same principle might on occasion require a limited aggression.[12] One cannot imagine Budé, much less Machiavelli, insisting that the prince must answer to God for 'each least drop of blood,' or urging that the Christian prince who cannot maintain his state without great loss of life ought rather to resign.[13] One who lived in the age of Henry VIII or Francis I and yet could say such things lays himself open, surely, to the charge of naivety.[14] Erasmus might have replied that moral standards set beyond the reach of sinful men are preferable to those within which people (or princes) can live comfortably.[15] As noted in chapter 2, one cannot exclude the possibility that Erasmus, hoping to trouble the consciences of the powerful, consciously chose to practise the folly which he elsewhere praises.[16]

When he describes to Beatus Rhenanus how Holland has been betrayed by its rulers, Erasmus does not name the guilty parties. Nonetheless it is not difficult to guess whom he has in mind. Sauvage's absence during this period – he had already sailed for Spain – removed from Charles's council its most important non-noble member. Later, explaining to various friends how the Black Band was spared, so that its members might be recruited if need be to keep the populace in subjection, Erasmus leaves no doubt as to his belief that this particular bit of treachery was due to 'the princes' in command at Venlo, including Nassau.[17] Elsewhere he suggests that youthful princes are prevented from becoming strong and effective kings because they are corrupted by tyrannical, self-serving *tutores* (Chièvres?) from among the *optimates*, men who 'strive by every means to prevent the public from enjoying peace' because they know more is permitted them in time of war.[18] One may infer, then, that his deep mistrust of the government was, more specifically, a mistrust of the great noblemen who served the realm as provincial governors and military commanders.

Erasmus and his friend More were set apart from many other humanists by their contempt for the traditional aristocracy and its mores.[19] Budé was willing to recognize in the chivalric sense of honour (recast in classical terms) the basis for a political ethic. In this respect he conformed to one of the basis assumptions of classical *paideia*, according to which man's capacity for anger – what Plato called *thumos* or 'spirit' – is the well-spring not only of the sense of honour, but also of virtue in general. Erasmus, perhaps because his vision of Christian *humanitas* left small room for the values of strife,[20] found in the whole culture of chivalry nothing of redeeming significance. But since he did believe that moral decisions flow from one's character, which in turn is formed by what one is taught in youth – for these too were basic premises of humanist pedagogy – he could never trust men who had been formed from youth in 'the stupid and tyrannical fables of King Arthur.' Not content with the observation, in itself sensible enough, that tales of ancient glory might whet the appetite of a bellicose young prince, Erasmus seems to have made a general rule: men steeped in humane letters (like Sauvage) might be expected to work for peace; but Chièvres and others of his class, military men by upbringing as well as by profession, could be expected only to foment war. One might speak here of a form of educational determinism,[21] a Renaissance humanist precedent, perhaps, of what Raymond Williams has called the cultural view of politics.[22]

But it was suggested in chapter 4 that Erasmus' interpretation of the Guelders war is most interesting not because it is wrong, and wildly so, but because it seems to have had some currency among his countrymen. There are some indications that others who mistrusted the government as deeply as Erasmus did so for the same reasons: the men of Hoorn, according to Velius, were quick to suspect that 'the lords' commanding them (including Ijselstein) were privy to the plans of the enemy, and Amsterdam found it necessary to prohibit its citizens from speaking out against 'the lords.'[23] The great families of the realm had at this time a power that might well be envied. So large were the revenues from their estates – sometimes including sizeable towns – that Netherlands nobles were in the position, perhaps unusual for men of their class, of being the government's main creditors.[24] With monotonous regularity members of the great families succeeded one another as provincial governors and military commanders; Chièvres, for instance, commanded one of the *compagnies d'ordonnance* in his capacity as Grand Bailli of Namur, as did Nassau as Stadhouder in Holland. (Even lesser nobles of the border region between France and the Netherlands enjoyed, as Erasmus recognized, an international reputation as commanders of mercenary bands.)[25] It is also true, of course, that the great towns of the Netherlands were strongly represented in the Estates, and that they had considerable financial and even military resources. But it may be that the tide of political influence was running in favour of the aristocracy. Historians used to speak of the early modern state as an alliance between crown and *bourgeoisie* at the expense of the traditional nobility; now they are perhaps more likely to speak of a 'rearistocratization' of society in the early sixteenth century.[26] The question has yet to be studied for the Low Countries, though one might take note of Walther's opinion that legist members of the provincial councils were at this time losing ground to their noble confrères.[27] On the other hand, it seems that families who once were creditors of the government were themselves becoming indebted by the end of Charles v's reign.[28] Whatever may be the verdict of future research, the position of the great nobles was clearly such that it would not have been possible for the towns to oppose the government effectively without their collaboration. But in this period, as scholars have found for other countries, resistance to the will of the prince often foundered on mutual mistrust between townsmen and noblemen.[29] From a later vantage point, Erasmus' vision of the great nobles concocting plots against the liberties of the people will appear not only fanciful in its details, but short-sighted and self-defeating in principle. But the wisdom of hindsight ought not obscure what remains clear and strong in his political vision. Not knowing what was to come, he understood well enough, it seems, what was happening before his eyes: 'The remnants of ancient democracy,' as he wrote Spalatin, were indeed passing from view.

Notes

INTRODUCTION

1 See chapter 2, notes 173–8. Eduard Füeter *Geschichte des europäischen Staatensystems von 1492 bis 1559*; Henri Hauser *Débuts de l'âge moderne*. Geoffrey Parker (*The Army of Flanders and the Spanish Road* 6–8) dates from the 1530s another quantum leap in army size.

2 J.R. Hale 'Sixteenth-Century Explanations of War and Violence'

3 See especially Gennaro Sasso *Niccolò Machiavelli, storia del suo pensiero politico* and Federico Chabod *Machiavelli and the Renaissance*.

4 Vittorio di Caprariis *Francesco Guicciardini, dalla politica alla storia*; Rudolf von Albertini *Das florentinische Staatsbewusstsein im Übergang von der Republik zum Prinzipat*

5 On More, see chapter 2, note 92. *Querela pacis* LB IV, 640EF: '... ubi vident Christianos sic inter sese concertare, levioribus de causis quam Ethnici, crudelius quam impii, machinis tetrioribus quam ipsi? Quorum inventum est bombarda? Nonne Christianorum?'

6 Machiavelli *The Prince and the Discourses* 129 (*Discourses* I, vi): 'I certainly think that if Venice could be kept in this equilibrium it would be the best political existence ... But as all things human are kept in perpetual movement, and can never remain stable, states naturally either rise or decline'; 13 (*The Prince* iii): 'The desire to acquire possessions is a very natural and ordinary thing, and when those men do it who can do so successfully, they are always praised and not blamed.' Guicciardini (*The History of Italy* 34) believed Lorenzo de' Medici (d. 1492) had seen to it that 'the Italian situation should be maintained in a balance' between the states. But the intrusion of transalpine powers into Italian politics introduced a new and fearful uncertainty.

7 *Paraclesis* in *Erasmus Ausgewählte Werke* 143–4'

8 Garrett Mattingly ('Some Revisions of the Political History of the Renaissance') notes of the first world war period that Renaissance scholars

seemed to lose interest in political history as political tensions in Europe increased.

9 Friedrich Meinecke *Machiavellism: The Doctrine of Raison d'Etat and Its Place in Modern History*. Albert Sorel *Europe in the Old Regime*, though it deals with the eighteenth century, well illustrates the importance of Machiavelli for historians in the late nineteenth century.

10 Above, note 6

11 The most effective defender of the plausibility of the 'moralist' response to early modern warfare has been Heinrich Lutz (*Ragione di stato und christliche Staatsethik im 16en Jahrhundert* and *Christianitas afflicta*). For opposing views see chapter 1 of Kurt von Raumer *Ewiger Friede: Friedensrufe und Friedenspläne seit der Renaissance* and J.A. Fernandez 'Erasmus on the Just War.'

12 For a sample of the growing literature see: Konrad Lorenz *On Aggression*; Josef Rattner *Aggression und menschliche Natur*; Roger N. Johnson *Aggression in Men and Animals*. See the discussion of Erasmus' idea of *humanitas* in my *Erasmus: The Growth of a Mind*.

13 Freud *Beyond the Pleasure Principle*; Aristotle *Politics* VII 7

14 Herding, introduction. The timely appearance of Professor Herding's fine work has spared the author of this study many errors, of both commission and omission. Also see Herding 'Isokrates, Erasmus, und die *Institutio principis christiani*'; Roland Bainton 'The *Querela pacis* of Erasmus, Classical and Christian Sources'; Georges Chantraine, SJ, 'Mysterium et sacramentum dans le *Dulce bellum inexpertis*'; and Robert Regout, SJ, 'Erasmus en de Theorie van de Rechtvaardigden Oorlog.'

15 Ferdinand Geldner *Die Staatsauffassung und Fürstenlehre des Erasmus von Rotterdam* 88) concludes that Erasmus was 'a democrat in theory, an aristocrat by preference, and, in the face of reality, a monarchist.' Geldner's work is in most respects superior to the more recent study by Eberhard von Koerber, *Die Staatstheorie des Erasmus von Rotterdam*.

16 See below, chapter 2, note 116.

17 Jerry H. Bentley 'Humanists and Holy Writ: A Comparison of the Pauline Scholarship of Erasmus and Lorenzo Valla'

18 Elise Constantinescu-Bagdat *La 'Querela pacis' d'Erasme*; Ines Thürlemann *Erasmus von Rotterdam und Juan Luis Vives als Pazifisten*; Vittorio di Caprariis 'Il *Panegyricus* di Erasmo a Filippo di Borgogna'

19 Chantraine (above, note 14); E.T. Kuiper 'Erasmus als Politiek Propagandist'

20 Jerome Busleiden to Erasmus, letter 244a, lines 13–20, I, 491 (this and subsequent references to Erasmus' correspondence in this form are to Allen unless otherwise stated). By contrast, see More to Budé, ca. June 1520, in *The Correspondence of Sir Thomas More* ed Elizabeth Rogers, letter 96, lines 13–22, 246.

21 Allen I, appendix VIII, the Deventer letter-book

22 On world citizenship, see below, chapter 2, note 189. Robert T. Adams (*The Better Part of Valor: More, Erasmus, Colet and Vives on Humanism, War and Peace*) points the way for the kind of study to be undertaken here. His account of the English background stands up well to examination, save that his view of divisions in the royal council between friends of the new learning and their opponents is too schematic: see below, chapter 2, note 90.

23 The 'landen van herwarts over,' very roughly equivalent to the modern Benelux countries, were so called in distinction to the Duchy of Burgundy and other possessions of the Burgundian dukes lying to the south.

24 It is commonly agreed, for example, that the Estates were in this period losing ground to the principle of direct government by the prince: see below, chapter 2, note 187, and chapter 4, note 4.

25 A.F. Pollard *Wolsey*; J.C. Scarisbrick *Henry VIII* 46ff.; Jocelyne Russell 'Wolsey and the Campaign for Universal Peace.' See also below, chapter 5, note 16.

26 G. Dansaert *Guillaume de Croy, dit le Sage* has much anecdotal material from local archives, but is not analytic.

27 The contrast may be illustrated by his relations with Jean Sauvage (d. 1518) and his successor, Mercurino Gattinara, Chancellor of Castile. In return for Sauvage's promise of a bishopric in Italy or Spain, Erasmus suffered for a time the humiliating experience of paying court to his benefactor; during this period he was able to indulge, in a work commissioned by Sauvage (*Querela pacis*), anti-imperial views that were parallel to those of his patron (see chapter 3). Gattinara too admired Erasmus, intervening, upon request, to silence the great humanist's critics in Louvain; but he so little understood Erasmus' views that he requested of him, in recompense for this favour, a commentary on Dante's *De monarchia*, a treatise extolling the benefits of world monarchy. Not surprisingly, Erasmus declined (letters 1554, 1643, 1790a); cf Rafael Maria de Hornedo, SJ 'Carlos V y Erasmo.'

28 'The humanist [educational] program was politically, socially, and economically neutral' (Eugene F. Rice Jr 'The Patrons of French Humanism, 1480–1520' 701). Professor Baron, in whose honour the volume in which this paper appears was published, is well known for his advocacy of a contrary view, at least in regard to the republican flavour of Florentine humanism in the early Quattrocento (*The Crisis of the Early Italian Renaissance*).

29 Letters 1417, line 11; 2375, lines 102–3; and 2645, line 23, cited in J.J. Poelhekke 'Het Naamloze Vaderland van Erasmus'

30 For an account of some non-humanist critics of contemporary wars, see Walter F. Bense 'Paris Theologians on War and Peace, 1521–1529.' It

should be noted, however, that the theologian Josse Clichetove was also a humanist and seems to have been influenced by Erasmus' writings on peace.

31 Above, notes 18 and 22

CHAPTER ONE

1 Henri Pirenne *Histoire de Belgique* 3: 21–53

2 Leading members of the family, exiled by Charles the Rash, had been restored to their lands by Maximilian. On the Croys, see Richard Vaughan *Philip the Good* 140–1, 321–2; Andreas von Walther *Die Anfänge Karls V* 6–10; G. Dansaert *Guillaume de Croy, dit le Sage*.

3 Walther *Die Anfänge Karls V* 15–19; C.J.F. Slootmans *Jan metten Lippen, zijn Familie en zijn Stad*

4 In 1491 the French king, Charles VIII, intercepted Maximilian's betrothed, Anne of Brittany, on her journey to Germany and forced her to marry him; at the same time he repudiated his own fiancée, Maximilian's daughter, Margaret of Austria.

5 A quarrel (1496) between Maximilian and Busleiden is reported in 'Dispacci al Senato di Francesco Foscari' *Archivo Storico Italiano* (Florence) 7 (1844); 801.

6 AGN 4: 24–31; J.E.A.L. Struick *Gelre en Habsburg, 1492–1528* 8–50. Charles of Egmond was a distant cousin to the Egmonds of Holland and north Brabant – John of Egmond and his brother Frederick of Ijselstein – a circumstance which enhanced partisan and dynastic rivalries.

7 E.g., Brewer I:1, 89

8 Walther *Die Anfänge Karls V* 15–9; N.J.M. Kerling *Commercial Relations of Holland and Zeeland with England from the Late Thirteenth to the Close of the Fourteenth Century* Pirenne *Histoire de Belgique* 3: 86–7. See below, chapter 3, note 84.

9 Pirenne *Histoire de Belgique* 3: 64–8. Philip's infant son, Charles, was pledged in marriage to Claude of France, infant daughter of Louis XII. Claude's dowry was to include the Kingdom of Naples, currently disputed between Louis XII and Ferdinand of Aragon. The treaty would thus add to Philip's difficulties with his father-in-law.

10 Walther *Die Anfänge Karls V* 25–6

11 L.P. Gachard 'Les Anciennes Assemblées nationales de la Belgique' 17–18

12 Pirenne *Histoire de Belgique* 3: 64–8

13 On Santeranus, LB I, 453DE; *Hieronymi opera* 2: 189. Allen I, 50, lines 94–100 (on the authenticity on the *Compendium vitae*, see Tracy 'Bermerkungen zur Jugend des Erasmus' and CWE 4 400–3). For Erasmus' contacts with the Bishop of Utrecht, letter 28, lines 18–23, I, 118; and I, 588n; LB V, 808BE (Bishop David tested candidates for ordination on their knowledge of theology). See below, note 18.

14 *Chroniques de Jean Molinet* ed. J.A. Buchon, 5:45

15 Philip made his *joyeuse entrée* on 19 September 1494: Arthur Gaillard *Le Conseil de Brabant* I: 68. Letter 39, line 150–2; LB V, 72D. See also Willem Hermans to James Batt, letter 35, lines 47–65, I, 132–3 (the follies of courtly love; this letter can be taken as representative of Erasmus' thoughts because it resembles at many points his 1494 *Antibarbarorum liber*).

16 Except for references to civil wars between the century-old Hoek and Kabiljauw factions which ravaged Holland between 1477 and 1489 or 1492 (LB VIII, 547C, 550C; LB V. 1249A); cf Letter 35, lines 43–51, I, 132. See H.P.H. Jansen *Hoekse en Kabiljauwse Twisten*.

17 *De Egmondsche Abtenkroniek van Johannes a Leydis* ed Victor J.G. Roefs, O. Carm, 238–43. The party of monks opposed to reform included sons of noble families hostile to the Egmonds, while John of Egmond and his brother Frederick of Ijsselstein supported the reformers. Erasmus' friend Cornelius Aurelius was to be part of a group of Dutch monks called to reform two monasteries near Paris (1496–7; see letter 52), and was later on good terms with the reform party at Egmond Abbey and a supporter of the Egmond family on political issues: below, chapter 4, note 119. See also below, note 67.

18 'When certain men urged that he should allow a coadjutor bishop to be appointed to help him, owing to the increasing burden of age, Bishop David replied that he was "discouraged from doing so by the example of St Anthony, who began to be neglected almost as soon as Roch, a more recent saint, came into fashion"' (LB II, 927B, adage 2838; St Roch, a southern French nobleman who died tending plague victims in the 1320s, was, like St Anthony, invoked in time of sickness). For some time the Dukes of Burgundy had sought to establish their influence in Utrecht by securing the appointment of coadjutor bishops with right of succession. David himself had originally been appointed in this way through the influence of his father, Duke Philip the Good. In 1493 the Utrecht chapter received emissaries from Frederick III, Maximilian, and Philip, each of whom had his own candidate for appointment as coadjutor bishop (S.B.J. Zilverberg *David van Bourgondie, Bisschop van Terwaan en van Utrecht*).

19 Letter 39, lines 113–14, I, 141

20 Erasmus complained frequently that the bishop gave little: letter 48, lines 25–6, I, 160; letter 75, lines 18–22, 202; letter 157, lines 16–18, 363.

21 On Batt, see C.J.F. Slootmans 'Erasmus en zijn Vrienden uit Bergen-op-Zoom' *Taxandria*.

22 See Allen's notes to letter 80.

23 Letters 143–5

24 Allen I, 357

25 Baron de Reiffenberg *Histoire de l'ordre de la toison d'or* 234: the order at

its January 1501 sitting initiated an inquiry into why the Grand Bastard had failed to return the collar of the French Order of St Michel given him by Louis XI (d. 1483). Why the issue was raised at this time is not clear.

26 CWE letter 157, lines 22–4, II, 39 (except as noted, translations *in extenso* of letters 1–445 are from CWE). Cf. Allen, letter 151, lines 10–11, 355: 'De D.P. semper mihi male praesagit animus, sed haec ab exitu spectabuntur.' Allen takes D.P. to mean 'Dominus Praepositus,' that is, Nicholas of Burgundy, Provost of St Peter's in Utrecht.

27 Allen I, 372

28 Letter 154 (July 1501), lines 1–4, I, 359, with Allen's note; see above, note 20.

29 CWE letter 157, lines 68–72, II, 41; Henri De Vocht *Jerome de Busleiden, His Life and Writings* 33: Jerome left for Italy the summer of 1501 and returned by late 1503. Letter 172 (September 1502), lines 3–4, 381; cf. letter 178 (November 1503), lines 11–15, 394: 'Conciliaui mihi, vel potius se mihi conciliauit Hieronymus Buslidanus, archidiaconus Cameracensis, frater Episcopi [Francis was Archbishop of Besançon], vir vtriusque linguae callentissimus. Is subinde dictitat me fortunatum fuisse futurum, si vir ille redisset incolumis; spes certe mihi omnis in eo viro sita fuerat.'

30 De Vocht *Jerome de Busleiden* 13–14

31 Letter 737, lines 7–12, III, 167 (Allen concurs with Reich's suggestion that the addressee is John of Bergen). Erasmus' friend John of Borsselen did not obtain the position for which he recommended him. This may explain his later request (letter 805, lines 12–14, 259) that Borsselen's having been a 'cliens' of the Busleiden family not be held against him ('ne illi fraudi sit').

32 De Vocht *Jerome de Busleiden* 41; letter 178, lines 12–13, I 394; letter 157, line 60, 364

33 *Apologia de precellentia protestatis imperatorie ditionis* (Antwerp, Hillen 1503), sig. AIII^{v}–AV^{v} (copy in the Newberry Library, lacking several pages from quires B and C). Bruni's letter to Ciriaco d'Ancona is reprinted by Anthonisz.

34 *De precellentia* sig. AVII–AVII^{v}. The first part of the treatise resembles the traditional Ghibelline arguments of Dante's *De monarchia*.

35 Ibid sig. DIV^{v}–DVI; sig. FVI^{v}–GI: 'Dicit praeterea Bar. in d. i Hostes unde hec porro majori parte sumpta sunt Si quis diceret imperatorem non esse universalem dominum & monarcham esset hereticus qui diceret contra determinationem sancte matris ecclesie & contra evangelium Exiit edictum a Caesare Augusto ut describeretur universis orbis. Luc. ii.'

36 Ibid sig. AIV

37 Cornelis Reedijk 'Erasmus' Versen op het Overlijden van Hendrik van Bergen, Bisschop van Kamerijk'

38 CWE letter 153, lines 10–11, II, 32; letter 173, lines 55–63, 73–6, II, 62.

Cornelis Reedijk (*The Poems of Erasmus* 265) notes that Erasmus probably contributed an epigram (dated 12 February 1503) as well as a preface to the book: 'Christianum orbem tuenti qui fauetis Caesari / Huic fauebitis libello qui tuetur Caesarem.' The epigram seems non-committal.

39 Letter 171, lines 10–15, I, 380 (see under Paludanus in the *Biographie nationale de la Belgique*); letter 178, lines 39–42, 394.

40 Letter 180, lines 177–81, I, 403; letter 175, lines 10–1, 389; letter 176, lines 3–4, 390

41 Letter 177, lines 10–11, I, 391; letter 205, lines 40–1, 435. Just after the archduke passed through Louvain (8 November), Erasmus dedicated to Ruistre a translation of one of Libanius' *Declamations*. Ruistre then received him at table and made him a gift of ten gulden: letter 178, lines 1–9, 393; Antoine de Lalain, Sieur de Montigny *Voyage de Philippe le Beau en Espagne* 336.

42 Letter 179, lines 13–16, I, 396

43 Letter 179, lines 24–32, I, 397; letter 180, lines 149–53, 402.

44 Letter 181, lines 54–6, I, 405; letter 180, lines 12–15, (with Allen's note) and 29–115, I, 398–401.

45 Herding 6–7, citing letter 337, lines 89–94, and LB V, 728E

46 Herding 7–9

47 Herding 29, lines 91–9 (= LB IV, 509); cf below, chapter 2, note 124.

48 Herding 53, lines 860–1; 82, lines 815–16; 80, lines 745–56 (= LB IV, 540F–541A)

49 Herding 77, lines 649–56 (= LB IV, 539); cf below, chapter 3, 59–65.

50 James D. Tracy *Erasmus: The Growth of a Mind* chapter 5; Herding (page 7) has noted some striking contrasts on particular points between the *Panegyricus* and the *Enchiridion militis christiani*, published in the same year or shortly before.

51 Herding 23, line 15n; 81–2, lines 801–8 (= LB IV, 541F–542A): 'Proinde tu tua pignora non nisi piis et integris nutricibus virisque sapientibus et incorruptis mandas … Iamdudum autem (vt audio) circumspicis aliquem litteris ac moribus spectatum virum delecturus ex vniuersa patria, cui teneros adhuc alumnos in gremium tradas iis disciplinis, quae principe dignae sint, erudiendos.' As Herding elsewhere notes (page 105), the educational nature of Erasmus' duties as 'councillor' in 1516 is made clear by letter 657, lines 46–60, III, 79.

52 Herding 69, lines 384–5 (= LB IV, 543A)

53 'In quibus dominatus ac seruitutis plurimum est, libertatis atque aequalitatis minimum' (Herding 88–9, lines 51–8 [= LB IV, 546]); cf 32, lines 204–6 (= LB IV, 511): 'Ad haec legerat audieratque Hispaniam vix vlli terrarum amoenitate cedere, regnum opibus virisque florentissimum, regem ac reginam tui cupientissimos, gentem principibus suis obsequentissimam mireque deditam.' Why Spain at this time should seem to a Netherlander a country where 'seruitus' prevailed is not clear, since the

Estates (Cortes) in the two Spanish realms were by no means powerless. The contrast between 'seruitus' and 'aequalitas' might refer to the survival of serfdom in Aragon (see Jaimé Vicens Vives *An Economic History of Spain*. Later (see below, chapter 3, notes 143–5) Erasmus found something sinister – perhaps servile – in the ceremonious ways of Spanish courtiers.

54 Herding 64, lines 199–205 (= LB IV, 530CD)

55 *De Precellentia*, sig. cviii^v: 'Ex quibus omnibus patet quod imperium non sonat legitimam sed principalem & supremam potestatem.'

56 *Nicolai Everardi consiliorum opus* no. xxxi, 97–102. On the late medieval concept of covenant, see William Courtenay 'Covenant and Causality in Peter d'Ailly.'

57 Herding 71–80 (= LB IV, 535–40); cf also the recurring contrast between Caesar's *gloria* and that of Philip (references given below, chapter 2, note 37). Even a passage which Herding (page 7) seems to include among Erasmus' extravagant concessions to chivalric culture has, in context, the opposite intention: 'Denique super haec omnia, vt donemus bellicam gloriam illustriorem esse, certe pacis optabilior est.'

58 Herding 83, lines 870–3 (= LB IV, 543BC): 'Etenim vt contemnenda videantur, quae quondam in tuo natali homines genethliaci praedixerunt & hodie syderum periti magno consensu de tuis ingentibus factis vaticinantur (nam semper horum artem pestiferam bonis principibus iudicavi) ...' Cf LB V, 15A; letter 1005, lines 1–7, IV, 41; and *The Latin Epigrams of Thomas More* ed and trans Leicester Bradner and Charles Arthur Lynch, nos 42–7. A.C.F. Koch (*The Year of Erasmus' Birth* 40–3) points out that Erasmus in later life expressed anxiety about the approach of his grand climacteric year (letter 1994a, lines 51–7, VIII init.). But letter 911, III, 468, does not imply, as Koch thinks, that Erasmus consulted an astrologer in 1519. Cf also M.M. Phillips 'Erasmus' horoscope' (*Erasmus in English* 3 24) and her review of Koch's book (*Erasmus in English* 6 14–15).

59 Herding (40–1, lines 490–2 [= LB IV,-516E]; 50, lines 769–70 [522AB]; 54, lines 902, 913–14 [524DF]; 66, lines 275–7 [531F]) makes explicit the link between astrology and the term *fatalis*. In *Institutio principis* Erasmus was less indulgent to astrologers: 'Longe pestilentius est magorum ac diuinorum genus, qui regibus longaeuitatem victorias triumphos voluptates et imperia pollicentur ... Ad hunc ordinem pertinent prognostae, qui ex astris futura praesagiunt, quorum an vlla sit ars, nos est huius loci discutere' (Herding 177, lines 337–42 [= LB 586A]).

60 Herding 64, lines 204–6 (= LB 530CD): 'Neque te clam est imperium haut vitae strepitu et colligendis vectigalibus contineri, sed munus esse publicum sic administrandum, vt si non aliis, certe tibi ipsi repetenti, certe deo repetundarum acturo quaeas rationem reddere.' Cf *Institutio principis* (Herding 159, lines 703–4): among Christians 'principatus administratio est, non imperium et regnum beneficium est, non tyrannis,' a

reference to *De civitate Dei* XIV, 28; XIX, 14.

61 Herding 74, lines 559–71 (= LB 537): 'Num Christianus dux, quem oportet esse clementissimum, quo non modo *numen* aliquod esse *iustumque memorque* [*Aeneid* iv 521] credit, verum etiam mox illi de minutissima quoque guttula sanguinis exactissimam rationem esse reddendam intelligit.' Herding (pages 108–10) finds Erasmus' views on war in the *Panegyricus* and in the *Institutio principis* relatively consistent.

62 For other indications of a religious horror of bloodshed on Erasmus' part, see below, chapter 2, note 37 and chapter 4, note 89.

63 Herding 46, lines 653–5 (= LB IV, 519); 74, lines 550–5 (= LB IV, 538): 'Denique quos mala mens malus animus tanquam ad facinus genitos sic extimulat, vt capitis etiam periculo ista fuerint ausuri nedum impunitate proposita nedum obiecta etiam mercede. Hac hominum colluuie bella gerenda, haec sentina in vrbes atque in domos recipienda, cuius fetorem ne solida quidem aetas queat e ciuium tuorum moribus expurgare.' On mercenaries, see below, chapter 4, 88–90.

64 Herding 12; 55–6, lines 935–52

65 Di Caprariis 'Il *Panegyricus* di Erasmo a Filippo di Borgogna' 208–10

66 Reiffenberg *Histoire de la toison d'or* 266–7; Naturel won the election (November 1504).

67 CWE letter 178, lines 47–54, II, 76–7. See above, notes 6 and 17. Hermans perhaps accepted the invitation: see below, chapter 4, note 119.

68 Herding 61–2, lines 118–30 (= LB IV, 528F–529D); Erasmus to Paludanus, letter 180, lines 181–5: 'Quin in ipso operis progressu quum alia quaedam, tum illud in primis suggessisti, id quod ego libenter arripui, vt honorifica mentione ornatissimi patris Francisci Buslidiani, archiepiscopi Byzontini, viri nunquam satis laudati, memoriam qua possem ab obliuione situque assererem.' Herding (page 12) asks the right questions: 'Stand im Hintergrund des *Panegyricus* eine profranzösische burgundische Friedenspartei, deren Impulse Desmarez [Paladunus] vermittelt hätte? ... Ob auch das schon erwähnte Schweigen über Egmont [Ijselstein] mit ihnen irgend zu tun hatte?' But given the strong partisan (i.e. imperialist) identity of the Egmond family (see below, chapter 4, notes 37, 41, 42), it is most unlikely that, even with Francis Busleiden dead and Henry of Bergen in disgrace, 'die Bahn nach oben' (page 5) was now open to Ijselstein.

69 Herding 58, lines 10–21 (= LB IV, 526E–527A): The common folk say 'that for many centuries there has been no duke who refrained from violence against churches, monasteries, and men dedicated to God (as you do and shall do), who has not enjoyed great success in his affairs. Conversely, whoever has dared violate church law in a tyrannical manner, and abused his power against the clergy, has, by a wretched and early death, rendered due satisfaction to God the avenger.' The last sentence evidently refers to Charles the Rash and his struggle with the clergy over mortmain. See Isaac Le Long *Historische Beschryving van de Reformatie der Stad*

Amsterdam 379–82. The passage is peculiar because a / in writings contemporary to the *Panegyricus* (e.g., *Enchiridion militis christiani*, LB V, 26E–27A), Erasmus attacked the popular belief that piety was rewarded by material blessings in this life; and b / Erasmus was not a notable defender of clerical privilege. More typical of Erasmus, albeit of later date, is one of the 1515 *Adagia*, 'Sileni Alcibiadis': 'Omne fulmen torquetur in illos, hostes Ecclesiae vocantur, ac propemodum haeretici, qui Sacerdotum crumenam nummulis aliquot fraudarint. Equidem non adsum fraudatori, ne quis hoc interpretetur, verum cedo, siquidem hostem Ecclesiae juvat odisse, num esse possit hostis Ecclesiae perniciosior, aut capitalior, quam impius Pontifex?' (LB II, 775F).

70 Herding, 63, lines 171–80. See below, chapter 3, 68–9.

71 Allen I, 403; letter 185, lines 5–7, 414, with Allen's note

72 *Deuxième Voyage de Philippe le Beau en Espagne* 1: 390–2

73 CWE letter 185, lines 14–16, II, 99

CHAPTER TWO

1 John S.C. Bridge *A History of France from the Death of Louis XI* vol 1; H. Lemonnier *Les Guerres d'Italie: la France sous Charles VIII, Louis XII et François I* 131ff; Eduard Füeter *Geschichte des europäischen Staatensystems von 1492 bis 1559* 1–3, 68–79. Louis XI conquered the Duchy of Burgundy in 1477; Britanny was subdued early in the reign of Charles VIII.

2 Lodovico il Moro, having usurped the ducal title from a nephew whose father-in-law was King of Naples, felt his position among Italian rulers to be insecure (Francesco Guicciardini *The History of Italy*).

3 The others were Louis XII (1498–1514), Francis I (1515–47), and Henry II (1547–59).

4 Bridge *History of France* vol 3. The Dukes of Orléans were descended in the female line from the Visconti rulers of Milan, whose family died out in the male line in 1447.

5 Ludwig Pastor *A History of the Popes* 6: 259–300

6 Henri Pirenne *Histoire de Belgique* 3: 75–7; AGN 4: 39ff; Andreas von Walther *Die Anfänge Karls V* 85–7. Pastor believes the pope did not resolve to join the coalition until Venice spurned his offer of compromise in April 1509. See below, note 80.

7 See below, notes 83–90.

8 Brewer I:1, 1307; D.S. Chambers *Cardinal Bainbridge in the Court of Rome, 1509–1514*

9 Chambers *Cardinal Bainbridge* 26–7: in an audience with the pope in December 1509, Bainbridge cautiously broached a proposal for a league against France, which he then reported to Henry as if it had been suggested by Julius.

10 Ibid. 29
11 Brewer I:1, 401, 432
12 Ibid 483. Good relations between the two countries had recently been restored by Henry's marriage (spring 1510) to Catherine of Aragon, widow of his brother, Arthur.
13 Ibid 965 (November 1511); cf Chambers *Cardinal Bainbridge* 38.
14 Brewer I:1, 325, 333, 355 (correspondence of Thomas Spinelly, Henry's agent in negotiations with Margaret); 884, 989, 992. See also Walther *Die Anfänge Karls V* 96 citing a letter of Margaret to Henry ca. February 1511, printed in L.Ph.C. van den Bergh *Gedenkstukken tot Opheldering der Nederlandsche Geschiedenis* (3 vols, Leiden Luchtmans 1845) 2, no 103: 247–50; and J.E.A.L. Struick *Gelre en Habsburg 1492–1528* 195.
15 Pastor *History of the Popes* 3: 801–54; O. de la Brosse *Le Pape et le Concile: la comparaison de leurs pouvoirs à la veille de la Réforme* 57–78
16 Brewer I:1, 812, 829: see below, note 88.
17 Brewer I:1, 889, 939
18 Ibid 1326.
19 Heinrich Ullmann *Kaiser Maximilian I* 2: 456: Maximilian feared a breach with France might endanger Verona and Bresica, his chief conquests in the Veneto.
20 Brewer I:1, 1334. Burgundy was the patrimony of Maximilian's father-in-law, Charles the Rash: see above, note 1.
21 Brewer I:1, 1370, 1437, 1554
22 Ullmann *Kaiser Maximilian I* 2: 461 (the battle of Novara, 6 June 1513)
23 So Bainbridge warned Henry (Brewer I:2, 2029; Chambers *Cardinal Bainbridge* 45–7).
24 C.G. Cruickshank *Army Royal: An Account of Henry VIII's Invasion of France* 13–24
25 Ullmann *Kaiser Maximilian I* 2: 467ff. The emperor wished to march on Paris, but Henry insisted on a more limited campaign to enlarge the English pale around Calais.
26 Brewer I:2, 2170, 2172. See below, note 53.
27 Brewer I:2, 2186, 2208; Cruickshank *Army Royal* 117–18. See below, note 100.
28 Brewer I:2, 2294; Cruickshank *Army Royal* 134
29 Brewer I:2, 2670, 2705
30 Ullmann *Kaiser Maximilian I* 2: 474–6, 487–93: any advantage Maximilian may have gained from the destruction of Thérouanne was nullified when the Swiss, paid to invade Burgundy (above, note 20), came to terms with Louis XII (September 1513).
31 Brewer I:2, 2160, 2448, 2611, 2658, 2928; Chambers (*Cardinal Bainbridge* 58–61) notes that Wolsey's agent in Rome for these negotiations was Silvestro Gigli, Bishop of Worcester, known to be an enemy of Bainbridge (Brewer I:2, 2926, 2928). On Foxe, see below, note 90.

32 Brewer I:2, 2820, 3009, 2918, 3020. See below, note 41. Canossa survives in literature as one of the interlocutors in Castiglione's *The Courtier*.
33 Brewer I: 2, 3146; Walter C. Richardson *Mary Tudor, the White Queen*
34 See especially Augustin Renaudet *Erasme et l'Italie*; also my *Erasmus: The Growth of a Mind* chapter 6. Erasmus had long desired to visit Italy and readily accepted an invitation to accompany two sons of Giovanni Boerio, Henry VII's physician, to the University of Bologna.
35 LB VI, 455F (*Paraphrasis in acta apost* 5: 14): 'Ipse spectavi primum Bononiae, deinde Romae, Julium Pontificem Romanum, ejus nominis secundum, splendidissimos agentem triumphos, ac prorsus tales, ut cum Pompejanis aut Caesarianis triumphis conferri possent.' Roland Bainton has found a convincing parallel between the description of Julius' entry into Bologna in *Julius exclusus e coelo* ed Wallace K. Ferguson, *Erasmi opuscula* 85, and a vehement attack on the splendour of the Jewish High Priest in Erasmus' 1524 paraphrase of Mark, chapter 11 ('Erasmus, Luther, and the Dialogue *Julius exclusus*').
36 CWE letter 205, lines 41–3, II, 128. Cf the portion of *Hieronymi opera* edited by Erasmus I, 4v: 'Negat Fabius a nomine duci idonea argumenta, quanquam valent in exhortando: ueluti, si quis Julium Pontificem exhortans ad bellum suscipiendum aduersus Gallos, dicat: Julius es, Julium agas oportet.'
37 Friedrich Gundolf *Caesar: Geschichte seines Ruhmes* 107–33; see also Hans Baron 'The Evolution of Petrarch's Thought' in *From Petrarch to Bruni*. LB II, 111B (from the 1515 *Adagia*). Of seven references to Caesar in the *Panegyricus*, only one reflects something of the conventional admiration for this hero of antiquity – Herding 37, lines 367–70: 'Vt nobilitate Cecropem ... vt victoriis C. Caesarem, vt triumphis Pompeium praecedas [sc. Philip], nihil tamen maius dare possint superi, quam hunc talem in te amando tuorum consensum.' Three others occur in passages urging Philip to seek his glory in the arts of peace, not, like Caesar, in war and conquest – Herding 54–5, lines 913–17: as Caesar was endowed with a 'fatal' force of personality, which struck fear into his enemies, Philip is blessed with the same quality 'ad excitandam beneuolentiam'; 72, lines 472–6: Philip's surest protection is in the love of his subjects, for 'Vbi nunc igitur Alexander Magnus ... Vbi C. Caesar, qui se vno tantum die vinci potuisse praedicauit?'; and 77, lines 662–6: 'dispeream ... si non C. Caesari longe plus attulit famae paucis donata vita quam tot milibus hominum aerepta vita' (Herding elsewhere cites a parallel thought in More to Erasmus, letter 601, lines 42–5). The remaining three are critical of Caesar – Herding 50, lines 754–9: 'Nam per deum immortalem quid erat omnino Macedonis illius profectio, nisi saeua quaedam tempestas ac turbo fatalis, quoquo versum ingrueret bello tumultu terrore cede sanguine permiscens omnia. A qua quidem specie haud ita procul aberat C.

Iulii decennis illa Galliarum Germaniae Britanniaeque vexatio, quum tu [Philip] interim quoquo te conuerteres veluti sol quidam iucundo affulgens lumine'; and 59, lines 53–9: 'In C. Caesare simulata fuit clementia.' Most instructive is what Erasmus does (75, lines 576–83, LB IV 537) with a classical reference which a marginal note traces to Cicero's *Pro Marcello* (8: 25). In context, Cicero is addressing Caesar, who alone can compose the troubles arising from the late civil war: 'Itaque illam tuam praeclarissimam et sapientissimam vocem invitus audivi: "Satis diu vel naturae vixi vel gloriae." Satis, si ita vis, fortasse naturae, addo etiam, si placet, gloriae: at, quod maximum est, patriae certe parum' (*Orationes* vol 2, ed. Clark). Erasmus read or remembered this passage in the light of his own religious horror of bloodshed: 'An diligenter potius pensiculans [sc. Christianus dux] atque aequis lancibus expendens hinc commodum illud, quod petitur, illinc diluuium malorum omnium, quod excitatur, in hanc ibit sententiam, vt statuat nullum omnino bellum sibi suscipiendum esse, quod quauis ratione possit euitari. C. Caesar, qui gloriae cupiditate tantum bellorum exhauserat, extremis aliquot annis de relinquenda vita cogitasse legitur, tum et mente coepisse destitui nimirum agitante iam eum scelerum conscientia ac manibus eorum, quos interemerat semper ob oculos obuersantibus.' (The last thought plainly has more in common with *Macbeth* than with Cicero's description of Caesar.) This harsh view of Caesar recurs in Erasmus' later works: see, for example, below, note 43; *Institutio principis* Herding 180, lines 460–2; and letter 760, lines 9–13, III, 197.

38 Carl Stange (*Erasmus und Julius II: Eine Legende* 12–16) believes the comparison with Caesar in letter 205 is meant to honour the pope; to corroborate this view he cites Erasmus' statement to his abbot, Servatius Roger (letter 203, line 11, I, 433), that Venice has occupied towns which are 'owing to' (*debitis*) the Pope. But one should not interpret what Erasmus says to Busleiden in light of what he tells his abbot. See below, note 69.

39 Allen I, 37, lines 7–14; LB II, 968C (*Antipolemos* 'quem ad Julium ... conscripsimus'). E.V. Telle ('Le *De copia verborum* d'Érasme et le *Julius exclusus*') notes that a list of reasons why Julius should not make war on Venice is given among sample argument outlines in *De copia*, LB I, 86D–87A. Roland Bainton (*Erasmus of Christendom* 89) points to a sketch of arguments to the same end in Erasmus' manual of preaching, *Ecclesiastes* (1535), LB V, 898B–899C. The two lists are similar but not identical.

40 G. Hoogewerff 'Erasmus te Rom in de Zomer van 1509'

41 Letter 222, I, 459–62. For two years both Erasmus and Ammonio stayed with More. When Erasmus returned from Paris, after publishing *Moriae encomium*, More had remarried and his scholar friends had to move out.

J.K. Sowards ('The Two Lost Years of Erasmus') conjectures that the gap in Erasmus' correspondence for this period may be due to the suppression of letters dealing with Julius II.

42 LB IV, 484D; Gerard Lister's footnote makes the reference to Julius explicit.

43 The authenticity of this poem has but recently been established (Cornelis Reedijk, 'Een Schimpdicht van Erasmus op Julius II').

44 The idea of tyrannicide occurred to others in connection with Julius II: cf Machiavelli *The Discourses* I, xxvii. Ferdinand Geldner (*Die Staatsauffassung und Fürstenlehre des Erasmus von Rotterdam* 109) says Erasmus always rejected the doctrine of tyrannicide. But *Tyrannicida*, a reply to Lucian's declamation on behalf of a citizen claiming the reward for tyrannicide, argues not that there should be no reward for tyrannicide, but merely that there should be none in this case, since the citizen in question acted from private motives. See Charles Rayment 'The *Tyrannicide* of Erasmus: Translated Excerpts with Introduction and Commentary.'

45 *Erasmus in Cambridge: The Cambridge Letters of Erasmus* trans D.F.S. Thomson, intro H.C. Porter

46 Clemente Pitti *Un Amico di Erasmo: Andrea Ammonio*

47 CWE letter 245, lines 25–32, II, 205

48 Erasmus to Ammonio, letter 240, lines 32–3, I, 483, 'De rebus Italicis mihi parum laeta nuncias, non studio Galli, sed odio belli.'

49 Cf my article 'Erasmus Becomes a German.'

50 Pitti *Andrea Ammonio*; Erasmus to Ammonio, letter 245, line 19, I, 492: 'Quid ais? *ho archiereus* ad Lauretanam? *ō tēs eusebias*.' See also letter 243, lines 22–32, 486–7.

51 Letter 236, line 43, I, 476; cf Erasmus to Leo X, letter 335, line 82, II, 82.

52 Letter 252, lines 1–8, I, 498

53 *The Latin Epigrams of Thomas More* ed and trans Leicester Bradner and Charles Arthur Lynch, nos. 77, 170, 171, 174–9, and 193. Brewer II:1, 2483: the speech of a French envoy to Brussels did not have as much 'brag' as the English envoy Cuthbert Tunstall thought it would. Cornelis Reedijk *The Poems of Erasmus* no. 93 'In fugam Gallorum' 304: 'Cato foeminas videre non potest, Gallus/ viros.' To Ruthall, letter 325, lines 15–18, II, 52. Erasmus took a different view of the battle in a comment published after he left England: *Hieronymi opera* (1516) I, 40^{v}: 'Nec unquam ad manus uentum est, neque enim unicum illud prelium, quo proceres aliquot Gallorum in Britanniam abducti sunt, nominatim eximius Iuvenis, dux Longueuillensis, & praefectus Claremontaus, prelium appellari potest.'

54 Above, note 48

55 For the state of the question, see James K. McConica, CSB 'Erasmus and

the "Julius"' in Charles Trinkaus (ed) *The Pursuit of Holiness in Late Medieval and Renaissance Religion*. My own reluctance to accept Erasmus' sole authorship (*The Growth of a Mind* 137) has been based in particular on the fulsome praise (Ferguson *Erasmi opuscula* 97) of Cardinal Georges d'Amboise (d. 1510), a man Erasmus did not meet and never mentions, and whose motives are not thought to have been so pure as the author of *Julius exclusus* maintains. But in the excited atmosphere of Paris in 1511, it is possible Erasmus accepted this description of Amboise from friends who had been in his service, or who were promoting what had been his project, the anti-papal Council of Pisa: see below, notes 70–4.

56 See the discussion of Erasmus' concept of *humanitas* (with its religious implications) in my *Erasmus: The Growth of a Mind*.

57 Cf Dante's attack on what was thought to have been the gift of temporal power to the popes by Constantine (*Inferno* canto 19). In contrast to Erasmus' views on the renunciation of power, Dante places Celestine v – the pope who escaped the moral ambiguities of power by resigning his office – among those sinners too contemptible even to be admitted to Hell proper (canto 3).

58 On 'Sileni Alcibiadis,' see Ernst Benz 'Christus und die Sileni des Alcibiades.'

59 LB II, 781E

60 LB II, 780F. Cf Machiavelli *The Prince* xi.

61 LB II, 778F

62 Twenty years later, in *Ecclesiastes* (LB V, 807BC), Erasmus admits that the temporal power of German prince-bishops may once have been necessary 'because of the wildness of the Germans.'

63 LB II, 779F–780A

64 As early as 1370 the popes collected licence fees for the export of Romagnol salt (John Larner *The Lords of Romagna* 222).

65 Jacob Burckhardt *The Civilization of the Renaissance in Italy* 1: 134, contrasting Julius with Alexander VI (father of Cesare Borgia) and others of his immediate predecessors. For background, see D.P. Waley *The Papal State in the Thirteenth Century* and Peter Partner *The Papal State Under Martin V*. Also see John Arthos 'The Ambiguities of Pope Julius and His Rome' in Trinkaus *The Pursuit of Holiness* (above, note 55).

66 The argument here is presumed to be similar in structure to the passage in *Institutio principis* (chapter 3, note 136) which says that the Christian prince who can hold office only by much bloodshed ought to resign.

67 On Bombasio, LB II, 221AB; Mario Cosenza *Biographical Dictionary of the Italian Humanists* 1: 640

68 He was attracted to Venice by the printing house of Aldus Manutius, which published a greatly expanded version of his *Adagia* in 1508.

69 See above, note 39. He argues, for example, that Venice has been of great service to Christendom against the Turk; that in seizing (Romagnol) towns the Venetians merely moved into an area that had historically been governed ill, if at all, by the popes; and that some of the disputed towns had been occupied by Venice for 'ages' (Ravena, for example, fell to Venetian control in 1441). See above, note 63.

70 On the Council of Pisa, see above, note 15.

71 N. van der Blom 'Fausto Andrelini Forlivensis, Poeta Regius'

72 Letter 636, lines 14–17, III, 58

73 *Adversus Fabrum* LB IX, 19 CD; Augustin Renaudet *Préréforme et Humanisme à Paris pendant les premières guerres d'Italie* 606–11. It was probably in Paris at this time that Erasmus heard an account (*Lingua*, ed. Schalk, 276, lines 373–9; LB IV, 684AB) of how the conflict was inflamed when Julius heard that Louis XII had called him a drunkard, 'id quod nemo Romae nesciebat esse verum.' Cf his statement (LB II, 553E) that Julius would have destroyed France had he lived.

74 For the younger Briçonnet, see A. Herminjard *Correspondance des réformateurs des pays de langue française* vol 1; *Novum instrumentum* (Basel, Froben 1516) 554 ('Louis XI'; in the 1519 edition, page 454, the correction is made to 'Louis XII').

75 Pastor (*History of the Popes* 6: 261) believes that Giovanni's wife and sons 'made the name of Bentivoglio thoroughly detested in the city by their tyranny and violence.' But cf ibid 7: 133–4. Ferguson (*Erasmi opuscula* 83–4) finds *Julius exclusus*'s assessment of citizen loyalty to the regime 'scarcely true,' though Giovanni was 'a very able ruler.' C.M. Ady (*The Bentivoglio of Bologna*) presents a generally favourable view of Giovanni but also cites (pages 129–31) arbitrary acts which created a significant political opposition in the city.

76 Ferguson *Erasmi opuscula* 84, lines 345–6

77 Pastor *History of the Popes* 6: 283; *Adagiorum Chiliades* (Basel, Froben 1515) 215–16, 'A mortuo tributum exigere' (LB II, 338A)

78 Letter 240, lines 35–7, I, 483; Reedijk ('Een Schimpdicht' 200–2) discusses a poem on the same theme, possibly by Erasmus, in Gerard Geldenhouwer's *Collectanea*. Letter 333, lines 55–9, II, 70.

79 Ferguson *Erasmi opuscula* 75, lines 211–17; cf letter 335, lines 109–15 and LB II, 553E.

80 F. Seneca *Venezia e il Papa Julio II*; Luigi Simeoni *I Signorie* 2: 791–3. Seneca's conclusion is supported by historians of the Netherlands (above, note 6), who attribute the initiative in forming the League of Cambrai to Margaret of Austria or to Chièvres.

81 Cruickshank *Army Royal* 11; letter 288, lines 82–6, I, 553: 'Suscipiendi belli praetextus erat Iulius periclitans; sublata est causa belli [by the death of Julius] nec tamen cessat bellum.'

82 Ferguson (*Erasmi opuscula*) assesses some of the charges made in *Julius exclusus*: that the pope bought votes in order to be elected (page 73) is well attested; that he was illegitimate (page 81) or preferred schism to a church council (page 102) is quite implausible; that he died of syphillis (page 72) or practised homosexuality (page 77) is supported by malicious gossip among his enemies, not by any evidence.
83 A.F. Pollard *Wolsey* 11
84 Warham obtained for him the living of Aldington in Kent (Allen I, 62, lines 224–35), which Erasmus held as an absentee.
85 Jervis Wegg *Richard Pace, A Tudor Diplomatist*
86 Fisher (cf letter 182; letter 216, line 21, I, 453) was by his own suggestion sent to Henry VIII as the bearer of certain letters from Julius II, Easter 1510 (Chambers *Cardinal Bainbridge* 30–2).
87 *The Better Part of Valor: More, Erasmus, Colet and Vives on Humanism, War and Peace* 58
88 On Bonvisi, above, note 16. *Lingua*, ed. Schalk, 277, lines 387–401; LB IV, 684BD) '... Italus quidam ... legatus veniret Julii nomine, quo regem ad bellum in Gallos accenderet. Is posteaquam in concilio perorasset ex more, eique regis nomine responsum esset: regis quidem animum vehementer propensum [Schalk has "porpensum"] esse ad propugnationem dignitatis pontificiae, caeterum Britanniae regnum iam diuturna pace desuevisse bello, & rem fore cum rege potentissimo, itaque non posse repente fieri quod peteretur, sed opus esse temporis spatio ad tanti belli apparatum: ille magis incaute quam scelerate, cum nihil esset necesse quicquam addere, subiecit sese eadem praedicasse Julio. Ea vox excepta mox suspicionem iniecit magnatibus, quod pontificis oratorem professus, nonnihil faveret Gallo. Deinde cum observatus, deprehenderetur cum oratore Gallorum nocturnis horis miscere colloquium, abductus est in carcerem, omnibusque fortunis exutus est, ne vita quidem incolumi, si venisset in manus Julii. Atqui hic linguae lapsus effecit, ut rex, qui forte prorogando negotio dissidium compositurus erat, bellum acceleraret.' If the French spy in papal service who called himself 'Abbatis' (Brewer I:1, 793; cf 812, 829) was indeed Bonvisi, as Brewer's index surmises, Erasmus was incorrect to think Bonvisi spoke 'magis incaute quam scelerate.' His charitable view of the matter may reflect the fact that More was a friend of the Bonvisi family (*The Correspondence of Sir Thomas More* 87–8). Probably at this time Erasmus inserted in *De copia* (published 1512; see above, note 39) the outline of a speech dissuading a young king from war with France (LB I, 87BD).
89 'Ea vox excepta mox suspicionem iniecit magnatibus,' above, note 88. Speaking of a slightly later date (1514), J.C. Scarisbrick (*Henry VIII* 55) describes Charles Brandon, soon to become Duke of Suffolk by Henry's favour (cf letter 287, line 12, I, 550), as the king's *'alter ego*

and companion in belligerence.' But cf above, chapter 1, notes 70, 72.

90 In 1510 both Christopher Fisher (above, note 86) and the Aragonese ambassador reported from London that Foxe had changed his mind and now supported a military alliance against France (Brewer I:1, 476; Chambers *Cardinal Bainbridge* 34). Robert T. Adams, who believes Foxe consistently supported peace from 1509 until 1516 (*The Better Part of Valor* 58), tends, like Erasmus, to identify friends of humane learning as men of peace. Adams cites a description of Foxe by the same Aragonese envoy, but dated in 1514 when the circumstances, and Foxe's views, were different: see above, note 31.

91 Wegg *Richard Pace* 3: Pace once wrote that he had been sent into the world for the ruin of France.

92 Three, if one accepts the argument of Adams (*The Better Part of Valor* 75–8) that in his epigrams on the French war (above note 53), 'More did much more than beat the common patriotic drum.' More's epigram on the fall of Tournai (no. 238), which Henry captured more easily than Caesar had done, can, according to Adams, be interpreted, as 'in veiled terms, identifying Henry with that figure of the tyrant.' Moreover, those of his poems which are directed against 'Chordigera,' an heroic poem by the French humanist Germain de Brie on a naval battle of 1512 (nos. 170, 171, 174–9, 193), 'should be read not as patriotic in inspiration, but as an attack by More on the decadent literary conventions of chivalric romance.'

93 Adams *The Better Part of Valor* 64–5, quoting *Edward Hall's Chronicle* ed H. Ellis (London 1809) 526. Brewer I:1, 1642, 1780; I:2, 2019, 2163. More (letter 388, lines 86–8) saw nothing political in Warham's retirement from the chancellorship in December 1515, but Erasmus' comment (letter 414, line 1) is more ambiguous.

94 Letter 1211, lines 557–616, IV, 524–6. Adams (*The Better Part of Valor* 71) discounts a story, tracing from Archbishop Parker, that Colet subsequently relented and preached a fiery patriotic sermon in favour of the war. Colet was prosecuted for heresy by the Bishop of London, Richard Fitzjames, in connection with his convocation sermon a year earlier (1512) attacking the vices of the clergy (P.S. Allen 'Dean Colet and Archbishop Warham'). Erasmus believed Warham supported Colet's adversaries (letter 414, lines 2–5, II, 246).

95 LB II, 870CD

96 *Querela pacis* LB IV, 640EF: 'Quorum inventum est bombarda? Nonne Christianorum? Et quo res sit indignior, his induuntur Apostolorum nomina, insculpuntur Divorum imagines' (cf Cruickshank *Army Royal* 74–6). The cannon were probably cast by the 'military' friend who once received the dedication of Erasmus' manual of piety, the *Enchiridion militis christiani*, but was not much changed by it (Otto Schottenloher

'Erasmus, Johann Poppenruyter, und die Entstehung des *Enchiridion militis christiani*.' Henne (2:13) traces the 'Twelve Apostles' to a Mechelen cannon-founder, Johann 'Poppinger.' But Poppenruyter, also of Mechelen, had many English contracts during this period (Brewer I:1, 324, 355, 1529).

97 Ferguson *Erasmi opuscula* 111–12, lines 889–902

98 Allen I, 6; Reedijk *The Poems* nos 45 and 46

99 Pace *De fructu qui ex doctrina percipitur* ed and trans Frank Manley and Richard Sylvester 141. Wegg (*Richard Pace* 117–20) discusses Erasmus' dislike of Pace's book.

100 *Hieronymi opera* (1516) I, 40^{v}: 'postea nostris, opinor agentibus, oppidum indigne deletum est.' This was the view at least of some contemporary observers: see above, note 27.

101 Erasmus to Henry VIII, letter 964, lines 43–8, III, 580. Adams (*The Better Part of Valor* 75) seems to make too much of this statement.

102 The chronicler Robert Macquereau (cited by Cruickshank *Army Royal* 133–4) related that Henry resolved to attack Tournai because the Tournaisiens were 'an incorrigible, ill-disposed lot, lampooning their neighbours, and even making fun of me.' Cf Schalk, 276–7, lines 385–7, LB IV, 684B: 'Neque satis feliciter cessit, Nerviis quos hodie *Tornacos* vocant, quod dicaces quidam in Caesarem Maximilianum praetereuntem scommatum nescio quid torserint.' For Erasmus' view of the emperor, see below, note 137.

103 Erasmus to Gonnell, 14 February 1514, letter 287, lines 8–10, I, 550: '... de pace inter Principes tractaturus; sed frustra. Is magis, ni fallor, suum aget negocium quam nostrum.' Cf Brewer I:2, 2632: the Venetian ambassador complained on February 7 that Caraffa had not yet seen the king.

104 Letter 2599, IX, 417–19

105 Letter 2599, lines 20–4, IX, 418: '"Non expediebat" inquam "fieri mentionem pacis." "Quamobrem?" "Quoniam pax" inquam "subito coire non potest. Atque interea dum monarchae tractant de conditionibus, milites ad odorem pacis peiora moliuntur quam in bello. Per inducias autem subito cohibentur militum manus."' Brewer I:2, 2660, 2820: Leo seems to accept Wolsey's idea of a general or universal peace; 2917 (May 1514): he says he is sending Canossa to treat of a peace or a truce.

106 Letter 541, lines 9–13, II, 487–8; letter 542, lines 12–18, 493, mentions Charles and Maximilian, but after Leo and Francis. Letters 333, lines 10–12, 69 (to Cardinal Riario) and 335, lines 76–83, 82 (to Leo) are more complimentary to the pope. But like many contemporaries, Erasmus changed his mind about the Medici pope as time went on.

107 To Anthony of Bergen, CWE letter 288, lines 88–100, II, 281–2. LB II, 966C: letter 288 was reworked into the adage 'Dulce bellum inexpertis.' Cf letter 2177, line 9; LB IV 609B, 636B, and LB V 831A, cited by Otto

Schottenloher ('Erasmus und die respublica christiana' *Historische Zeitschrift* 210 [1970]: 295–323). Herding (216–17, line 542n) points out that Erasmus hoped for the popes to play a role in preventing war, not merely, as in the traditional view, to arbitrate disputed issues of legal right.

108 The bitterness with which Erasmus later speaks of Leo X (see below, chapter 5, notes 22–7) may well be the counterpart of his idealized view of the pope's role in 1514.

109 To this list 'Sileni Alcibiadis' (above, notes 58–63) might be added, though it deals more with religious reform than with civil government. For the character of the 1515 *Adagia*, see Margaret Mann Philips *The Adages of Erasmus*; letter 421, lines 83–8, II, 254.

110 Erasmus revised his *Adagia* at Cambridge in 1512 (letter 264, lines 1–8). But 'Dulce bellum inexpertis' was a reworking of letter 288 (to Anthony of Bergen, August 1514). 'Scarabaeus aquilam quaerit' clearly refers (LB II, 872AB) to the bargain (January 1515) by which Maximilian agreed to emancipate his grandson Charles in return for a large subsidy from the Estates: see below, note 138. The adage 'Aut regem, aut fatuum nasci oportet' is taken from Seneca's *Apocolocyntosis*: 'nam is nuper in Germania repertus, in lucem emersit' (LB II, 106D). This text was first published in Rome in 1513, on the basis of a German manuscript. In 1515 Beatus Rhenanus reedited and annotated it as part of Erasmus' edition of Seneca's works, published by Froben (*The Satire of Seneca on the Apotheosis of Claudius* ed Allen Perley Ball, 92–4). Thus Erasmus cannot have written this adage before 1513, and probably not until he met Rhenanus at the Froben press (fall 1514). 'Spartam nactus es' (553D–554A) refers to events of 1513 (the death of Julius II, the battles of Novara and Flodden) and seems to refer to Charles as duke, a title he would not have had until his emancipation in January 1515 (553A, 'Carolus [the Rash] Burgundionum dux, hujus proavus'). 'Ut fici oculis incumbunt' first appears in the 1515 edition, but contains no political commentary until the 1520 edition. 'Sileni Alcibiadis' contains no indication of composition date, though the implied criticism of Julius II (above, notes 58–63) is more likely to have been written after the pope's death early in 1513.

111 Herding 123–4, citing page 162, line 838; cf Karl Schätti *Erasmus und die Römische Kurie* 75–7, citing letter 1039, lines 97–101, IV, 115.

112 *Institutio principis* Herding 187, lines 672–8 (= LB IV, 592)

113 Ibid 164–5, lines 910–18 (= LB IV, 577F–578A). Cf LB II, 654BC: 'Perspicuunt [sc. optimates] praecipuam reip. felicitatem in hoc sitam, si Principem habeat integrum, cordatum, vigilantem, hoc est, vere Principem. Itaque miro studio curant tutores, ne unquam vir sit Princeps.'

114 Herding (pages 123–4) rightly criticizes the view expressed by Renaudet (*Erasme et l'Italie* 9).

115 Herding, 162–3, lines 843–51 (= LB IV, 576). Cf introduction, note 15.

116 Herding (page 126) emphasizes the importance for Erasmus of the principle of *consensus*, but (wrongly, as it will be argued here) does not think he had in mind a particular institutional framework, such as the limitation of a prince by his Estates. One might, for example, find in page 146, lines 317–18 ('Hac lege populus in tua iurauit verba') an allusion to the Brabançon *joyeuse entrée* (cf above, chapter 1, note 54). J.A. Fernandez ('Erasmus on the Just War' *Journal of the History of Ideas* 34 [1973]: 210–16) asserts that Erasmus scorns the *populus* and places all his hope in the prince, who has no need of constraint by Estates; he perhaps has in mind page 151, lines 475–8 (= LB IV, 569F), '... Vna superest veluti sacra ancora incorruptus principis animus,' which must be evaluated in light of the work in which it occurs: see below, notes 147–9 and Erasmus to More, letter 543. What is 'flimsy' is not Erasmus' conception of the state, but Fernandez' understanding of Erasmus: see below, conclusion, note 3.

117 Above, note 110

118 Craig Thompson *The Translations of Lucian by Erasmus and St Thomas More*; Lucian 'A True Story,' in *Selected Satires of Lucian* trans Lionel Casson (Garden City, N.Y., Doubleday Anchor Books 1962), 13–57. See below, note 132.

119 Contrast Herding 180, lines 460–2 ('Cum Achillem audis, cum Xersem Cyrum Darium Iulium, ne quid te rapiat magni nominis praestigium. Magnos ac furiosos latrones audis. Sic enim illos aliquoties vocat Seneca' = LB IV, 588) with the source given by Herding (*De beneficiis* II, 18, 6: 'eodem loco latronem pone, piratam, regem animum latronis ac piratae habentem'; or *Dialogi* V, 16, 3). See above, note 37.

120 See below, notes 173–8.

121 *The Latin Epigrams of Thomas More* ed and trans Bradner and Lynch, no. 1 (to Henry VIII on his coronation), page 18: 'Eneruare bonas immensa licentia mentes / Idque etiam in magnis assolet ingeniis.'

122 Compare LB II, 109CD with More, epigram 182, page 83, on the failings of hereditary monarchy as compared with an elected senate.

123 See Marie Madeleine de la Garanderie *La Correspondance d'Erasme et de Guillaume Budé*.

124 Contrast epigram 1 (to Henry VIII), page 17: 'Mille inter comites excelsior omnibus extat' with 'Aut regem, aut fatuum nasci oportere,' LB II, 108A: '... stultam plebeculam, omnia potius suscipere in Regibus, quam id quod solum erat requirendum ... Procerus est, & ab humeris inter omnes eminet.' This characteristic was perhaps a part of the medieval myth of monarchy; cf Joinville's description of St Louis: Jean Sieur de Joinville *The Life of St Louis* in *Chronicles of the Crusades* trans M.R.B. Shaw (Baltimore, Penguin Books 1963) 222. But cf chapter 1, note 47. On More's caution, see also introduction, note 20.

125 My *Erasmus: The Growth of a Mind* 90–8, 144–50, 160–1, 167–9

126 LB II, 110C. See above, chapter 1, note 60.

127 LB II, 773F

128 LB II, 871A. Budé (*De l'institution du prince* 64) speaks of divine judgments, based on 'l'authorité de puissance universelle absolue, laquelle seule proprement est monarchique & souveraine, appellée avec elle Providence.' Anthonisz (*De precellentia*, sig. AVII[v], FVI) uses the term *monarchia* to refer to the universal dominion of Alexander the Great. See below, note 141.

129 LB II, 109CE. As Geldner notes, however, he adds an important qualification: 'Sed esto, receptius est, quam ut convelli possit.'

130 *Institutio principis* Herding 136, lines 27–31 (= LB IV, 561)

131 LB II, 111B. 'Scarabaeus aquilam quaerit,' LB II, 869D, refers in Homeric terms to the *thumos agēnor* of royal eagles. For Erasmus' generally negative judgment of what Plato called *thumos* (the spirited or irascible part of man, source of the passion for honour), see the comments on 'spiritus' in my *Erasmus: The Growth of a Mind* 11, 99, 187, 205–6.

132 Homer's traditional stature as teacher of morals seems to be mocked also in Seneca's *Apocolocyntosis* (*The Satire of Seneca* ed Ball, V, 120): '[Hercules] ipse Homerico versu Caesarem se esse significans ait: *Iliothen me pherōn anemos Kikinessi pelassen*. Erat autem sequens versus verior, aeque Homericus: *ethna d'ego polin eprathon, ōlesa d'autous*.'

133 LB II, 106E–107B

134 *De conscribendis epistolis*, ed. Margolin, p. 294, lines 4–7, commenting on 'Most Christian King' and other royal titles: 'Quis hanc titulorum superstitionem inuexit in mundum? Nimirum pharasaicum illud hominum genus, quod aliis quoque ceremoniis, et falsae religionis praestigiis, diu mortalium generi nimirum credulo imposuit.'

135 Herding 63, lines 173–80 (LB IV, 529F–530A); 173, lines 205–9 (LB IV, 583CD)

136 What Erasmus understands by *scarabaeus* is made clear in the adage 'Abominandus scarabaeus' LB II, 686D: '*Cantharides* vermiculi sunt letali veneno ... In Sacris quoque Litteris, *Vermis* abiit in proverbium contemptus. Quod genus est illud in Psalmis mysticis: "Ego autem sum *vermis* & non homo."' 'Scarabaeus' is thus linked to what was traditionally understood as a messianic passage. The image of Christ as 'scarabaeus' suggests in turn an interesting parallel in thought structure between 'Sileni Alcibiadis' and 'Scarabaeus aquilam quaerit.'

137 LB II, 872AB (see above, note 110). *Dulce bellum inexpertis* ed and trans Yvonne Remy & René Dunil-Marquebreucq, 28, lines 182–5, also contained a veiled reference to Maximilian: 'Nos, Deum immortalem, quam friuolis de causis, quas bellorum tragoedias excitamus! Ob inanissimos titulos, ob puerilem iram, ob [interceptam] mulierculam, ob causas his quoque multo magis ridiculas.' The word in brackets, added only for the

1523 edition, makes it clear, as the editors note, that Erasmus was thinking of Maximilian's perennial *casus belli* against France: in 1491 Maximilian's bride, the Duchess Anne of Brittany, was stopped on her journey across France and compelled to marry King Charles VIII instead.

138 Spinelly to Henry VIII, 29 January 1515, Brewer II:1, 70; the personal grant to Maximilian is confirmed by an 'acceptation' (by the prince) 'of the consent' (by the Estates), dated 12 April 1515, in the *Root Boek van de Staten van Brabant* 50^{v} (see Alfred d'Hoop *Inventaire sommaire des archives des Etats de Brabant* 18). The Froben *Adagia* appeared in April 1515 (see *Bibliotheca Erasmiana* for a listing of editions). Erasmus does say in a letter of 24 January 1515 'Eduntur Adagiorum chiliades,' but he does not mean the work is completed, for he uses the same word (*eduntur*) of Froben's *Hieronymi opera*, which did not appear until January 1516. Erasmus felt he had been particularly free in speaking his mind in 'Scarabaeus': '... Nam in proverbio *Kantharos aeton maieuetai* [= Scarabaeus aquilam quaerit] plane lusimus ingenio' (Erasmus to Budé, letter 421, lines 83–9, II, 254 [cf below, note 152]).

139 'Scarabaeus aquilam quaerit' LB II, 871D. Pliny's discussion of eagles (*Hist. Nat.* X, 3–5, ed. E. de Saint Denis) offers details on which Erasmus seems to have built; e.g., the first of six species of eagles Pliny mentions ('sola aquilarum fetus suos alit – caeterae ... fugant') (cf LB II, 872B). Pliny's comment that cranes, unlike other birds, do not choose a leader for their migrations may have inspired LB II, 874D: 'Nec cum gruibus satis convenit, opinor ob id, quod illis impendio placeat Democratia, vehementer invisa Monarchis, a quibus tamen ingenio superantur.' I am indebted for these references to Professor Joseph Schork, now of the Classics Department of the University of Massachussetts in Boston.

140 LB II, 872C, 870EF; cf 962EF, 111E. The same passage from Homer is cited in the *Panegyricus* and the *Institutio principis* (Herding 64, line 212; 160, line 749).

141 Cf Erasmus' important letter to Luther's friend John Lang in October 1518: letter 872, lines 16–18, III, 409–10 (italic portions in Greek): 'Video *tēn tou Rhomanou Archieros* (ut nunc est ea sedes) *monarchian* pestem esse *Christianismi*.'

142 To Anthony of Bergen, CWE letter 288, lines 34–6, II, 280 (the passage is expanded in 'Dulce bellum inexpertis' LB II, 968EF).

143 'Ut fici oculis incumbunt' LB II, 654B

144 'A mortuo tributum exigere' LB II, 338C: 'Denique cum haec tam multa non possint explere vere pertusum dolium, h. e: Principum fiscum, bellum Praetexitur, colludunt Duces, populus infelix ad medullas usque exsugitur.' Also letter 288, line 55, I, 553 ('ne iam commemorem ex-

pilationem populi, ducum collusionem,' 'Sileni Alcibiadis' LB II, 775DE, and *Querela pacis* LB IV, 633CD.

145 'Ut fici oculis incumbunt' LB II, 654C; see above, note 44.

146 Above, note 129

147 LB II, 111E, 654B. Cf LB V, 354E, and *Querela pacis* LB IV, 634BC and 642C; the first and third passages are cited in this connection in Ines Thürlemann *Erasmus von Rotterdam und Juan Luis Vives als Pazifisten* 42–6. On Estates, see also below, chapter 4, note 105 and chapter 5, note 38.

148 *Julius exclusus, Erasmi opuscula* ed Ferguson 93–4, lines 508–22. Cf More's epigram 182, a comparison between a senate and a king, to the disadvantage of the latter.

149 A passage added to 'Ut fici oculis incumbunt' for the 1520 *Adagia* (Basel, Froben 1520), 494; Kurt von Raumer *Ewiger Friede: Friedensrufe und Friedenspläne seit der Renaissance* 18

150 In his notes to Jerome's *Epistolae* Erasmus lamented the fall of Tournai, 'ciuitas alioqui libera: cuiusmodi sunt aliquot in confinijs Francae ditionis & Burgundicae' (*Hieronymi opera* 40^{v}).

151 Louis Delaruelle *Guillaume Budé: les origines, les debuts, les idées maîtresses*; David O. McNeil *Guillaume Budé and Humanism in the Reign of Francis I*; see also the chapter on Budé in Donald R. Kelley *The Foundations of Modern Historical Scholarship*.

152 'Nam in prouerbio *Kantharos aeton maieutetai* ['Scarabaeus aquilam quaerit'] plane lusimus ingenio.' A translation like 'give free play to my thoughts' fits the context better than 'I was being hardly serious' (CWE letter 421, lines 95–6, III 307) or 'einen blossen Scherz,' suggested by Otto Herding in his introduction to *Institutio principis* (page 97).

153 Letter 403, lines 1–2, 121–30, II, 228, 232; letter 421, lines 75–88, 254 (my translation); letter 435, lines 45–60, 273–4: '... ibi tu nonnihil simile inueníes, licet impar, iis quae in tuis Silenis scripsisti'; CWE letter 435, lines 47–64, III, 330. Rogers *Correspondence of Thomas More* letters 65, 66, pages 124–34; More's letter does not specifically mention the digressions of *De asse*, but it may be that Budé (letter 66, lines 100–4) is referring not to letter 65, but to another letter, now lost. The correspondence between Erasmus and Budé, much of which was in Greek, is translated and annotated by Marie Madeleine de la Garanderie (*La Correspondance d'Erasme et de Guillaume Budé*). On the digressions of *De asse*, see Delaruelle *Guillaume Budé* 158–78; McNeil *Budé and Humanism* 29–36; and Marie-Madeleine de la Garanderie 'L'Harmonie sécrète du *De asse* de Budé.' After reading Budé's digressions Erasmus praised their content, but rather ungenerously commented that they distracted one from the main theme of the book (letter 480, lines 194–213, 255–68, II, 368–9).

154 *De asse*, in *Opera omnia* (5 vols, Basel, Episcopius 1557; reprinted by

Gregg, London 1966) 2: 168–9, 26. Cf *Utopia* trans Edward L. Surtz 40–2 and *Institutio principis* (Herding 208, lines 282–5).

155 *De asse* 165–6; Bridge *History of France* 4: 88

156 *De asse* 29: 'O beatam futuram te Francia, si intra te tantum felix esse uoluisses. Nam ex quo tempore extra fines auitos prosilire tibi uisum est, cum charissima pignora longissime amandasti, ad te nunquam reditura, tum uelut abdicatis tuis, alienis sinum pandere destinasti. Quod si in rem atque existimationem tuam futurum uidebatur, ut ad te aut gente aut cognatione potentatus pertinenteis omni ope reposceres, idque quando nisi Marte disceptante atque arbitro consequi nullo modo posses, uirium tuarum specimen facere extra fines oportebat: oportuerit sane, quandoquidem arduum est rebus temperare prosperis. Sed quis te superum infensus ita praeposteram egit, ut choragis pastophoris pyrricham saltare praeclarum esse duceres?'

157 *De asse* 176: 'Sic paucis annis factum, ut inuersis ordinibus patricii ad plebem, & plebeii ad patricios plausibiliter traducerentur'; 178: those in power overlook 'uiros eximios, qui aut ingenii ornamentis, aut praerogatiua natalium, aut innocentiae & doctrinae suffragio renunciari sperent'; 180: 'Etenim qui satis secundas partes implere nequeunt, qua (malum) fronte primas tenere contendunt? praesertim quum tot egregios actores inter cuneos inerteis exactosque sedere uideamus, & decus scene proceres longissime submotos?'

158 *De asse* 313

159 *De asse* 167, commenting on the Treaty of London (August 1514), by which Mary Tudor was pledged to wed Louis XII: 'Quid ni enim has ego superum inducias potius quam pacem uocandas esse putem, cum aspectum in caelum nos referre non uideam? Simul ab istis galeripetis metuo (ut aperte loquamur) qui nos semper e tranquillo in aestum atque in scopulum auferunt, fatali Franciae calamitate.'

160 *De asse* 271: '… sacerdotes, quos nunc ferme solos secundum reges & principes opulentos esse cernimus …' Above, note 157.

161 Delaruelle (*Guillaume Budé* 168–71) has rightly identified Amboise as the powerful figure who is so bitterly attacked in *De asse* 23–6 for his patronage of Italians. Italians who found favour at the court during Louis XII's reign included the historian Paolo Aemilio and Eramus' poet friend Fausto Andrelini: see above, note 71.

162 *De asse* 26; cf 29, 168.

163 Ibid 28–9

164 Delaruelle (above, note 161) identifies the other two leading figures Budé mentions on page 25 as the two chancellors, Guy de Rochefort (whom Budé praised) and Germain de Ganay. On Briçonnet and De Vesc, see Bridge, *History of France* 1: 237. See above, note 74.

165 *De asse* 23–4: 'Nam quum primores procerum, ignorantiam literarum

percupide sibi uendicent, ac nihil sui muneris esse in pacis artibus credant: euenit ut plurima aulae consulta ex paucorum commodo fiant, qui in rem ipsi suam suarumque necessitudinum concipere edicta principis consultaque didicerunt.'

166 Ibid 178, 24

167 Ibid 24, 288

168 Ibid 302–3, 175. For a sample of recent literature on Louis XI, see the essays by Chevalier and Pocquet du Haut-Jussé in P.S. Lewis (ed) *The Recovery of France in the Fifteenth Century*.

169 *De l'institution du prince* (Arriour, Nicole Paris 1547) 42, 64, 107–8; cf *De philologia* (Paris, Badius 1532) 40[v].

170 *De l'institution du prince* 79; above, note 168

171 Bertrand de Jouvenel *On Power* 124

172 Federico Chabod *Storia di Milano nel Epoca di Carlo V* 40–7

173 The notion that one can speak of 'new monarchies' in the late fifteenth or early sixteenth century seems on the whole to be losing ground: see the bibliography in A.J. Slavin *The 'New Monarchs' and Representative Assemblies*. Yet there can be little doubt that kings of this period had better command of national resources than did their predecessors 100 or 200 years earlier.

174 Paul D. Solon 'Popular Response to Standing Military Forces in Fifteenth Century France'

175 F.L. Taylor *The Art of War in Italy, 1494–1525*

176 Cruickshank *Army Royal*; E.F. Jacob *Henry V and the Invasion of France* 64–8; Paul Leroy Holmer, 'Studies in the Military Organization of the Yorkist Kings' 116

177 Bridge *History of France* 2: 93–4; Ferdinand Lot *Recherches sur les effectifs des armées françaises, 1494–1562* 41–2

178 See the biographies of the four Valois Dukes of Burgundy (Philip the Bold, John the Fearless, Philip the Good, Charles the Rash) by Richard Vaughan.

179 Füeter (*Geschichte des europäischen Staatensystems* 77–9) points out that the argument that France had to seize Lombardy to prevent Spain from gaining control of it – in other words, the strategic notion of preventive war – presumes a situation which did not exist until France's Italian policy had become an established fact.

180 Lemonnier *Les Guerres d'Italie* 13–16, citing the work of Delaborde on Charles VIII with which he disagrees, holding that Charles VIII turned away from the 'politique nationale' of his predecessors.

181 Füeter *Geschichte des europäischen Staatensystems* 77; Bridge *History of France* 2: 11

182 Cruickshank *Army Royal* 1

183 Jean Giono *The Battle of Pavia* 43

184 Lucien Romier *Les Origines politiques des guerres de religion*

185 P.S. Lewis *Later Medieval France* 81–101; some of Lewis' conclusions are disputed, however, by Paul Solon ('Popular Response').
186 'Spartam nactus es' LB II, 553AB: evidently a reference to Charles's prolonged seige of Neuss, near Cologne, in 1474
187 P. J. Blok *Geschiedenis eener Hollandsche Stadt* 2: 25
188 See the discusssion of *humanitas* in my *Erasmus: The Growth of a Mind*.
189 In *Institutio principis* Erasmus speaks of feeling for the *patria* as a force that binds together prince and subjects, but urges that *ratio*, rather than *usus* or *experientia*, be the basis of statecraft (Herding 184, lines 582–90; 148–9, lines 393–406 = LB IV, 590, 568). Erasmus to Budé, letter 480, lines 250–5, II, 369.
190 Chabod *Machiavelli and the Renaissance* 74: 'The national significance of *The Prince* lies elsewhere. We find it above all in the reaffirmation of the necessity of open and uninhibited political strife, which alone can avail to revive the greatness and glory of a land that has been "ravaged, plundered, violated and reviled."'
191 Budé *De studio litterarum* (Paris, Badius 1532) 13
192 *De asse* 169: 'Nam ne nusquam belligeremus, inquies noster animus ferre nullo modo potest. Sic opes iam nimias conteri bello continenti necesse est, & referre dicunt nostrorum quorundam aerarii dispensatorum, principes a rebus bellicis nunquam esse feriatos, ne tranquillo rerum statu rationes ipsis recognoscere uacet.' Not untypically, Budé links, as if they were parallel, two antithetical views of the subject.
193 *De l'institution du prince* 79: 'Car la reverence & Maiesté Royale est adherente & inseperable de la couronne & de la personne, en laquelle elle est située: & est la reverence & authorité de legitime Monarchie conioincte avec icelle Maiesté, & à elle adherente, comme l'umbre avec le corps.'
194 *Montaigne's Essays and Selected Writings* ed and trans Donald Frame 115. This quotation from 'Of Cannibals' should not be taken as a full statement of the views Montaigne developed on monarchy, especially as the French civil wars progressed: see Frieda Brown *Religious and Political Conservatism in the Essays of Montaigne*.
195 Pascal *Pensées* nos 324, 325

CHAPTER THREE

1 Henri Pirenne *Histoire de Belgique* 3: 75–7; AGN 4: 39ff
2 AGN 4: 45–8
3 Andreas von Walther *Die Anfänge Karls V* 133–42. Margaret's position was further weakened when, at the request of Ferdinand of Aragon, she arrested a Castilian nobleman resident in Brussels, Juan Manuel. Since Manuel was a knight of the Golden Fleece, entitled to trial by his peers, his summary arrest rallied to his cause other members of the order, which

traditionally included the most powerful nobles of the realm (AGN 4: 48–50).

4 Henne 2: 90, 123–4: the Estates of Flanders voted 200,000 écus in March; the Estates of Brabant voted 450,000 florins in January (Brewer II:1, 70), payable over three years, but obtained in return an addition to the *joyeuse entrée* stipulating that no further subsidy would be demanded during those three years. See chapter 2, note 138.

5 The post of grand chancellor of Burgundy was the summit of the legist hierarchy in the Burgundian state, as the post of first chamberlain was the summit of the aristocratic hierarchy (Andraeas von Walther *Die burgundischen Zentralbehörden unter Maximilian I und Karl V*). Sauvage (1455–1518), born of a bureaucratic family in Bruges, was the first grand chancellor who was not a native of Franche-Comté.

6 Pirenne (*Histoire de Belgique* 3: 81–4) believes the terms of the treaty were dictated by France: the dowry for Renée of France (daughter of the deceased Louis XII) was to be the Duchy of Berry (not the Duchy of Burgundy, which had been seized in 1477 by Louis XI), over which the French king was to retain sovereignty. Walther (*Die Anfänge Karls V* 148) believes the treaty brought an important advantage to Charles, since Ferdinand of Aragon, who was suspected of scheming to prevent Spain from falling to Charles, had been seeking Renée as a bride for Charles's younger brother, Ferdinand, who was growing up in Spain.

7 Brewer II:1, 473. The 'Intercursus malus,' so-called in the Netherlands because its terms favoured England, was drafted when Philip was in haste to depart for Castile in 1506 (Pirenne *Histoire de Belgique* 3: 64–8; Georg Schanz *Englische Handelspolitik gegen das Ende des Mittelalters* 1: 30–1).

8 Jervis Wegg *Richard Pace, A Tudor Diplomatist* 71–3

9 Ibid 3. Some years later, however, Pace was a partisan of peace between England and France, as is clear from the letter to him which is printed first in Budé's Latin *Epistolae*. Heinrich Ullmann *Kaiser Maximilian I* 2: 673–80.

10 Brewer II:1, 1764, 1822

11 An additional secret clause evidently provided for the sale to France of Verona, one of Maximilian's conquests in 1509 (Adelheid Schneller *Der brüsseler Friede von 1516* 25–35).

12 Brewer II:1, 2450, 2663, 2685; II:2, 2909, 2958, 3178, 3180, 3210, 3223

13 Ibid II:1, 2450, 2463, 2486; II:2, 2911 (Tunstall on the crown imperial); Wegg *Richard Pace* 102

14 Schneller *Der brüsseler Friede* 43–55

15 Brewer II:1, 2700, 2715

16 Ludwig Pastor *A History of the Popes* 7: 161

17 Brewer II:1, 2713; II:2, 2863

18 Above, note 12
19 Brewer II:2, 3182, 3271: Henry and Maximilian were still exchanging private communications in May.
20 Pastor *History of the Popes* 7: 161–6, 210–11
21 Ibid 6: 299: the ostensible object of the League of Cambrai (1508) had been the union of Christian powers for a crusade against the Turks. For similar proposals in 1517, see Brewer II:2, 3375; Pastor, *History of the Popes* 7: 213–30.
22 J.S. Theissen *De Regering van Karel V in de Noordlijke Nederlanden* 48–9
23 Letter 266, lines 11–14, I, 519. Erasmus might have settled in England could suitable arrangements have been made. In September 1514 Lord Mountjoy obtained for him the promise of a canonry in Tournai, but Erasmus was not surprised when the appointment – which proved of little value, since Wolsey, the English nominee for bishop, was never accepted by the Tournai clergy – went instead to the son of a royal physician (Brewer II:1, 889, 890; letter 360, lines 15–20, II, 149–150; letter 371, 162–3).
24 Above, chapter 2, notes 137, 138
25 Letter 301, lines 35–8, II, 6: 'Offendi hic Praesidem Flandriae ... nam Caesarem et alios quosdam [friends of Erasmus in Ghent] antea noueram.'
26 Letter 332 (Allen's preface); Walther *Burgündische Zentralbehörden* (cf above, note 5).
27 Letter 332, lines 2–3, II, 67–8
28 Letter 370, lines 16–20, II, 161. *Novum instrumentum* (Basel, Froben 1516) 294 (called 268); letter 597, lines 26–8, III, 5; letter 621, lines 9–11, 43. Erasmus' salary was 300 florins, of which Sauvage on one occasion advanced him 200 out of his own pocket.
29 Letter 657, lines 46–60, III, 79
30 Allen I, 19, lines 24–33; II, 205
31 Allen's preface to letter 603
32 Letter 410, lines 1–5, II, 240
33 Letter 412, lines 51–5, II 243
34 CWE letter 436, lines 4–8, III, 333–4
35 Allen I, 44, lines 3–5
36 CWE letter 443, lines 19–21, III, 341
37 Letter 476, lines 22–4, II, 357. Roland Bainton (*Erasmus of Christendom* 111) accepts this statement. Allen (letter 475, line 4n, II, 355) believes Erasmus would have accepted a bishopric if he could have held it without residing, as did Sauvage's chaplain, Peter Barbirius (letter 476, line 12n). See below, note 38.
38 Letter 2613, line 7, IX, 441: 'A Syluagio pertractus contempsi fortunam

Anglicam.' Erasmus to Pirckheimer, 2 November 1517, letter 694, lines 7–17, III, 116–17: 'Proximo vere cum Angliam ob priuatum quoddam adissem negotium [see letter 577], Rex vltro me mira complexus est humanitate, atque item Cardinalis [Wolsey], Rex alter, vt ita loquar. Obtulerunt praeter aedes magnificas sexcentos florenos in singulos annos [see Allen's note; the actual offer was 100 marks]. Sic egi gratias vt nec acciperem conditionem oblatam nec reiicerem. Hic [Louvain] licet maximo meo sumtu viuam, tamen certum est menses aliquot desidere, partim vt absoluam quod est in manibus, partim vt videam quorsum euasurae sint spes amplissimae quas Principis nomine mihi discedens hinc ostendit Cancellarius Burgundiae, Ioannes Syluagius, vir vt eruditissimus, ita litteratorum omnium patronus.' It seems likely only a bishopric could have given Erasmus a larger income than he was promised in England.

39 Letter 475, lines 9–11, II, 355. Allen (II, 291–2) believes the appeal was linked to, among other things, Erasmus' hope for a bishopric.

40 See Allen's introduction to letter 447, II, 291–3.

41 Letter 475, lines 1–11, II, 354–5; letter 476, lines 9–26, 356–7

42 Letter 476, lines 1–3, II, 356; cf letter 475, line 13, 355; letter 474, lines 15–16, 354; letter 438, line 12, 278; letter 483, lines 18–20, 374.

43 Brewer II:1, 2463

44 Brewer II:1, 2640 (Tunstall to Wolsey, 6 December 1516), 2700 (Wolsey to Tunstall, 25 December). Tunstall held to his supicions. Brewer (II:2, 2765) notes that the following sentence from Tunstall's mid-January dispatch to the king was not deciphered by Brian Tuke: 'On the coming of the emperor it will be seen whether the Lady Margaret is altered or the ambassadors.'

45 Brewer II:1, 2702; II:2, 2756, 3128

46 Brewer (II, cxiii) is critical of Tunstall for transmitting the funds to Maximilian: 'His habitual caution and timidity foiled his first and better judgment.' Charles Sturge (*Cuthbert Tunstall* 38–46) argues, with very little evidence, that Tunstall made this decision to keep alive the possibility of an alliance with the empire, because he feared that France and the empire might combine to support Richard de la Pole, Yorkist claimant to the throne. Neither seems justly to appreciate the risk Tunstall ran in placing himself in opposition to Henry's desire for a coalition against France.

47 Brewer II:1, 2132

48 Ibid 2640

49 Ibid II:2, 2910, 2911. Despite his support of an anti-French coalition, Richard Pace took a similar dim view of Maximilian's offer: 'Whilst we worked for the crown imperial, we might lose the crown of England, which is this day more esteemed than the emperor's crown' (Wegg *Richard Pace* 102).

50 Brewer II:2, 2863, 2910, 2911, 2923; later, when he adopted Henry's belief that Margaret was 'truly minded,' Worcester no longer confided in Tunstall (2993, 3005).
51 Ibid 2923
52 Ibid 3128
53 Ibid II:1, 2685, 2270, 2671 (Tunstall on Maximilian)
54 See below, note 70.
55 Brewer II:1, 2484, 2663
56 Erasmus thought of himself as excessively free in speech (letter 2599, lines 47–50, IX, 418). But cf letter 628, lines 54–7, III, 52: 'Theatinus Episcopus [Gianpietro Caraffa] spe fortunae se suosque omneis sumptibus exhausit. Et delatus est apud Regem litterulis per notulas scriptis, quod ipse nondum nouit. Nec mihi tutum erat illi indicare, ne in periculum vocarem eos a quibus acceperam.' Although not always trusted by Erasmus (above, chapter 2, note 103), Caraffa was at this time his staunch protector (below, note 141). Pastor (*History of the Popes* 10: 404–5) cites for this period of Caraffa's life C. Bromato *Storia di Paulo IV* (Ravenna 1748).
57 Brewer II:1, 2685: when an unknown man purporting to be a messenger from Margaret of Austria presented him with written assurances concerning the plan to overthrow Chièvres, Tunstall professed ignorance of the scheme, believing (incorrectly) that the handwriting was not Margaret's; II:2, 3343: Tunstall interprets Juan de la Nucha's criticism of Chièvres as an effort to have him compromise himself by joining in the criticism.
58 Cf *Lingua* (1525) ed. Schalk, 273–4, lines 253–68 (= LB IV, 681E–682A): '... ita non debetur silentii fides, ei qui primus silentii foedus violauit. Ante complures annos coenabam cum viro prudenti juxta ac docto, qui tum apud nostros regis sui nomine legatum agebat. Interuenit quidam Dominicanus, qui Romani Pontificis negotia procurabat. Expetiit arcanum coloquium. Secessum est. Domincanus aiebat arcanum esse quod vellet communicare, non communicaturus tamen, nisi [legatus] iuraret se tactiurum. Alter negabat se iuraturum in re, cuius ipse cognoscendae desiderio non teneretur. "Si mihi" inquit "diffidis, ne communica: sin fidis, quid opus est iureiurando? Quod etiamsi intercessisset, & referret principem meum scire quod credidisses, non celarem. Neque enim iusiurandum hoc animo suscipitur a bonis viris, vt dum alteri fidem servat, principi suo fidem violet, cui ego" inquit "non simplici nomine fidem debeo, Primum vt civis, deinde vt legatus. Si tale fuerit vt citra impietatem et crimen violati officii sileri queat, polliceor silentium, non iuro: neque enim soleo iurare temere, et is sum qui silere possim: Sin secus, serva tibi mysterium." Hac oratione victus ille communicavit nugamentum, quod nec ad principem, nec ad legatum quicquam attinebat.' If this envoy to the Burgundian court was indeed Tunstall, the story is an interesting document of his sense of obligation as an ambassador.

59 Letter 571, II, 538–44
60 Herding 216, lines 548–50 (= LB 609CD)
61 Erasmus knew, of course, that England was not a party to the Cambrai meeting (see below, note 77). In this letter, written in 1523–4, he probably confused the Cambrai Conference with the Field of the Cloth of Gold near Calais in 1520, in which Henry VIII did participate (Allen IV, 296).
62 Ibid I, 18, line 29 to 19, line 3
63 Pastor *History of the Popes* 7: 161–5; LB IV, 636C
64 Letter 603, lines 24–9, III, 15: '... quidam, amicis quam hostibus grauiores ...' It is difficult to imagine who besides the English could be meant. For reasons why Erasmus may have chosen Philip of Burgundy to be dedicand of the *Querela pacis*, see below, chapter 4, note 115. Elsewhere (below, note 70) he links Henry with Maximilian as lukewarm proponents of peace.
65 Brewer II:2, 3174, 3271; Ullmann *Kaiser Maximilian I* 2: 689. The emperor had no reason for discontent with an agreement which would abandon French claims to the Kingdom of Naples, held by one of his grandsons (Charles of Castile), and create a kingdom for the other (Ferdinand) in Tuscany and the Veneto.
66 Letter 541, the famous letter to Wolfgang Capito hailing the birth of a new age (see lines 6ff.), lines 42–8, II, 488–9
67 Bartholinus to Erasmus, sending along Velius' *Genethliacon Erasmi*, letter 548, lines 3–4, II, 499, with Allen's note. Allen dates this letter (c. March 10) to bring it into proximity with Erasmus' reply to Bartholinus, dated March 10. But Velius' poem was composed c. February, and there is no reason why Erasmus cannot have received it before writing Capito (above, note 66) on February 26.
68 Letter 669, lines 12–13, III, 92; letter 670, 93; letter 688, lines 12–13, 111
69 See Herding 101–2 for evidence, several months after Erasmus' just-quoted letters to More, of a plan to make him Ferdinand's teacher.
70 LB IV, 642BC: 'Vocat ille non titulo tantum Christianissimus Galliarum Rex Franciscus, qui pacem nec emere gravatur, nec usquam suae majestatis habet rationem, modo publicae paci consulat: hoc denique vere splendidum ac Regium esse docens, de genere humano quam optime mereri. Vocat huc clarissimus Princeps Carolus, incorruptae indolis adolescens. Nec abhorret Caesar Maximilianus, nec detrectat inclytus Angliae Rex Henricus.' The description of Francis I as willing to 'buy' peace seems an allusion to the impecunious emperor's habit of selling his friendship dear: see above, chapter 2, note 138. Henry VIII had 'purchased' Maximilian's participation in a league against France in 1512 (chapter 2, note 14) and again in 1516 (Tunstall's mission). The passage might be taken as a hint that Erasmus knew, perhaps through Tunstall or Schinner, that Henry was attempting once more to buy the emperor's allegiance.

71 LB IV, 638DE; see Pierre Mesnard *L'Essor de la philosophie politique au XVIe siècle* 133–5 on the argument for amity between France and the Netherlands based on a lack of natural frontiers. Mesnard cites a variant reading from a 1518 edition which makes explicit that Flanders was being claimed (falsely) as a part of Germany. Cf letter 421, lines 31–4, II, 253; and below, note 74.

72 LB IV, 640C: 'Vis hanc aut illam ditionis partem vindicare, quid istud ad populi negotium? Vis ulcisci qui filiae renunciavit, quid hoc ad Rempublicam?' For the interpretation of this passage, see above, chapter 1, note 4.

73 So Tunstall believed (Brewer II:2, 2910). See Paul Egers 'Kardinal Matthäus Lang' 501.

74 Erasmus tended to think of his countrymen as Germans or 'Gauls,' depending on whether he was writing to Germans (Lang, Bartholinus' employer, was Bishop of Gurk) or Frenchmen (Johan Huizinga 'Erasmus über Vaterland und Nationen' 40–1). Huizinga's views in general are supported by J.J. Poelhekke ('Het Naamloze Vaderland van Erasmus').

75 Letter 549, lines 6–30, II, 501; LB IV, 633EF. The pro-French orientation of the *Querela pacis* has been discussed by Elise Constantinescu-Bagdat *La 'Querela pacis' d'Erasme* 15–19. See also chapter 4, note 113.

76 Herding 206, lines 226–43 (LB IV, 603AB); *Utopia* trans Edward L. Surtz, 117. Cf [Tunstall's?] attitude toward oath-taking, above, note 58.

77 Letter 505, lines 18–21, II, 424

78 Petrus Aegidius (Gilles) *Summae sive argumenta legum diversorum imperatorum* (Louvain, Martens [1517]), dedicatory preface to Sauvage. For Gilles' friendship with Erasmus, see Floris Prims, 'Aegidius' in his *Antwerpiensa, losse Bijdragen tot de Antwerpse Geschiedenis* 168–75; M.A. Nauwelaerts 'Un Ami anversois de More et d'Erasme, Petrus Aegidius.'

79 Letter 586, lines 245–51, II, 586

80 See above, chapter 2, note 47; see below, note 83.

81 Above, note 3; Herding 189, lines 742–6 (= LB IV, 593CD): 'Commodissima fuerit augendi vectigalis ratio, si princeps sumptus superuacaneos amputarit, si ministeria ociosa reiecerit, si bella et his simillimas peregrinationes vitauerit, si officiorum rapacitatem cohibuerit, et si magis studeat recte administrandae ditioni suae quam propagandae.' For a story of how Maximilian dealt with peculation by his officials, see the colloquy 'Convivium fabulosum' (LB I, 764BF).

82 Herding 184, lines 582–9; 209, lines 335–41 (= LB IV, 590, 606)

83 *Querela pacis* LB IV, 637B: 'Nunc hujusmodi matrimoniorum vicibus fit, ut apud Hibernos natus, repente imperet Indis, aut qui modo Syris imperabat, subito Rex fit Italiae.' The last example could be a veiled reference to secret negotiations at Cambrai (above, note 16) which called for a kingdom to be created in Tuscany or the Veneto for Ferdinand.

84 George of Thiemsecke, provost of Cassel. Letter 412, lines 51–2: Erasmus found Thiemsecke and the papal legate Cajetan at dinner with Sauvage when he went to greet the chancellor. More, one of the English negotiators (above, note 7), felt Thiemsecke was of crucial importance (Henne 2: 150n, citing an article by Baron De Reiffenberg in *Nouvelles Archives historiques pour le Pays Bas* 5: 94). Brewer II:1, 581: Thomas Spinelly, the English agent in Bruges, learned from private conversation with Thiemsecke that the government wanted English merchants to resort to Bruges. Georg Schanz (*Englische Handelspolitik gegen das Ende des Mittelalters* 1: 41–8) rightly complains that Spinelly's 'gossipy' correspondence is the only source for these negotiations. He notes that Thiemsecke, as a prominent citizen of Bruges, had a personal stake in that port's prosperity. Spinelly's report of the conversation concludes with a reference to the danger of rebellion by the men of Antwerp: 'And rather than the English men should have remission of these tolls, which is the cause of your passing their country and leaving them, they would rage and be ready to an insurrection' (Brewer, II:1, 581). The fact that Antwerp should insist on maintaining the 'Zeeuwse toll' (cf *Nicolai Everardi Consiliorum opus* III, 7–8, a defence of Bergen's exemption from the Antwerp toll) supports the argument that earlier notions of a contrast in economic philosophy between 'free trade' Antwerp and 'protectionist' Bruges were overdrawn: see W. Brulez 'Brugge en Antwerpen in de 15e en 16e Eeuwen: een Tegenstelling?' Further evidence that the economic policy of Chièvres' government was somewhat favourable to Flanders may be found in an *ordonnance* dated in Bruges just as these negotiations began (8 May 1515): in response to a petition from the Four Members of Flanders, the merchants of Antwerp and Bergen are instructed to stop holding their fairs for longer periods of time than were allowed by the *ordonnance* of 15 May 1498 (*Recueil des anciennes ordonnances de la Belgique 2e Série, 1506–1700* 1: 398–400).

85 Herding 200–1, lines 50–9 (= LB IV 599EF). More *The Epigrams* no. 1, 16, 18; Everardi *Consiliorum opus* III, 7–10: 'Ius recipiendi vectigal ... a mercatoribus vel nautis ... est quaedam servitus.' Hubertus Schulte-Hebrüggen (*Sir Thomas More: Neue Briefe*) suggests that More's visit to Erasmus' friend Peter Gilles in Antwerp – it was at Gilles' house that More began his *Utopia* – was connected with the trade negotiations. Was Gilles perhaps a partisan of the solution eventually agreed on in 1516, whereby the Zeeuwse toll was no longer to be collected from English merchants?

86 Herding 190–2, lines 781–8 (= LB IV, 594), with Herding's note. On the system of taxation in Holland, see H. Terdenge 'Zur Geschichte der holländischen Steuern im 15en und 16en Jahrhundert' and Robert Fruin 'De Verpandingen van 1496 en 1515 en haar Voorbereidung.'

87 Herding 192–4, lines 824–40 (= LB IV 595F–596B): '... At cum aduentante principe ciues, si quid est elegantius in supellectile abdunt, filias

insigni forma recludunt, adolescentes ablegant, opes dissimulant ...' The language suggests Erasmus is here thinking of the prince as accompanied by mercenaries or recruiting agents as well as by tax-assessors. On mercenaries, see chapter 4, pages 88–90; also chapter 1, note 63.

88 Letter 1469, lines 222–44, V, 504; letter 421, lines 83–91, II, 254. Cf Allen I, 19, lines 30–3: 'Et tamen huius libelli libertate nemo magnatum offensus est. Ferunt boni principes liberam admonitionem, seditiosam licentiam non ferunt.'

89 Miriam Chrisman *Strasbourg in the Age of Reform* 195. In 1530, the city council sought to arrest the Anabaptist Melchior Hoffman because of a book which compared the emperor to the Beast of the Apocalypse (Cornelius Krahn *Dutch Anabaptism* 91). Sebastian Franck *Chronica, Zeytbüch und Geschÿchtbibel* cxix–cxxv: 'Vorred auff des Adlers ... Art ... das allermeist aus dem Sprichwort Erasmi Scarabeus ... entnemen.' Franck borrowed also from the adages 'Aut regem aut fatuum nasci oportet' and 'Sileni Alcibiadis.' See Rudolf Kommoss *Sebastian Franck und Erasmus von Rotterdam* 90. Though famed for its tolerance, Strasbourg at this time – a Protestant city – wished to avoid offending Emperor Charles V.

90 Letter 608, lines 12–17, III, 21: Erasmus classes Adrian with Standish and Briselot, men he considered resolute enemies of 'good letters.' But see also letter 171, lines 10–13, I, 380.

91 Henri De Vocht (*Jerome de Busleiden, His Life and Writings* 315–17) concludes that Adrian's duties as Charles's teacher probably began in 1510.

92 Loys Gallut, cited in Henne 2: 80–1

93 AGN 4: 61–4. O. Cartellieri (*Am Hofe der Herzöge von Burgund* 187–95) notes that Charles the Rash tended to prefer the heroes of antiquity to those of chivalric legend. As Count of Charolais, before succeeding his father Philip the Good as Duke of Burgundy, he commissioned tapestries celebrating the deeds of Hannibal and Alexander. Vasco de Lucena's *Faictz et gestes d'Alexandre*, based on Quintus Curtius, was but one of several vernacular renderings of ancient histories done at his behest. Charles himself studied Caesar's *Commentaries* and Xenophon's *Cyropaideia*, while his councillor Humbertcourt frequently read to him at bedtime from other ancient works. *Perceforest*, which brings together Alexander the Great and the Knights of the Round Table, also dates from this era. On the 'Trojan' origins of the Habsburg-Burgundian house, see Olivier de la Marche (d. 1504) *Mémoires* ed H. Beaune & J. d'Arbaumont, 1: 17–22. Cf Earl Rosenthal '*Plus ultra, non plus ultra* and the Columnar Device of the Emperor Charles V': Charles's 1516 device, 'Plus Oultre,' had its sources in fifteenth-century chivalric literature, not in the classics.

94 See Charles N. Cochrane *Christianity and Classical Culture*.

95 *De l'institution du prince* 32–3
96 *De asse* 28, 23–4
97 *De l'institution du prince* 33, 43; cf *De philologia* (Paris, Badius 1532) 34^{v}, 42^{v}, 67–8.
98 *De l'institution du prince* 9
99 *De philologia* 23–23^{v} on previous writers of French history: 'Qui postquam se in mari (ut vocant) historiarum ingurgitarunt, rerum gestarum commenta miserabilia in coetu imperitorum fundunt. His nos historias suas interdum serio & graviter memorantibus (qui iamdiu emersimus ex eo fabularum figmentorumque pelago) velut scurrilibus acroamatis auscultare solemus: easque nugas eo loco habere, quo mythistorias illas nobiles mensae orbicularis, quae tamen ipsae lectores scita & artifici varietate delectant, mirisque illecebris commemorationum, hominum attentionem illiteratorum retinent.' Donald Kelley (*Foundations of Modern Historical Scholarship* 76–8) notes that Budé, in his regard for French history and culture, departed from conventional humanist ideas about the unique superiority of classical civilization.
100 On *De l'institution du prince*, see the last chapter of Louis Delaruelle *Guillaume Budé: les origines, les débuts, les idées maîtresses* and, of less value, Milosch Triwunar *Guillaume Budés 'De l'institution du prince'*.
101 *De l'institution du prince* 99
102 Ibid 142, 114, 116–17, 121
103 Ibid 63, 144
104 Ibid 193–4; Triwunar *Budés 'De l'institution du prince'* 65–6
105 *De l'institution du Prince* 97, 38; cf Erasmus' attitude towards the mendicant friars and, earlier, Poggio Bracchiolini's *De avaritia* and *Contra fratres ipocritas* and Lorenzo Valla's treatise (unpublished till the nineteenth century) *De votis monasticis*. Budé also wrote, however, a treatise *De contemptu rerum fortuitarum*.
106 *De l'institution du Prince* 96, 145
107 Ibid 73, 17–19
108 *De transitu hellenismi ad christianismum* 12^{v}, 18^{v}–19, 30^{v}–31, 41^{v}–42, 54, 58^{v}, 60^{v}–64, 72, 75–75^{v}, 79–79^{v}, 92: *prudentia* has several meanings, not all negative. Cf Josef Bohatec *Budé und Calvin: Studien zum Gedankenwelt des französischen Humanismus*.
109 *Institutio principis* Herding 140, lines 139–42 (= LB IV, 563)
110 Herding 77, lines 649–65 (= LB IV, 539)
111 CWE letter 337, lines 32–5, III, 112 (on personal glory); Herding 164, lines 889–891 (= LB IV, 577CD)
112 Herding 176, lines 312–20 (= LB IV, 576)
113 See above, note 93.
114 CWE letter 126, lines 49–52, I, 257 (cf LB I, 89C); Herding 140, lines 149–50 (= LB IV, 564A). On the *Institutio principis*, see Herding 'Isok-

rates, Erasmus, und die *Institutio principis christiani'* ; and Herding's introduction to the Rotterdam edition.

115 Herding 148–9, lines 393–406 (= LB IV, 568), above, note 97

116 Herding 182, lines 499–503 (= LB IV, 588F–589A); *The Education of a Christian Prince* trans Lester K. Born, 203

117 *Enchiridion militis christiani* LB V, 29BE; *Institutio principis* Herding 180, lines 458–62, and 179–80, lines 420–30 (= LB IV, 588B, 587CB). See above, chapter 2, note 133.

118 Budé *De philologia* 43–59; More *The Epigrams* no. 19, p. 27; *Moriae encomium* LB IV, 442A–441B. Marcelle Derwa ('Trois Aspects humanistes de l'épicurisme chrétien' *Colloquium Erasmianum* 124) notes that Valla undertook a 'demystification of heroism' in his *De voluptate*, and that Erasmus and More shared in his Epicurean rejection of aristocratic 'shame-culture.'

119 Herding 146, lines 296–302 (= LB IV, 566); Charity Cannon Willard 'The Concept of True Nobility at the Court of Burgundy' *Studies in the Renaissance* 14 (1967): 33–48

120 Above, note 96; chapter 2, note 157

121 Herding 197–8, lines 950–82 (monks and nobles; = LB IV, 597F–598A). Cf ibid 154, lines 558–71, with Herding's insightful comment.

122 Ibid 144, lines 257–9 (= LB IV, 563, 565)

123 Ibid 144, lines 237–9 (= LB IV, 565)

124 'Sileni Alcibiadis' LB II, 774EF

125 Above, note 121

126 The contrast between *fortuna* and the Christian doctrine of providence, indeed *praedestinatio*, occurs throughout Budé's works, but especially in *De transitu hellenismi ad christianismum*. See Bohatec's groundbreaking study (above, note 108) of the development from Budé to Calvin.

127 *Novum testamentum* (Basel, Froben 1527) 215, note to 1 Tim. 3:16, the 'mystery of godliness'

128 *Panegyricus* Herding 59, lines 47–52 (= LB IV, 527): 'Etenim quum princeps inter mortales quasi numinis vice fungatur, nihil autem deo vel ad beneficentiam propensius vel a saeuicia alienius neque quicquam aliud omnino sit deus, vt ait Plinius, quam *iuuare mortalem*, profecto quo quisque maius gerit imperium, hoc oportet propius ad istam imaginem accedere.'

129 *Institutio principis* Herding 150, lines 450–7 (= LB IV, 569); also 'Sileni Alcibiadis' LB II, 775BD . J.A. Fernandez ('Erasmus on the Just War' *Journal of the History of Ideas* 34 [1973]: 217–18, citing 'Sileni Alcibiadis' [no column reference]) believes Erasmus felt that a Christian prince could not legitimately assume *imperium*, meaning the power to make war. If he has in mind LB II, 780AF, he has failed to note the context, in which Erasmus is discussing the wisdom of the acceptance of *imperium*

in Italy by the popes (above, chapter 2, notes 58–63).

130 Herding 214–15, lines 501–11; *Querela pacis* LB IV, 633AB, 640EF

131 *Querela pacis* LB IV, 630A: 'Sit ultionum Deus, modo vindictam accipias, vitiorum correctionem, ut cruentas strages, quibus Hebraeorum libri referti sunt, non ad laniandos homines, sed ad impios affectus e pectore profligandos referas'; *Institutio principis* Herding 147, lines 354–6 (= LB IV, 567): 'at post mortem iudicium haud aequum est omnibus, in quo cum nullis seuerius agetur quam cum potentibus'; 194, lines 845–9 (= LB IV, 596); see above, chapter 2, note 37 (last passage quoted).

132 Herding 146–7, lines 327–36 (= LB IV 567)

133 Herding 159, lines 698–704 (= LB IV 574AB). As a source for this passage, Herding cites Augustine *De civitate Dei* XIV 28; XIX 14. For Erasmus' generally critical views of Biblical literalism, see *Hieronymi opera* 5, 61; letter 1006, lines 206–38, IV, 48–9; and LB IX, 834–5. Herding 'Isokrates, Erasmus, und die *Institutio principis*' 101–2.

134 Herding 165–6, lines 930–78 (= LB IV, 578–9). Cf Ephesians 6:5–9.

135 Herding 166–7, lines 979–95 (= LB IV, 579)

136 Ibid 148, lines 367–87 (= LB IV, 568AB)

137 Geldner *Die Staatsauffassung und Fürstenlehre des Erasmus von Rotterdam* 149; Herding, 'Isokrates, Erasmus, und die *Institutio Principis*' 101–2

138 Cf his concept of the *humanitas* of Christ as described in my *Erasmus: The Growth of a Mind*.

139 Fernandez ('Erasmus on the Just War') makes this point in regard to his *Utilissima consultatio de bello turcis inferendo* (1530).

140 Hans Hillerbrand *Die politische Ethik des oberdeutschen Täufertums* 58–60. Before pressing the comparison further, one ought to examine the question whether Erasmus is presenting in *Institutio principis*, on pedagogical or rhetorical grounds, a moral ideal he expects never to be fulfilled. Herding has found fourteen references to Plato's *Republic*, and Erasmus seems to admit in one place, in connection with his comments on dynastic marriage, that he has no hope his advice will be followed (209, lines 340–1 = LB IV, 606). One must not forget that Erasmus' friend More was the author of *Utopia*.

141 Letter 539, lines 1–10, II, 484. Erasmus had given offence to some Louvain theologians by his *Moriae encomium* and by his 1516 edition of the Greek New Testament.

142 Letter 532, lines 23–6, II, 476; letter 543, lines 9–10, 494

143 Letter 694, lines 4–7, III, 116: (Erasmus remains in Louvain) 'Id malui quam Principem Carolum in Hispanias comitari; maxime cum viderem aulam in tot sectam factiones Hispanos, Maranos, Ciuericos, Gallos, Caesareanos, Neapolitanos, Siculos et quos non.' What Walther (*Die Anfänge Karls V* 153–5) calls the Castilian nationalist party was aligned against Ferdinand's Aragonese partisans. The fact that Erasmus speaks of

'Marranos' rather than Aragonese suggests he may have been listening to Ferdinand's enemies.

144 Erasmus to More, letter 545, lines 15–17, II, 497: 'Si [Juan Luis] Viues crebro fuit apud te, facile coniectabis quid ego passus sim Bruxellae, cui cotidie cum tot salutatoribus Hispanis fuerit res, praeter Italos et Germanos.' Letter 700, lines 3–4, III, 125: 'Sed id temporis ex aula Bruxellensi profugeram, Hispanorum improbis consalutationibus pene extinctus.' See above, chapter 1, note 53.

145 F. Kossman 'Een Vergeten Lofdicht van Erasmus op de Ordre van het Gouden Vlies door Alvar Gomez 1517.' The poem is reprinted in Cornelis Reedijk *The Poems of Erasmus* 324–6. Gomez' *De militia principis Burgundi quam velleris aurei vocant*, together with Erasmus' poem, was first printed in Toledo in 1540. Gomez introduced himself to Erasmus (letter 506) with a poem in honour of Marliani, who had just been named Bishop of Tuy in Galicia, and who, as De Vocht notes (*Jerome de Busleiden* 358–61), preached before the Chapter of the Golden Fleece held in Brussels on 27 October 1516. Erasmus praises Gomez' 'magniloquente camoena' (line 8), his 'graniloquo ... versu' (line 11), and the 'sacrumque furorem / Carminis Hispani' (lines 15–16), stylistic and psychological characteristics which he otherwise always deprecated. A further touch of irony can be found in 'ter magno ... Charlo' (line 12), an allusion to 'Thrice-great Mercury,' (Hermes Trismegistus), the supposed author of the late classical collection of magical writings which was gaining popularity among some humanists. Erasmus was displeased when a friend called him 'ter maximum' (G. Clutton 'Ter Maximum, a Humanist Jest'). Cf 'Ter Maximi Pontifices,' added to the 1515 *Moriae encomium* (my 'Erasmus Becomes a German' 287).

146 *Querela pacis* LB IV, 628CD

147 Letter 2613, lines 7–13, IX, 441

148 Letter 526, II, 452: noting Tunstall's departure from Brussels, Peter Gilles expected Erasmus in Antwerp at the beginning of February. Gilles was Erasmus' perennial host in Antwerp during these years; above, note 78.

149 Letter 625, lines 15–18, III, 49; above, note 38

150 Letter 597, lines 3–16, III, 4

151 Henne 2: 84; letter 85, line 10, I, 222

152 Letter 628, lines 24–7, III, 51; letter 597, lines 3–16, 4

153 Letter 597, lines 8–10; for the translation, letter 641, lines 5–7, 63

154 *Institutio principis* Herding 176, lines 331–5 (= LB IV, 585EF)

155 Letter 597, lines 10–12, III, 4

156 Alonso Manrique (then Bishop of Bajadoz) to Cardinal Ximénes de Cisneros, 8 March 1516, *Bulletins de la Commision royale d'histoire* ed L.P. Gachard (1st series, vol 10, 1845): 24: 'El principal que govierna, y por cuya mano se hace todo, es monsieur de Xebres.'

157 See above, note 141.

158 See above, note 62.

159 'Aut regem, aut fatuum nasci oportere' LB II, 107C. The phrase is again applied to Chièvres in letter 628, line 59, III, 52. Cf a similar passage in Budé's attack (*De asse*, 1557 *Opera* II, 25) on Georges d'Amboise, Louis XII's chief minister: 'omnia iam infra supra nutu uerti suo uolens ...'

160 Above, note 143

161 Letter 628, lines 59–61, III, 52; see also 68. Cf above, note 112.

162 *Institutio principis* Herding 179, lines 420–6 (= LB IV, 587CD)

163 *Querela pacis* LB IV, 634F–635A: 'Ante paucos annos, cum fatali quodam morbo mundus ad arma raperetur, Euangelici praecones, hoc est, Minores ac Dominicani quidam e suggesto sacro classicum canebant, & ultro ad furiam propensos magis accendebant. Apud Britannos animabant in Gallos, apud Gallos animabant in Britannos.' He had in mind the English Franciscan Edmund Birkhead (letter 1211, lines 561, 602, IV, 524–6), among others. But see above, chapter 2, note 90.

164 Above, notes 118–25

165 *Die Anfänge Karls V* 127–32, speaking especially of Peter Martyr d'Anghiera

166 Robert T. Adams 'Pre-Renaissance Courtly Propaganda for Peace in English Literature'; Maurice Keen *The Laws of War in the Middle Ages*

167 Commines *Mémoires* ed Joseph Calmette, I, iii, 26. Cf LB II, 959C: 'cum incertum sit, quo sit alea belli casura.'

168 Chapter 1, note 72

CHAPTER FOUR

1 Ludwig Duncker *Fürst Rudolf der Tapfere von Anhalt und der Krieg gegen Herzog Karl von Geldern 1507/1508*; J.E.A.L. Struick *Gelre en Habsburg, 1492–1528* 58–65

2 Le Baron Guillaume *Histoire des bandes d'ordonnance des Pays Bas* 3–57

3 Duncker *Fürst Rudolf der Tapfere* 17–37. See below, note 83.

4 See, for example, Henri Pirenne *Early Democracies in the Low Countries*; B. Chevalier 'Le Roi Louis XI et les bonnes villes: le cas de Tours'; Rudolf von Albertini *Das florentinische Staatsbewusstsein im Übergang von der Republik zum Prinzipat*; and José Antonio Maravall *Las Comunidades de Castilla*.

5 C.C. Bayley *War and Society in Renaissance Florence*; Gennaro Sasso *Niccolò Machiavelli, storia del suo pensiero politico*; F.L. Taylor *The Art of War in Italy, 1494–1525*

6 Paul D. Solon 'Popular Response to Standing Military Forces in Fifteenth-Century France'; Chevalier 'Le Roi Louis XI et les bonnes villes'

7 [Pieter de la Court] *Historie van Holland onder de Gravelijke Regering* 151–2

8 Struick *Gelre en Habsburg* 50

9 Josse de Weert *Chronycke van Nederlant, besonderlyck der Stadt Antwerpen, 1097–1565* 85
10 Hadrianus Barlandus *Historia rerum gestarum a Brabantiae ducibus* 139–40, 'cum armato milite'
11 J.S. Theissen *De Regering van Karel V in de Noordlijke Nederlanden* 37–8
12 Aelbertus Cuperinus *Chronicke* 79–81
13 Solon 'Popular Response' 107–9; Brewer II:1 1895 (Spinelly, 16 May 1516, reporting a comment by John of Bergen)
14 Henri Pirenne *Histoire de Belgique* 3: 10–13
15 H.P.H. Jansen *Hoekse en Kabiljauwse Twisten* 92–8; F.W.N. Hugenholz 'Het Kaas- en Broodvolk'
16 AGN 4: 24–6
17 *Nieuwe Ordinancie op der Wachte der Stadt van Loven*
18 [Cornelius Aurelius] *Cronycke van Hollandt, Zeelandt & Vrieslant* (the so-called *Divisie Cronycke*) sig. Ee5v; Theodorus Velius *Chronyk van Hoorn tot het Jaar 1630* ed Sebastian Centen 197. Velius may depend here on the *Divisie Cronycke*, since his account agrees with it in all details, save that he has the men called up sent to Sparendam rather than Haarlem.
19 Willem Hermans *Hollandiae Gelriaeque bellum* 327: 'Hagensis inde Curiae promulgatur edictum, uti armarentur agrestes.' Cf Maximilian's instructions to Margaret, July 1508 in Le Glay, *Correspondance de L'Empereur Maximilien I et de Marguerite d'Autriche* 1: 55.
20 L.M. Rollin Couquerque & A. Meerkamp van Embden 'Goudse Vroedschaps-Resolutien betreffende Dagvaarten der Staten van Holland en de Staten Generael, 1501–1524' no. xxi, 73
21 Theo Reintges *Ursprung und Wesen der mittelalterlichen Schützengilden* 51–4. Of 750 towns listed in Reintges' index as having such guilds, some 300 were in the Low Countries (including Guelders).
22 *Recueil des anciennes ordonnances de la Belgique 2e Série, 1506–1700* 1: 379 (confirmation in 1515 of the privileges of the Ghent arquebus guild founded in 1489); see also 62–3, 120–1, 434–6, 198–200, and 290
23 H. Brugmans *Geschiedenis van Amsterdam* 1: 292–300; [De la Court] *Holland onder de Gravelijke Regering* 147. Reintges (*Ursprung und Wesen* 80–2) believes that the *schutters* guilds originated with the coming to power of the craft guilds and that patricians joined the guilds only later.
24 Hermans *Hollandiae Gelriaeque bellum* 328. Reyner Snoy *De rebus Batavicis libri XIII* 186–8: the burgers of Weesp, spurning the aid of a mercenary company, fail to destroy a bridge and so lose their city; two years later, the men of Utrecht do not fear the approach of Ijselstein and his troops, 'dicereque mercenariis se esse digniores,' but the town is captured nonetheless. The fact that Snoy cites (185–6) the 'fable about the kite who saw and devoured both fighters,' which is reminiscent of Her-

mans' fable about the crow (see below, note 35; both passages refer to dissension among the cities of Holland during the siege of Poederoy), suggests that his account (which ends in 1517) may have been influenced by Hermans.

25 Jervis Wegg *Antwerp, 1477–1559* 50: the victory (supported by some German mercenaries) over the Flemish rebels in 1485 was 'one of the last military achievements in the field of the Antwerp guilds.' Cf Charity Cannon Willard 'The Concept of True Nobility at the Court of Burgundy' 47, citing a poem of 1507 by Jean Lemaire des Belges.

26 See above, note 22.

27 Hermans *Hollandiae Gelriaeque bellum* 333–4; Cuperinus *Chronicke* 73; Duncker *Fürst Rudolf der Tapfere* 60–5

28 See below, note 152.

29 Duncker *Fürst Rudolf der Tapfere* 14; Brewer II, 3441, 3442; Brewer I:1, 1241, 1245. Le Glay *Correspondance de L'Empereur Maximilien* 1: 55: in July of 1508 Maximilian spoke of coming to the Netherlands and raising sixteen thousand men-at-arms in Flanders, Brabant, and Holland; but this must be reckoned among his more chimerical schemes.

30 Geoffrey Parker *The Army of Flanders and the Spanish Road* 29–30; Henne 1: 15–16: 'On sait le concours actif des Walons dans les guerres de Philippe le Bon et de Maximilien contre les communes de la Flandre et du Brabant.' Cf De Weert's account of riotous behaviour in Antwerp by five hundred 'ruyters Namuroisen' (*Chronycke van Nederlant*).

31 Edward Füeter *Geschichte des europäischen Staatensystems von 1492 bis 1559* 112, citing only a Venetian ambassador's report of 1546, says Netherlands rulers preferred German troops because the native infantry was inferior in quality.

32 Duncker *Fürst Rudolf der Tapfere* 12–14; L.P. Gachard, 'Les Anciennes Assemblées nationales de la Belgique' *Revue de Bruxelles* 3: (1839) 20–1. There are no printed sources for the Estates General from 1477 to the 1560s, and Gachard remains the only secondary account; he found in 1839 that the relevant documents were scattered among twenty local archives. Gachard, followed by Duncker and others, assumes that sums voted by the Estates General were grants of money. It is clear from the *Root Boek* of the Estates of Brabant, however (see below, note 61), that sums voted by the Estates General were subject to approval by the provincial Estates, according to a prearranged quota system. Votes by the Estates General were in themselves of no effect. (See Gordon Griffiths *Representative Government in Western Europe in the Sixteenth Century* 298.)

33 Duncker *Fürst Rudolf der Tapfere* 49–70

34 Cuperinus *Chronicke* 73–4; the author notes that in 1510 the city refused its share of a subsidy voted by the Estates of Brabant, alleging its im-

poverishment from war expenses; Duncker *Fürst Rudolf der Tapfere* 24; J.L. van Dalen *Geschiedenis van Dordrecht* 2: 1093. It was at this time disputed whether Dordrecht and its surrounding area owed one ninth (6,000 gulden) or one twelfth (5,000) of Holland's annual subsidy to the prince (Robert Fruin 'De Verpandingen van 1496 en 1515 en haar Voorbereiding').

35 Fruin 'De Verpandingen van 1496 en 1515'; Van Dalen *Geschiedenis van Dordrecht* 2: 1090–1 (for a discussion of the fourteenth-century origins of these disputes, see the chapter in Jansen *Hoekse en Kabiljauwse Twisten*); Hermans *Hollandiae Gelriaeque bellum* 334.

36 AGN 4: 43

37 [De la Court] *Holland onder de Gravelijke Regering* 145–51

38 Struick *Gelre en Habsburg* 26

39 Hugenholz 'Het Kaas- en Broodvolk'

40 Van Dalen *Geschiedenis van Dordrecht* 2: 1090–1; Duncker *Fürst Rudolf der Tapfere* 20

41 Struick *Gelre en Habsburg* 195

42 Brewer I:1, 1566. Spinelly's comment must be evaluated in the light of the fact that Ijselstein was among the nobles (Brewer II:1, 70) who agreed to work against the influence of Chièvres, and that Spinelly himself was later suspected by Wolsey of having fallen under the influence of Chièvres (Brewer II:1, 2700). [De la Court] *Holland onder de Gravelijke Regering* 143: at the Estates General in Ghent in 1482, the Holland deputies, since they were Kabiljauws, requested Maximilian to appoint as Stadhouder not the 'foreigner' Engelbrecht of Nassau, but John of Egmond (Ijselstein's uncle), head of their party.

43 Barlandus *Historia rerum gestarum* 147–8

44 Le Glay *Correspondance de l'Empereur Maximilien* 1:15

45 AGN 4:41–2; Duncker *Fürst Rudolf der Tapfere* 14

46 AGN 4:39; Andreas von Walther *Die Anfänge Karls V* 85–7; Pirenne *Histoire de Belgique* 3: 75–7

47 Robert Fruin 'Korte Autobiographie van Mr. Floris Oem van Wijngarden' 151–2

48 Walther *Die Anfänge Karls V* 89–103; Struick (*Gelre en Habsburg* 195) believes Margaret determined on war only after the Duke of Guelders refused to surrender the town of Harderwijk.

49 Struick *Gelre en Habsburg* 197; 'Goudse Vroedschaps-Resolutien' no xxxiii, 9 May 1513

50 Gachard 'Les Anciennes Assemblées' 23–4

51 Barlandus *Historia rerum gestarum* 171; Cuperinus *Chronicke* 76–7. On Barlandus' historical works, see Etienne Daxhelet *Adrien Barlandus, Humaniste belge, 1486–1538* 92–117.

52 'Cornelius Aurelius ad suam Bataviam' in his *Batavia, sive de antiquo*

veroque situ eius insulae quam Rhenus in Hollandia facit 78:

At quum tanta potes terraque marique, dolendum est
Ut minimat laudem Gelria sola tuam
Ergone visa ni est secordia tanta Senatus,
Robur ut antiquum fluxerat omne tibi?

See below, note 119.

53 Brewer II:1, 1706

54 Thiessen *Regering van Karel V* 31–42; Struick *Gelre en Habsburg* 235–41. The origin of the Black Band is obscure. Walther Rose ('Die deutschen und italienischen Schwarzen (Grossen) Garden im 15en und 16en Jahrhundert') believes, on the basis of statements by Du Bellay and Paolo Giovio, that it was recruited for French service by Robert de la Marck and others at least by 1512, possibly as early as 1495. But Rose is not aware of Netherlands evidence that the Black Band fought for the Habsburgs in Frisia before taking part in Francis I's victorious Italian campaign (September 1515).

55 Theissen, *Regering van Karel V* 31–42: Bernard Bucho ab Aytta (uncle of the young humanist lawyer who was to be Erasmus' good friend, Viglius Zuichemius ab Aytta), pastor in Leeuwarden and councillor to both Saxon and Habsburg governments in Frisia, believed at first that a peaceful settlement was possible, but then concluded that Ijselstein had been right in recommending a military solution.

56 Struick *Gelre en Habsburg* 243; Brewer II:1, 538. Nassau was not among those (Brewer II:1 70) who agreed in January 1515 to work against Chièvres; his marriage to the Princess of Orange should be seen in the light of Chièvres' policy of easing partisan friction (Walther *Die Anfänge Karls V* 148–53). Moreover, it was not the first time that the central government had sought to replace an Egmond with a Nassau as Stadhouder of Holland: see above, note 42.

57 Henne 2: 124

58 *Root Boek van de Staten van Brabant* 50^{v}, 12 April 1515

59 Fruin 'De Verpandingen van 1496 en 1515' 148

60 Charles Hirschauer *Les Etats d'Artois de leurs origines à l'occupation française, 1346–1640* 1:224–5

61 Gachard ('Les Anciennes Assemblées' 27) and Henne (2: 157) interpret this vote of March 1516 by the Estates General as an actual grant of money. But the *Root Boek* of the Estates of Brabant (page 54, 15 April 1516) records Brabant's 'consent vander quote van Brabant inde vier hundert duysent philippus guldens by alle de landen geconsenteerd den Eertshertog Carol, om te volbringen syne reyse naer Spagnien.' A Gouda *Vroedschaps-Resolutie* (see above, note 20) for 3 April 1516 gives that city's deputies to the Estates of Holland leave to respond as they see fit to the 'petitie' for the 400,000 gulden for Charles's journey. Both texts clearly indicate that the vote by the Estates General became effective only

when each of the provinces, through its Estates, approved its quota of the sum. In 1509 Margaret promised the Estates of Holland that their consent to Holland's share of a subsidy of 500,000 gulden asked of the Estates General (Gachard 23) would not take effect unless the other provinces consented too (P.A. Meilink *Archieven van de Staten van Holland: Eerste Deel, voor 1572* no 261).

62 Guillaume *Histoire des bandes d'ordonnance* 70; Brewer II:1, 2417 (not wholly accurate); Henne 2: 169; Gachard 'Les Anciennes Assemblées' 28

63 Brewer II:1, 2529

64 Henne 2: 123

65 Struick *Gelre en Habsburg* 243–6; Aurelius *Divisie Cronycke* sig. EE[4]–EE[5]; J.J. Kalma *Grote Pier van Kimswerd*

66 Count [Henry] of Nassau to Arend van Duuvenvoorden, 7 September 1516, Algemene Rijksarchief, The Hague, inventory no. 2413 (Staten van Holland voor 1572), item 38, calendared in Meilink *Archieven van de Staten van Holland* 'Regestenlijst' no. 329. See J. ter Gouw *Geschiedenis van Amsterdam* 4: 22. Duvenvoorde, Nassau's appointee, had been requested by Amsterdam and other cities in a war against Lübeck in 1511 (papers of Albrecht van Loo, Advocaat of the Estates of Holland, calendared in Meilink 282). He may have been a scion of the ancient Hoek family of the same name.

67 H. Ullmann *Franz von Sickingen* 48–54; cf Robert de la Marck, Sieur de Florange *Mémoires du Maréchal de Florange* 1: 214–15.

68 Aurelius *Divisie Cronycke* sig. EE[5]

69 Brewer II:2, 3033, 3044, 3054, 3075. Previous English sources (Brewer II:1, 1434, 1479, 1498) knew that the Black Band had fought for the French at Marignano (September 1515) and again in Lorraine the following spring. But the correspondence of 20–30 March 1517 suggests that emissaries of the band had, understandably enough, presented themselves to Schinner and to Worcester and Tunstall without mentioning their recent French association.

70 Robert Macquereau *Chronique de la maison de Bourgogne* in J.A.C. Buchon *Choix de chroniques et mémoires sur l'histoire de France* 4, v: 69–70. It was Chièvres' decision 'd'en riens faire; puisque on scavoit leurs [the French] secretz, et que on avoit leur fiance, on estoit bien au deseure de leur vollenté.' On Macquereau, see C. von Höfler 'Kritische Untersuchungen über die Quellen der Geschichte Philipps des Schönen.'

71 Brewer II:2, 3175

72 *Recueil des anciennes ordonnances de la Belgique* 1: 546–7

73 *Root Boek* session for '27 March 1516 before Easter,' i.e., 1517 new style, 57^{v}–58

74 Ibid, session for 23 February 1517, 56^{v}–57. The deputies normally went home, allowing town governments time to deliberate, and then reconvened to give their response to the government's request. In this case

the affirmative response was given at the March 27 session, recorded on pages 57v–58. For the previous request to the Estates General for money to support the king's 'horse' (*peerden*), see above, note 62.

75 'Goudse Vroedschaps-Resolutien' no. xliv, 83, 21 February 1517

76 Since the Great Privilege of 1477, and the accompanying special charters to various provinces, major towns in Flanders (Pirenne *Histoire de Belgique* 3: 13), Brabant (Cuperinus *Chronicke* 73–4), and Holland (Fruin 'De Verpandingen van 1496 en 1515') claimed liberty not to be bound by decisions taken by a majority of the Estates of their respective provinces. See below, note 142.

77 Aurelius *Divisie Cronycke* sig. Ee5–5v; Velius *Cronyck van Hoorn* 194; Kalma *Grote Pier van Kimswerd*

78 Above, note 18; Ter Gouw *Geschiedenis van Amsterdam* 4: 23–5

79 Henne 2: 214; Cuperinus *Chronicke* entry for 5 April 1518; *De Egmondsche Abtenkroniek van Johannes a Leydis* ed Victor J.G. Roefs, O. Carm, 256. The divergences among these accounts are discussed below, note 151.

80 Velius *Cronyck van Hoorn* 195–6: Ijselstein 'siende den Vyand vast trekken / seyde tegen d'omstanders / ten was soo niet gesegt / 't welk eenige burgers hoorende duyden de woorden verkeert / en verdachten de Heeren / als of sy van desen aenslag voor heen yet geweten hadden' (197).

81 Ter Gouw *Geschiedenis van Amsterdam* 4: 24–6: ''T is verboden kwaad te spreken van de Heeren ...' Ter Gouw takes the phrase to refer to the 'lords' of the city government in Amsterdam itself.

82 Donald Wilcox *The Development of Florentine Humanist Historiography* 90

83 Barlandus *Historia rerum gestarum* 169: 'Quod mirum videri potest, ita in totam illam regionem grassanti per dies complures, hosti nullae sunt objectae ex Brabantia copiae.' See above, note 3: Duncker notes that Anhalt was at this time instructed to avoid giving battle.

84 Above, note 70

85 Aurelius *Divisie Cronycke* sig. Ee3, Ee4v, Ee5–5v; Velius *Cronyck van Hoorn* 194

86 P.J. Overmeer 'Het Staande Leger en de Huurbenden in de Nederlanden, 1471–1584' *Navorscher* 59 (1910): 181–93; Ter Gouw *Geschiedenis van Amsterdam* 4: 33–4

87 Letter 1122, lines 3–4, IV, 304; Struick *Gelre en Habsburg* 50. On Bruni's *De militia*, see Bayley *War and Society in Renaissance Florence*. Erasmus was familiar with Bruni's works: letter 173 (the preface to Anthonisz' *De precellentia potestatis imperatoriae*, discussed in chapter 1), lines 96–9, I, 384.

88 LB IV, 640BC, 633CD; cf 632C, 635B.

89 LB IV, 633D; cf 630C, 634E, 638A, 639F. By way of contrast, see the dis-

cussion of 'Jewish ceremonies' in my *Erasmus: The Growth of a Mind*. See above, chapter 1, notes 61 and 62.

90 Kurt von Raumer 'Erasmus, der Humanist und der Friede' in *Ewiger Friede: Friedensrufe und Friedenspläne seit der Renaissance* 14; see above, note 6.

91 Letter 2599, lines 20–4, IX, 418

92 CWE letter 412, lines 5–10, III, 291; CWE letter 413, lines 46–51, III, 295; see above, note 67.

93 LB IV, 640 BC

94 Cf *Dulce bellum inexpertis* ed and trans Yvonne Remy & René Dunil-Marquebreucq 28, lines 182–5; see above, chapter 2, note 137.

95 Letter 597, lines 16–17, III, 4; Allen cites a passage from Erasmus' *Apologia qua respondet invectivis ed. lei* describing Tunstall's collaboration with him in Ghent.

96 M.A. Nauwelaerts 'Un Ami amversois de More et d'Erasme, Petrus Aegidius'

97 Allen I, 356; letter 147, line 58n, 350

98 Lucie de Keyser 'Cornelius Grapheus, Humaniste anversois, Etude bio-bibliographique'

99 Letter 616, line 14n, III, 33–4

100 Letter 543, lines 23–5, II, 495, with Allen's note

101 Letter 545 (to More), lines 5–6, II, 496: 'Est Antuuerpiae senator cui vsqueadeo placet [More's *Utopia*] vt eam memoriter teneat.'

102 Letter 474, line 3, II, 353; letter 570, line 2, II, 537

103 Petrus Aegidius *Summae sive argumenta legum diversorum imperatorum* and *Lamentatio in obitum Caesaris Maximiliani*; Nicholas Buscodensis (ed) *Hugonis sancti victoris quaestiones concinnae quicquid est in divi Pauli obscurum mira brevitate elucidantes*; and *Richardi sancti victoris in apocalypsim commentarii*; Cornelius Grapheus *Androtheogonia*

104 Petrus Aegidius and Cornelius Grapheus *Hypotheses sive argumenta spectaculorum quae Caesari Carolo civitatis Antverpiensis antistites sunt edituri* sig. A^{2v-3}; cf sig. A^{4v}-B1. According to the title page 'Petrus Aegidius scribebat' and 'Cornelius Grapheus characteres faciebat.' In view of Grapheus' known talents as a designer of such festivals (see the discussion of this point in De Keyser 'Cornelius Graephaeus'), this is a division of labour one might expect. For purposes of comparison, see *Remi Du Puys, La Tryumphante Entrée de Charles prince des Espagnes en Bruges, 1515* with introduction by Sydney Anglo. In contrast to the Spanish and Italian pageants, which vaunted the theme of world empire, the Brugeois pageants, as Anglo says, 'resisted the temptation to flatter or exhort [the prince] at every turn'; but nothing is said about tyranny. Guy de Tervarent *Attributs et symboles dans l'art profane, 1450–1600*

129–31: the 'couronne murale' or 'tourelée' was mentioned in classical literature as an attribute of the goddess Cybele, or of Terra (e.g., Lucretius *de rerum natura* 2: 606–7). Prior to the Antwerp triumphal arches for Charles v (not mentioned by Tervarent), the motif was taken up by Renaissance artists only in Italy (two medals, a painting by Mantegna). It was also used by the painter Abraham Janssens (late sixteenth century) for an allegorical representation of the city of Antwerp. Frances Yates (*Astraea: The Imperial Theme in the Sixteenth Century*) provides valuable background, but does not mention Gilles or Graphaeus.

105 Letter 543, lines 15–21, II, 494–5

106 Above, notes 61, 73

107 *Root Boek* session of 23 February 1517, page 57: '... ende behalvens de costen die hy [the Prince] hadde gedaen int oprusten vande scheppen tot syne reyse van Spaegnien ende alsnu te vergeefs waren ...'

108 Above, note 74

109 C.J.F. Slootmans *Jan metten Lippen, zijn Familie en zijn Stad* 168–71

110 Above, note 72; see also notes 68, 69. By March 20 (Brewer II:2, 3033) rumours were circulating in Brussels about the four thousand *landsknechte* who had been dismissed from Habsburg service; they were reported to be in the neighbourhood of Besançon, and it was thought they might be used by France against Tournai or by Franz von Sickingen against Maximilian.

111 Letter 413, line 44, II, 245: 'sed incertum erat a quo mitterentur.' Letter 543, lines 19–20, 495: 'et vnde aut cuius nomine veniant incertum.' See below, note 131.

112 Above, note 69

113 Letter 584, lines 27–33, II, 577; see above, note 95.

114 See above, chapter 3, notes 70–5.

115 Letter 584, lines 33–5, II 577; see letter 603, III, 13–5. Philip of Burgundy had resigned from the council in protest in 1511 because the regent, Margaret of Austria, had apparently stalled peace negotiations with Guelders (Walther *Die Anfänge Karls V* 89–103). R.R. Post ('Een Ontwerp van een Bischoppelijke Toespraak Gemaakt door Erasmus') argues plausibly that the brief *oratio* to be pronounced by a bishop on the occasion of his formal reception by his subjects (LB IV, 633–4) was written for Philip of Burgundy's *blijde inkomst* as Bishop of Utrecht in 1517. But the *oratio* treats solely of the spiritual duties of bishops and is, as Post observes, conspicuous for a lack of attention to politics.

116 Letter 584, lines 23–7, II 576–7. Schinner and Erasmus probably discussed his New Testament work more than politics, for it was most likely on this occasion that the Cardinal of Sion urged him to paraphrase the Gospels as he had done the Epistles (Allen I, 20, lines 32–3; VI, 103).

117 See above, chapter 2, note 110.

118 P.C. Molhuysen 'Cornelius Aurelius' and 'Nieuwe Bescheiden over Cor-

nelius Aurelius'; H.A. Enno van Gelder 'Cornelius Aurelius te Lopsen'; Bob de Graaf *Reyner Snoygoudanus: A Bio-Bibliographical Study*

119 Molhuysen 'Cornelius Aurelius' 15, 20. See above, note 52. *Batavia*, from which this passage is quoted, has been dated 1514–15. *Batavia* (pages 89–94) contains undated letters to Jacobus Lochorst, Aurelius' patron and the governor (*praetor*) of Leyden, and to Nassau. Both letters relate to a lost patriotic poem. To Lochorst: 'Hoc opusculum tuo nomini peculiariter dicare, dignum enim esse arbitror, ut qui a Carolo rege Catholico, nostroque principe, militaris gloriae insignia accepisti, eius etiam vicario [Nassau] quem nostris praefecit in oris, sincerissime, pro victoria quam apud Novioportum strenue confecit, gratuleris … Leges igitur in hoc carmine quid tibi & civibus, quid patriae debeas & superis.' Nassau is compared to Judas Macchabeus, 'dum non solum Augusti castrum [I cannot identify], sed et Augustini claustrum [identified in a note by Vulcanius as Hemsdonck] tuo gladio protexisti.' See also Willem Hermans *Hollandiae Gelriaeque bellum* 334. It will be recalled from chapter 1 that Erasmus told Hermans he could put him in touch with Ijselstein (note 67). In fact, urged by 'Magister Antonius, vir literatissimus,' Hermans did dedicate to Ijselstein some fables of Aesop later published by Martin van Dorp (*Fabulae Aesopi*). Hermans' translation appears to predate his *Hollandiae Gelriaeque bellum* since the story of the mouse and the frog snatched by a crow (or kite) has a more pointed moral in *Bellum* than in the translation: 'Itidem evenire solet factiosis civibus … dum inter se certant fieri magistratus, opes suas, plerunque etiam vitam in periculo ponunt.' 'Magister Antonius' could be a name for Erasmus: cf 'Antonius Baldus' of *Encomium matrimonii*, published in 1518 but first written in 1498.

120 Snoy *De rebus Batavicis* 192: Holland was 'milite omni ac praesidio tum vacuam.'

121 On Everardi, see below, chapter 5, note 77.

122 Bob de Graaf 'Alardus Amstelredamus'; A.J. Kölker *Alardus Amstelredamus en Cornelius Crocus, twee Amsterdamse Priester-Humanisten*

123 Letter 433, lines 35–8, II, 271; letter 485, lines 52–3, 378. Alard was in close touch with Cornelius Aurelius and describes Willem Hermans as his former teacher. Alard was also (letter 676, lines 39–40, III, 100) a kinsman of Meinard Mann, Abbot of the Benedictine monastery of Egmond from 1509, who was apparently among the reformist party of monks supported by the Egmond (Ijselstein) family (*De Egmondsche Abtenchroniek* ed Roefs 239–43, 252: Mann succeeded Hendrik van Witenhorst, the first reformed abbot, and was elected in the presence of representatives from the monasteries from which Egmond's reformed monks had come), and who encouraged Cornelius Aurelius in his antiquarian researches (*Batavia* 17).

124 De Graaf 'Alardus Amstelredamus' 72–81: a letter of Murmellius to

Alard dated 17 September 1516 was printed in Murmellius' edition of Persius. See D. Reichling *Johannes Murmellius: sein Leben und seine Werke* 120–8.

125 Letter 485, lines 30–41, II, 376–7. Otto Nübel (*Pompeius Occo*) does not mention the Guelders war.

126 Letter 676, III, 98–100; De Graaf 'Alardus Amstelredamus' 82

127 Letter 628, lines 6–27, 28–48, 62–4, III, 51–2. Because of its importance to the argument, the crucial passage in this letter, lines 28–48, may be given in full: 'Est quaedam hominum colluuies quam Nigram vocant Manum. Ea Alcmariam, satis florens Holandie oppidum, cepit ac diripuit; vbi mire seuitum est in mulieres quoque et in pueros, quod acriter se defendissent. Quod si vel sexcentos habuissent milites in praesidium, tuti fuerant. Atque hii ipsi paulo ante pro nobis pugnabant contra Phrysios. Hec dum timebantur euentura, et ob id missi qui praesidium a Principe peterent, admissi non sunt, nec data venia vt se vel suis opibus atque armis tuerentur, imo interdictum sub poena capitis, ne spoliati a Ghelriis Ghelrios vicissim inuaderent. Post hanc tam atrocem cedem primariae ciuitates iam sibi timentes adeunt Regem. Vix data venia vt de suis sumptibus tueantur, sed hac lege vt rursus Principem nouo instruant viatico, quod vetus iam absumptum sit; cum ian soluerunt quod post tres annos debebatur. Id quoniam Holandi grauabantur facere, de composito immissa tempestas. Nemo technam non intelligit; verum nec mederi facile nec dicere tutum. Nuper coniecti sunt in carcerem aliquot, quod dixissent, si omnes ii qui sunt apud Principem, tam syncere amarent illum quam ego amo, non sic tractrarentur illius oppida. Vix ad D. Margaretae preces emissi post ebdomades tres. Suspitio est horum artificio agi, ne Princeps abeat; quod timeat ne ciuitates absente eo non ferant hec ludibria diutius.'

128 To Tunstall, letter 643, lines 29–34, III, 65

129 Letter 829, lines 7–17, III, 295; Erasmus was particularly concerned because he was contemplating a journey up the Rhine to Basel.

130 Letter 832, lines 12–27, III, 303

131 Letter 1001, lines 63–82, IV, 32. Here again (see above, note 111) phrases like 'incertum quo duce, cuius iussu, aut quorsum tendens' (lines 69–70) are used in a context which suggests that mysterious troop movements are to be explained by Habsburg policy. For the context of Erasmus' correspondence with Spalatin, see chapter 5, note 44.

132 Nassau to Arend van Duuvenvoorden (above, note 66)

133 Aurelius *Divisie Cronycke* sig. Ee^{5}

134 'Goudse Vroedschaps-Resolutien' no. xxxviii, 3 April 1516: Gouda's deputies receive full power to deal with the petition for 400,000 gulden for the prince's journey to Spain; 16 May 1516, they are instructed to reject a request to *anticipate* the St John's day payment of Holland's

portion of the 400,000 gulden; ibid xl and xlii, 21 May 1516, authorize anticipation of the St John's day payment.

135 Treasurer Philippe Haneton, 2 June 1517, instructs Willem Ghondt, Receiver of Aids of Holland, to pay out, as specified in a request from Nassau, 21,000 gulden for military expenses, to be taken from the St John's day (June 24) payment of Holland's regular subsidy, and a further 6,000 gulden to revictual Frisian towns loyal to Prince Charles, to be taken from the Christmas payment of the Holland subsidy (Algemene Rijksarchief, The Hague, inventory no. 2413 [Staten van Holland voor 1572], item 38, calendared in Meilink *Archieven van de Staten van Holland* 'Regenstenlijst' no. 330.) These instructions, especially the latter, make no sense unless the sums to be drawn on were already paid into the treasury.

136 'Goudse Vroedschaps-Resolutien' no. xlv, 26 June 1517. One of the conditions for a 1515 three-year subsidy granted by the Estates of Brabant was that the government not 'anticipate the sum now agreed on ... or shorten the terminal dates [of payment] in any manner' (*Root Boek* 51, 12 April 1515).

137 *Root Boek* 56v; see above, note 105.

138 Ibid 'continuatio vande voorgaende bede van 150,000 guldens voor andere drye jaeren.'

139 See above, note 59.

140 See above, notes 62, 63.

141 *Root Boek* 51: a further condition of the April 15 grant was that should war arise, 'de resterende penningen souden worden betreckt totten selven oorloge.'

142 Haneton to Willem Ghondt (above, note 135): part of the funds Nassau requested were 'au remboursement de VIm F[lorins] dudict pris que aucunes villes de Hollande ont payées et desbourssées pour les affaires du Roy et la deffense desdict pays.'

143 'Goudse Vroedschaps-Resolutien' no. xliv, 21 February 1517: '... ende wederstaen die contributie van de Lm Philippusgulden over alle de landen van harwaerts over begeert by de C.M., daer wy nyet in geconsenteert en hebben. Ende indien men dat nyet wederstaen en can, dat men in den Hage reysen sal in de ghyselinge aleer men daerto consenteren sal.'

144 Guillaume *Histoire des bandes d'ordonnance* 70

145 Aurelius *Divisie Cronycke* sig. Ee5–Ee5v; Haneton (for the council) to Ghondt (above, note 135). See also Velius *Chronyck van Hoorn* 194, with caveat mentioned above, note 18.

146 'Goudse Vroedschaps-Resolutien' no. xlvii, 8 July 1517

147 Velius *Chronyck van Hoorn* 198

148 Paul Rosenfeld 'The Provincial Governors from the Minority of Charles v to the Revolt' 26

149 Above, note 81
150 Above, notes 47, 143
151 Cuperinus *Chronicke* 5 April 1518: 'Den swarten hoop, acht oft negen duysent sterck wesende, van alle landen vergadert wesende, ende lagen op den huysman die geheele vasten ende aten vlesch, speck, booter, eyer en al wat sy vonden; ende alzoe zyn vergadert die herren van Nassauw, Ravestyn, Cleve end andere Rynsche heeren en zyn tsamen veraccordeert ende zyn daer onder geslagen met assistencie vanden huysman aldaer wonende, geweecken wesende vuyte meyerye vanden Bosche naer Venloo, dat op een cleyne plaetse zyn gebleven en doot geslagen 1800, en die anderen zyn al ewech geloopen ende sommighe aen bomen gehaengen.' Continuator of Johannes a Leydis (*De Egmondische Abtenkroniek* 255–6): [Nassau recaptured Asperen] 'et eosdem etiam in terra Gelrensi insecutus fuit, et civitatem Arnhemensem [!] circumdedit et multa iacula in eandem misit. Sed per literas Karoli archiducis Austrie et regis Hispanie revocatus, ad ulteriora procedere prohibitus extitit, procurantibus, ut dicitur, aliquibus nobilibus ex Francia, qui ea tempestate in Arnhem praesentes erant.' See also Snoy *De rebus Batavicis* 192. I have not been able to obtain the extract from the Chronicle of Erkelenz cited by Allen III, 295, 9n.
152 Brewer II:1, 4117
153 Letter 288, lines 55–6, I, 553: 'ducum collusiones'; LB II, 338C: 'Denique cum haec tam multa non possint explere vere pertusum dolium, h. e. Principum fiscum, bellum Praetexitur, colludunt Duces, populus infelix ad medullas usque exsugitur'; LB II, 654B: on the 'Tyrannis potentium … Sentiunt in pace minimum sibi licere, cum res legibus & consiliis agitur, non dolis, aut armis. Proinde modis omnibus id agunt, ne populus publica pace gaudeat.' See above, chapter 2, note 144.
154 Letter 948, lines 27–36, III, 542; letter 962, lines 25–30, 577; letter 991, lines 37–47, 623. These passages refer to Erasmus' fears concerning his theological critics during the heated controversies of 1519 and later. But he seems also to have been suspicious by nature: see, for example, letter 133, lines 22–70, I, 309–10.
155 Above, notes 80, 81
156 He is thus not quite the detached intellectual presented by E. Rottier (*La Vie et les travaux d'Erasme considérés dans leurs rapports avec la Belgique*) 'Chez Erasme, on ne trouve aucune trace de ces colères populaires' [in Holland].
157 See above, chapter 2, note 145, for the invocation to Brutus in LB II, 654C. In the 1526 edition of the *Adagia* (Basel, Froben), as in LB II, 654CD, the passage reads: 'O Brutorum genus jam olim exstinctum! o fulmen Jovis aut caecum, aut obtusum! Neque dubium est, quin isti Principum corruptores [the 'Principum optimates' of 654A, the 'tutores' of 654CD], poenas Deo daturi sint, sed sero nobis. Interim ferendi sunt, ne Tyrannidem

excipiat anarchia, malum pene perniciosius. *Quod* complurium rerum publicarum experimentis comprobatum est, & nuper etiam agricolarum per Germaniam exortus tumultus nos docuit, aliquanto tolerabiliorem esse Principum inhumanitatem, quam *anarchian* omnia *confundentem'* (my italics). In the 1520 Froben edition (494), 'Ut fici oculis incumbunt' has, for the words from *quod* to *confundentem*, the following: *'Id* quod apud Eluetios usu uenisse uidemus, qui cum olim nobilitatem omnem tyrannide grauem, aut trucidarint, aut in exilium egerint, nunc ipsi mundo graues & formadibiles, fortassis et ipsisibi exitio futuri nisi se concordia *munirent'* (my italics). In the 1515 edition this adage is quite brief and has no political commentary.

158 E.T. Kuiper 'Erasmus als Politiek Propagandist'; Ferdinand Geldner *Die Staatsauffassung und Fürstenlehre des Erasmus von Rotterdam* 151 (cf above, note 157).

159 Above, notes 93, 113

160 Struick *Gelre en Habsburg* 241

CHAPTER FIVE

1 Ludwig Pastor *A History of the Popes* 7, chapter 4. See above, chapter 2, note 65.

2 Ibid, chapter 5. The crusade memorandum of 12 November 1518 is published in *Ulrichi Hutteni opera* ed Eduard Böcking, 5: 146–57.

3 In addition to Pastor, see Kenneth M. Setton 'Pope Leo x and the Turkish Peril,' especially 400, 407, 415. R.W. Scribner ('The Social Thought of Erasmus' 21) says Erasmus 'did not hesitate to expose the whole business as a sham,' but provides no argument that it was a sham.

4 Brewer II:2, 2761, 3119, 3163, 3816, 3973, 4023

5 Brewer II:2, 3350, 4068, 3950, 4128. For Schinner's difficulties with Leo x, 3495, 3589, 3685, and Pastor *History of the Popes* 7: 142–3. Leo released an old enemy of Schinner's from prison, then replaced him as nuncio to Switzerland with the more pliant Antonio Pucci: see below, note 30.

6 Pastor *History of the Popes* 7: 239–53; Brewer II:1, cclii–cclxiii

7 See above, introduction, note 25.

8 Jocelyne Russell 'Wolsey and the Campaign for Universal Peace'

9 Pastor *History of the Popes* 7:243; Brewer II:2, 4469, 4481

10 *Deutsche Reichstagsakten, jüngere Reihe* ed August Kluckhohn 1:1–140; Pastor *History of the Popes* 7, chapter 6; Brewer III:1, 240, 241

11 Paul Kalkoff (*Die Kaiserwahl Friedrichs IV und Karls V* cites the following sources for Frederick the Wise's election: a remark by Luther in 1522 that the old prophecies concerning Emperor Frederick's return to the throne were literally fulfilled in Frederick the Wise (Paul Kalkoff [ed] *Wormser Reichstag* 384, note 1); a statement in Spalatin's *Ephemerides* (ed B.J.

Struve *Corpus Hist. Germ.* 2:971, note 32) that Frederick 'tria habuit suffragia,' those of Brandenburg, Trier, and the Palatinate, meaning that his own vote would make a majority of four; and a report of 17 August 1518 by Antonio and Sebastian Giustiniani, Venetian ambassadors to France and England, that, according to Richard Pace, 'the Duke of Saxony was for three hours elected King of the Romans, but then abdicated' (reprinted in *Deutsche Reichstagsakten* 1: 828, note 1). Kluckhohn thinks 'tre ore' in this last document might be a mistake for 'tre vote,' but Kalkoff's rejection of this suggestion is confirmed by S. Giustiniani's September 1519 report to the Venetian Senate (Rawdon Brown, ed *Calendar of State Papers, Venetian* 2: 561): 'He stated that for half a day the Duke of Saxony had been elected King of the Romans.' Karl Brandi ('Die Wahl Karls v') argues that the absence of any hint of such an election in the official sources (such as the protocol kept on such occasions by the Frankfurt town council) makes it highly improbable, and rightly points out that many of Kalkoff's arguments strain credulity (for instance, his reconstruction of how the Elector Palatine must have received the hypothetical fateful message that caused him to change his vote). Brandi says nothing, however, about the possibility (see below, notes 44, 46) that several of the Electors did offer the crown to Frederick if he were willing to stand for election.

12 Brewer III:1, xxxii–lxxxix

13 Ibid, xc–clxi; Karl Brandi *The Emperor Charles V* 156

14 Allen IV, 295–6, 551

15 To Henry VIII, letter 964, lines 32–5, III, 580; to Wolsey, letter 967, lines 16–19, 587. In 1514, when Wolsey wanted peace and Leo preferred a truce, Erasmus thought the pope's position wiser: letter 2599, lines 20–4, IX, 418 (cited above, chapter 2, note 105, and chapter 4, note 91).

16 Letter 936, lines 77–82, III, 524; contrast letter 967, lines 24–5, 587–8 (to Wolsey).

17 Letters 948, lines 27–36, III, 542; 962, lines 25–30, 577; 991, lines 37–47, 623; 1040, lines 1–9, IV, 119; 1113, lines 3–4, 286

18 Letter 694, lines 21–31, III, 117; letter 778, lines 18–24, 221–2 (refers back to letters 558, 744, l. 14–37); letter 786, lines 22–3, 240; letter 1128, lines 9–11, IV, 320–1. See also letter 1233, lines 17–22, 576, where he speaks of certain men known to his correspondent (Budé) who seek to prevent concord between Charles V and Francis I, 'so as to put their own tyranny on a firm footing.'

19 Letter 948, lines 182–219, III, 546–7 (cf More's letter to Oxford, *The Correspondence of Sir Thomas More* ed Elizabeth Rogers, letter 60); letter 968, lines 11–19, 594; letter 999, lines 277–95, IV, 22; letter 1004, lines 135–47, 40. Cf his statements (letters 1031, 1032) that John of Bergen was sending his son to England because Henry's was the least corrupt of courts.

20 Erasmus had quite a low opinion of Pace's *De fructu qui ex doctrina percipitur* (letter 776, lines 1–21, III, 218–19; see above, chapter 2, note 99). On 6 December 1517 he was not sure whether Rhenanus shared this view: 'Paceus suis ad me litteris iactat libellum de Fructu Studiorum abs te laudatum' (letter 732, lines 52–3, 162). By 13 March 1518 (letter 796, lines 1–6, 251, 'De Pacaei frigidissimo libello ...') he knew he could speak his mind freely on this subject; hence he must have heard from Rhenanus in the interim. When writing to his English friends, Erasmus in each case justifies his critique of pope and princes by referring to the crusade. To Rhenanus (letter 796, lines 17–20) he merely expatiates on the wickedness of pope and kings. He must therefore have known that Rhenanus would understand whereof he spoke.

21 Letter 775, lines 5–8, III, 217; letter 796, lines 17–20, 251

22 Letter 775, lines 5–8, III 217

23 Letter 786, lines 23–9, III 240–1. See below, note 28.

24 Letter 784, lines 58–61, III 238

25 Letter 785, lines 21–39, III 239. In the crusade memorandum of November 1517 (above, note 2), which is evidently to be identified with the 'consilium de bello in Turcas suscipiendo' which Erasmus sent More with this letter, there is nothing at all like the detail Erasmus gives. It is of course possible that he quotes here from some unknown exhortation, but the absurdity of what he says makes it far more likely that he is indulging in parody. His reference to Dame Alice would seem to clinch the case. My previous treatment of this passage (*Erasmus: The Growth of a Mind* 176) is thus in need of correction.

26 Letter 781, lines 25–31, III 234, with Allen's note

27 Letter 796, lines 17–20, III 251

28 Letter 785, lines 36–9, III 239. See above, note 23.

29 See above, note 4.

30 See above, note 5. Several circumstances suggest that Schinner may have been one of Erasmus' informants: both he and the new nuncio, Pucci, were in Zurich at this time for the Swiss Diet, and one may presume that Pucci brought with him exemplars of the crusade memorandum, of which Erasmus forwarded a copy to England; his low opinion of Pucci was later shared by Erasmus (letter 1188, lines 27–8, IV, 447); and Erasmus' estimates of Schinner's rough candour (letter 584, lines 25–6, II, 577) would square with the uncomplimentary description of his Swiss sources in letter 781, line 29: 'Non fugit omnino res hec Eluetios, licet crassos' (though it must be said that such opinions of the Swiss were common).

31 See above, chapter 2, notes 106, 107.

32 Allen II, 69

33 Nesen to Bruno Amerbach, 21 June 1518, and Hummelberger to Bruno Amerbach, 19 November 1518, in Alfred Hartmann *Die Amerbachkorrespondenz* 2: 118–19, 139–40. Amerbach, son of the Basel printer who

had been Froben's partner, was a close friend of both Rhenanus and Erasmus.

34 Tracy 'Erasmus Becomes a German'; *Erasmus: The Growth of a Mind* 177–8

35 Letter 867, lines 75–116, III 396–7; letter 877, lines 16–31, 415–16

36 Neuenahr's presence at Augsburg is attested by Johann Haselberg (*Die Stend des hailigen römischen Reichs, so zu Augsburg erschinen* in *Ulrichi Hutteni Opera* 5: 290. Erasmus' comments about the Diet date from a month after his visit with Neuenahr, in letters written once he reached Louvain and recovered from the illness described in letter 867.

37 Letter 878 (to Neuenahr), line 5, III, 416; letter 893, lines 39–43, 431–2: Erasmus thought Charles was more likely headed for Naples (to defend against a Franco-Papal attack? see above note 26); both he and Neuenahr assumed that Ferdinand, not Charles, was the Habsburg candidate for the imperial crown.

38 To Pace, letter 887, lines 13–14, III, 426; to Colet, letter 891, lines 24–32, 429; to Warham, letter 893, lines 35–9, 431. Once again, save for the letter to Pace, in which the crucial phrase is in Greek, these comments were not published by Erasmus.

39 Letters 870–5, especially letter 872, lines 12–21, 409–10

40 For Jonas' visit and its impact, see Tracy *Erasmus: The Growth of a Mind* 181–2. On Frederick the Wise and Luther, see letter 963, lines 12–21, III 578; letter 1030, lines 49–51, IV, 94.

41 Letter 978, lines 7–9, III, 603–4; letter 1001, lines 43–51, IV, 31. That Erard worked in concert with Habsburg representatives in Frankfurt is attested in *Deutsche Reichstagsakten* no. 332, pages 767–8.

42 To Albert of Brandenburg, letter 1009, lines 1–41, IV, 56–7. Erasmus at one time thought well of the Archbishop of Mainz, but not after he accepted a cardinal's hat at the Diet of Augsburg (letter 891, lines 24–9, III, 429). He must have known that Albert's own vote had been bought at great price, but by the Habsburgs.

43 Letter 1001, lines 63–5, IV, 32; above, note 37. *Vivat Rex Carolus* (s.l., s.d., copy in the Royal Library, The Hague) includes a letter sent from Coblenz on June 5 to the Electors by the French envoys; an oration by Neuenahr 'pro invictissimo Carolo Romanorum Rege iam electo'; and a letter to Neuenahr by the Cologne humanist Jacobus Sobius. Against the French claim that Francis I, because of his victory at Marignano, is best suited to thrust back the Turks, Neuenahr maintains that what is necessary is a defensive, not offensive posture (B3V, B4V). Sobius (E4) quotes the adage 'Spartam adeptus, eam orna.' In view of Erasmus' contacts with both Neuenahr and Erard, it is interesting that Neuenahr (B5V) praises Erard as a prince of Gallic tongue who is loyal to the empire.

44 Letter 1001, lines 53–61, IV, 32 (for the comment on Asperen, see above, chapter 4, note 131); letters 968–70, III, 593–6.

45 Above, note 11
46 To Fisher, letter 1030, lines 53–64, IV, 94
47 Brandi ('Die Wahl Karls V' 112–13, note 1) criticizes Kluckhohn's view of the elector's refusal of bribes on the basis of documents published by Kluckhohn himself.
48 Tracy *Erasmus: The Growth of a Mind* 183–7; Paul Kalkoff *Erasmus, Luther und Friedrich der Weise*. The *Consilium* is edited by Wallace K. Ferguson, *Erasmi opuscula*.
49 The best study is Cornelis Augustijn *Erasmus en de Reformatie*.
50 See the discussion of *libertas* – pre-eminently a religious category for Erasmus – in Tracy *Erasmus: The Growth of a Mind* 144–51, 167–71.
51 On 'mendicant tyrants' and their role in the schism, see: the *Consilium cujusdam* ed Ferguson *Erasmi opuscula* 353; letter 694, lines 26–45, III, 117; letter 948, lines 27–36, 542; letter 1113, lines 23–8, IV, 287; and a marginal note (*ptochotyranni* = mendicant tyrants) to his *Hilarii opera* (Basel, Froben 1523) 2, sig. EE 3^{v}.
52 Letter 1256, lines 23–6, V, 8; letter 1901, lines 67–78, VII, 232
53 See the *Consilium cujusdam* ed Ferguson; letter 991, lines 27–36, III, 623.
54 On the Territorial Inquisition and those arrested, see: J.G. De Hoop Scheffer *Geschiedenis der Kerkhervorming in Nederland van haar Ontstaan tot 1531* 144–94; Paul Kalkoff *Die Anfänge der Gegenreformation in den Niederlanden*; and P.E. Valvekens *De Inquisitie in de Nederlanden in de Zestiende Eeuw* 164–205.
55 Letter 1603, lines 27–9, VI, 155
56 Tracy *Erasmus: The Growth of a Mind* 187–95
57 De Hoop Scheffer *Geschiedenis der Kerk hervorming in Nederland* 204–24
58 On the uprising in 's Hertogenbosch, see Aelbertus Cuperinus *Chronicke* 90–1, and Erasmus to Pirckheimer, letter 1603, lines 15–24, VI, 155.
59 Paul Fredericq *Corpus documentorum inquisitionis haereticae pravitatis Neerlandicae*. The documents in vol 5 (e.g., nos. 497, 544, 580, 586) give some particulars of the long and many-sided legal struggle among towns, provincial councils, and the central government.
60 H. Brugmans *Geschiedenis van Amsterdam* 2: 398
61 An exception was the regulation of monasteries by town governments: letter 1585, lines 86–100, VI, 114; letter 1598, lines 15–24, 150; letter 1603, lines 53–83, 156–7.
62 Letters 597, lines 3–16, III, 4; 628, lines 16–26, 51; 695, lines 40–2, 121; 794, lines 25–9, 247–8; 1040, lines 2–9, IV, 119
63 On Egmondanus and Latomus, see Allen III, 416, 13n, and 519, 3n, and the references in Allen's general index, vol XII.
64 Letter 1218, lines 7–19, IV, 541; letter 1263, lines 1–3, V, 27
65 Letter 739, lines 1–26, III, 169 (but cf letter 683, lines 51–7, 105); letters 1038, lines 14–20, IV, 112–13; 1040, lines 2–9, 119

66 Letters 1038, lines 14–16, IV, 112; 1545, lines 28–30, VI, 22; 1553, lines 46–9, 35; 1585, lines 49–52. See also letters 2906, lines 73–5, X, 358, and 2961, lines 47–8, XI, 32, both from 1534.
67 Letters 1166, lines 53–6, IV, 398; 1268, lines 61–70, V, 34. See below, note 74.
68 Above, note 54; letters 1299, lines 8–13, V, 85; 1345, lines 36–9, 235; 1417, lines 19–21, 396; 1434, lines 38–9, 425
69 Letters 1299, lines 89–101, V, 87; 1302, lines 83–6, 97
70 De Hoop Scheffer *Geschiedenis der Kerkhervorming in Nederland* 159ff.; Valvekens *De Inquisitie in de Nederlanden* 173–4
71 Letters 1299, lines 1–4, V, 85; 1717, lines 14–18, VI, 350–1; 2191, lines 25–39, VIII, 220–1
72 De Hoop Scheffer *Geschiedenis der Kerkhvorming in Nederland* 144–94
73 Letter 1358, lines 26–31, V, 276–7, with Allen's note
74 Letter 1467, lines 9–11, V, 497
75 Letter 1555, line 33, VI, 39
76 Henri De Vocht *History of the Collegium Trilingue Lovaniense* vols 1 and 2, passim
77 For example, Nicholas Everardi, President of the Council of Holland, endorsed Erasmus' plan to discredit the Bull excommunicating Luther and later invited him to Holland (letters 1165, lines 1–4, IV, 394; 1238, lines 1–5, 591). But letters 1469 and 1653 indicate that Erasmus subsequently had to convince Everardi of his orthodoxy.
78 Letter 1255, lines 24–33, V, 5 (letter dedicating the *Paraphrase of Matthew* to Charles V)
79 Vives to Erasmus, letter 1256, lines 23–46, 60–89, V, 8–10; letter 1269, 35–6
80 Tracy *Erasmus: The Growth of a Mind* 191–3
81 Letter 1302, lines 43–57, V, 96
82 Letter 1305, lines 17–18, V, 112
83 Letters 1320, lines 1–15, V, 138–9; 1334, lines 111–21, 175; 1345, lines 38–9, 235
84 Letters 1380, V, 312; 1417, lines 13–24, 396; 1434, lines 1–2, 37–48, 424–5
85 Letters 1549, lines 13–16, VI, 26; 1585, lines 45–9, 113; 1700, lines 25–9, 327
86 He had obtained from Adrian VI a letter silencing Egmondanus, but it was of no value after the pope's death (letter 1481, lines 62–6, V, 528).
87 Letters 1690, lines 118–23, VI, 312; 1717, lines 7–18, 350–1; 1747, lines 1–32, 406–7; 1784a, lines 8–14, 460
88 De Hoop Scheffer *Geschiedenis der Kerkhvorming in Nederland* 195
89 A.J. Kölker *Alardus Amstelredamus en Cornelius Crocus, twee Amsterdamse Priester-Humanisten*
90 Fredericq *Corpus documentorum* no. 586 (5: 205–8), dated April [1527].

The meeting of the Estates of Holland at which the accusation against Amsterdam was made took place in March 1527 (*Resolutien der Staten van Holland* 1: 35). Luyt (Lucas) Jacobs, the burgermaster who accompanied the town secretary to Mechelen, held office in 1527, but not in 1526 or 1528 (J. Wagenaar *Amsterdam in zijn Opkomst, Aanwas, Geschiedenis* vol 3, list of burgermasters). Lauweryns was President of the Grand Council till his death in November 1527 (Allen v, 84).

CONCLUSION

1 E.g., Kurt von Raumer 'Erasmus, der Humanist und der Friede,' in *Ewiger Friede: Friedensrufe und Friedenspläne seit der Renaissance* 19, citing Huizinga
2 Above, chapter 3, note 70
3 J.A. Fernandez, 'Erasmus on the Just War' 210, 215; von Raumer *Ewiger Friede* 6
4 Von Raumer *Ewiger Friede* 16; Pierre Brachin '*Vox clamantis in deserto*' 257–8, citing letter 480
5 Above, introduction, note 27
6 Fernandez 'Erasmus on the Just War' passim
7 Above, introduction, note 6; chapter 2, note 171
8 Jacqueline de Romilly *Thucydide et l'impérialisme athénien* part 3, chapter 3
9 Above, chapter 2, notes 172, 179
10 See J.R. Hale *Renaissance Europe, 1480–1520* 87–100.
11 Cf Gerhard Ritter *The Corrupting Influence of Power*, a comparison between Machiavelli's *Prince* and More's *Utopia*.
12 Above, chapter 2, note 156
13 Above, chapter 1, note 61, and chapter 3, note 136
14 Von Raumer *Ewiger Friede* 19
15 *Hieronymi opera* 3: 117: 'Demiror cur Hieronymus tam iniquus sit huic Stoicorum paradoxo, quo nihil esse possit Christianius, si quis recte interpretetur. Etenim si non assequaris, est tamen aliquid, ad id quod optimum est niti.'
16 Above, chapter 3, note 140
17 Above, chapter 4, notes 129–31
18 'Ut fici oculis incumbunt' LB II, 654BC: 'Siquidem animadverterunt hoc homines tantum ad nocendum oculati cordatique, unam hanc ancoram superesse publicae incolumitatis, si civium & civitatum honesta concordia, Tyrannis potentium coerceatur. Hanc igitur in primis dirimere cura est. Sentiunt in pace minimum sibi licere, cum res legibus & consiliis agitur, non dolis, aut armis. Proinde modis omnibus id agunt, ne populus publica pace gaudeat. Perspiciunt praecipuam reip. felicitatem in hoc sitam, si Principem habeat integrum, cordatum, vigilantem, hoc est, vere

Principem. Itaque miro studio curant tutores, ne unquam vir sit Princeps. Adnituntur optimates, ii, qui publicis malis saginantur, ut voluptatibus fit quam effoeminatissimus.' Cf above, chapter 3, note 112.

19 Above, chapter 3, notes 118, 125

20 Tracy *Erasmus: The Growth of a Mind* 142–4, 161–2

21 In the same way he mistrusted Luther because of the reformer's scholastic training.

22 Raymond Williams (*Culture and Society* 24) suggests a Renaissance background for the concept of culture whose history he traces from Burke through Arnold and beyond.

23 Above, chapter 4, notes 80, 81

24 Above, chapter 4, note 64

25 Above, chapter 4, note 88; cf Bryce Lyon *From Fief to Indenture*

26 Above, chapter 2, note 173; Fernand Braudel *La Méditerranée et le monde méditerranéen*

27 Above, chapter 3, note 5; Paul Rosenfeld 'The Provincial Governors from the Minority of Charles v to the Revolt'

28 Gordon Griffiths *William of Hornes, Lord of Hèze, and the Revolt of the Netherlands, 1576–1580*

29 Cf José Antonio Maravall *Las Comunidades de Castilla*

Bibliography

❧

ABBREVIATIONS

AGN *Algemene Geschiedenis der Nederlanden* vol 4. Antwerp, Standaard 1952

Allen *Opus epistolarum Des. Erasmi Roterodami* ed P.S. Allen. 11 vols. Oxford, Clarendon 1906–63

Brewer Brewer, J.S. *Letters and Papers, Foreign and Domestic, of the Reign of Henry VIII* rev ed. London, Public Record Office 1920–

CWE *Collected Works of Erasmus: The Correspondence of Erasmus* Toronto, University of Toronto Press 1974–7; vol 1: letters 1–141 trans R.A.B. Mynors and D.F.S. Thomson, annotated by Wallace K. Ferguson; vol 2: letters 142–297 trans R.A.B. Mynors and D.F.S. Thomson, annotated by Wallace K. Ferguson; vol 3: letters 298–445 trans R.A.B. Mynors and D.F.S. Thomson, annotated by James K. McConica; vol 4: letters 446–593 trans R.A.B. Mynors and D.F.S. Thomson, annotated by James K. McConica

Henne Henne, Alexandre *Histoire du règne de Charles Quint en Belgique* Vols 1 and 2. Brussels, Flatau 1858

Herding *Institutio principis christiani and Panegyricus* ed Otto Herding in *Opera omnia Des. Erasmi Roterodami* 4:1. Amsterdam, North Holland 1974

LB *Opera omnia Des. Erasmi Roterodami* Jean Leclerc. 10 vols. Leiden, Leclerc 1703–6

WORKS OF ERASMUS

Hieronymi opera Basel, Froben 1516

Erasmi opuscula ed Wallace K. Ferguson. The Hague, Nijhoff 1933

Erasmus Ausgewählte Werke ed Hajo Holborn. Munich, Beck 1933

The Education of a Christian Prince trans Lester K. Born. New York, Columbia University Press 1936

Dulce bellum inexpertis ed and trans Yvonne Remy and René Dunil-Marquebreucq (Collection Latomus 7). Brussels, Latomus 1953

The Poems of Erasmus ed Cornelis Reedijk. Leiden, Brill 1956

Erasmus and Cambridge: The Cambridge Letters of Erasmus ed H.C. Porter, trans D.F.S. Thomson. Toronto, University of Toronto Press 1963

La Correspondance d'Erasme et de Guillaume Budé trans Marie Madeleine de la Garanderie. Paris, Vrin 1967

De conscribendis epistolis ed Jean-Claude Margolin. *Opera Omnia Des. Erasmi Roterodami* 1:2 Amsterdam, North Holland 1971

Lingua ed F. Schalk. *Opera Omnia Des. Erasmi Roterodami* 4:1 Amsterdam, North Holland 1974

PRIMARY SOURCES

Aegidius, Petrus *Summae sive argumenta legum diversorum imperatorum* Louvain, Martens [1517]. Copy in University of Ghent Library

– *Lamentatio in obitum Caesaris Maximiliani* Strasbourg, Johann Scotus, s.d. Copy in the Newberry Library

Aegidius, Petrus, and Grapheus, Cornelius *Hypotheses sive argumenta spectaculorum quae Caesari Carolo civitatis Antverpiensis antistites sunt edituri* Antwerp, Hillen 1520

Algemene Rijksarchief, The Hague, Inventory no. 2413 'Staten van Holland voor 1572.'

Die Amerbachkorrespondenz ed Alfred Hartmann 8 vols. Basel, Universitätsbibliothek 1943–72

Anglo, Sydney, ed *Remi Du Puys, La Tryumphante Entrée de Charles prince des Espagnes en Bruges, 1515* New York, Johnson Reprints 1976

Anthonisz, James (Jacobus) *Apologia de precellentia potestatis imperatorie ditionis* Antwerp, Hillen 1503. Copy in Newberry Library

Aurelius, Cornelius *Batavia, sive de antiquo veroque situ eius insulae quam Rhenus in Hollandia facit* Antwerp, Christopher Plantin 1586

[Aurelius, Cornelius] *Cronycke van Hollandt, Zeelandt & Vrieslant* (the so-called *Divisie Cronycke*) Antwerp, J. Doesburg 1530

Barlandus, Hadrianus *Hollandiae Comitum Historia et Icones* Frankfurt, Jo. Wechelus 1585

– *Historia rerum gestarum a Brabantiae ducibus* Brussels, F. Foppens 1585

Brown, Rawdon, ed *Calendar of State Papers, Venetian*, London, Public Record Office 1867

Budé, Guillaume *De contemptu rerum fortuitarum* Cologne, Soter 1521

– *De philologia* Paris, Badius 1532

– *De studio literarum* Paris, Badius 1532

– *De transitu hellenismi ad christianismum* Paris, R. Estienne 1535

– *De l'institution du prince* Arriour, Nicole Paris 1547

– *De asse et partibus eius* in *Opera omnia* 5 vols. Basel, Episcopius 1557; reprinted London, Gregg 1966

Buscodensis, Nicholas, ed *Hugonis sancti victoris quaestiones concinnae quicquid est in divi Pauli obscurum mira brevitate elucidantes* s.l., T. Martens, s.d. Copy in University of Ghent Library

– *Richardi sancti victoris in apocalypsim commentarii* Louvain, Martens 1513. Copy in the Plantijn Museum, Antwerp

Commynes, Philippe de *Mémoires* ed Joseph Calmette, in *Les Classiques de l'histoire de France au moyen age* ed Louis Halphen, vols 3, 5, 6. Paris, Champion 1924

M. Tulli Ciceronis Orationes vol 2, ed Albertus Curtis Clark. Oxford, Clarendon, 2nd ed 1918 (reprinted 1970)

Cuperinus, Aelbertus *Chronicke* in C.R. Hermans, ed *Verzameling van Kronyken, Charters en Oorkonden betrekkelijk de Stad en Meierij van 's Hertogenbosch* vol 1: *De Stad 's Hertogenbosch* 's Hertogenbosch, P. Stockvis 1848

Deutsche Reichstagsakten, jüngere Reihe vol 1, ed August Kluckhohn. Gotha, Berthes 1893

Deuxième Voyage de Philippe le Beau en Espagne ed Gachard *Collection des voyages* (see under Lalain) I

van Dorp, Martin *Fabulae Aesopi* Louvain, Martens 1513

De Egmondsche Abtenkroniek van Johannes a Leydis ed Victor J.G. Roefs, O. Carm. Sittard, Alberts 1942

Nicolai Everardi consiliorum opus Louvain 1571

Mémoires du Maréchal de Florange (Fleuranges) ed Robert Guibaux and P.A. Lemoisne (Publications de la société pour l'histoire de France 363, 406) Paris, Renouard 1913, 1924

'Dispacci al Senato Veneto di Francesco Foscari e di Altri Oratori presso l'Imperatore Massimiliano I nel 1496' *Archivo Storico Italiano* VII:2a (Florence 1844): 721–948

Franck, Sebastian *Chronica, Zeytbüch und Geschÿchtbibel* Strasbourg, B. Derk 1531

Fredericq, Paul *Corpus documentorum inquisitionis haereticae pravitatis Neerlandicae* 5 vols. Ghent, Vuylstene 1895–1902

Gachard, L.P. 'Les Anciennes Assemblées nationales de la Belgique' *Revue de Bruxelles* 3 (1839):1–79

Gallee, J.H., and Muller, Fz., S. 'Berijmd Verhaal van het Beleg van Ijsselstein door Gelder en Utrecht en 1511' *Bijdragen en Mededelingen van het Historisch Genootschap gevestigd te Utrecht* 4 (1881):665–704

Grapheus, Cornelius *Androtheogonia* Antwerp, Martens 1514; reproduced Aalst 1964. Copy in the Royal Library, Brussels

Guicciardini, Francesco *The History of Italy* New York, Macmillan 1969

'Goudse Vroedschaps-Resolutien betreffende Dagvaarten der Staten van Holland en de Staten Generael, 1501–1524' L.M. Rollin-Couquerque and A. Meerkamp van Embden, eds *Bijdragen en Mededelingen van het Historisch Genootschap gevestigd te Utrecht* 37 (1916):61–182

Hermans, Willem *Hollandiae Gelriaeque bellum* in Ant. Mathesius, ed *Veteris aevi analecta* The Hague, G. Block 1738

Herminjard, A. *Correspondance des réformateurs des pays de langue française* 9 vols. Paris, Lévy 1878–9

Ulrichi Hutteni opera ed. Eduard Böcking, 5 vols. Leipzig, Teubner 1861

de Lalain, Antoine, Sieur de Montigny *Voyage de Philippe le Beau en Espagne* ed. L.P. Gachard *Collection des voyages des souverains des Pays Bas* Brussels, Hayez 1876

Le Glay, M., ed *Correspondance de l'Empereur Maximilien I et de Marguerite d'Autriche* (Publications de la société pour l'histoire de France 7) Paris, Renouard 1839

Machiavelli, Niccolò *The Prince and the Discourses* New York, Library of the Liberal Arts 1950

Macquereau, Robert *Chronique de la maison de Bourgogne* in J.A.C. Buchon, ed *Choix de chroniques et mémoires sur l'histoire de France* 5 vols. Paris, Desrez 1838

Olivier de la Marche *Mémoires* ed H. Beaune and J. d'Arbaumont (Publications de la Société pour l'histoire de France 71) Paris, Renouard 1883

Chroniques de Jean Molinet ed J.A. Buchon. 5 vols (Collection des Chroniques nationales françaises 43–7) Paris, Verdière 1927–8

Montaigne's Essays and Selected Writings ed and trans Donald Frame. New York, St Martin's 1963

The Correspondence of Sir Thomas More ed. Elizabeth Rogers. Princeton, Princeton University Press 1947

The Latin Epigrams of Thomas More ed and trans Leicester Bradner and Charles Arthur Lynch. Chicago, University of Chicago Press 1953

More, Thomas *Utopia* trans Edward L. Surtz. New Haven, Yale University Press 1964

Schulte-Herbrüggen, Hubertus *Sir Thomas More: Neue Briefe* Münster, Aschendorff 1966

Nieuwe Ordinancie op der Wachte der Stadt van Loven Louvain, Geerardt Rivius 1521. Louvain, Stadsarchief no 1558

'Korte Autobiographie van Mr. Floris Oem van Wijngarden,' Robert Fruin, ed *Handelingen en Mededelingen der Maatschappij der Nederlandse Letterkunde te Leiden* (1866):143–53

Pace, Richard *De fructu qui ex doctrina percipitur* ed and trans Frank Manley and Richard Sylvester. New York, Ungar 1967

Blaise Pascal *Pensées* New York, Dutton 1958

Pliny the Elder *Histoire naturelle* book 10, ed E. de Saint Denis. Paris, 'Les Belles Lettres' 1961

Recueil des anciennes ordonnances de la Belgique, 2e Série, 1506–1700 vol 1, ed Ch. Laurent, Brussels, Gomaere 1893; vol 2, ed J. LaMeere, Brussels, Gomaere 1898

Resolutien der Staten van Holland vol 1. Amsterdam, 1789. Copy in the Bell Collection, University of Minnesota

Root Boek van de Staten van Brabant Algemene Rijksarchief, Brussels, catalogue no R. 199/16

The Satire of Seneca on the Apotheosis of Claudius ed Allan Perley Ball. New York, Columbia University Press 1902

Smit, H.J. *Bronnen tot de Geschiedenis van den Handel met Engelland* vol 2, part 1, 1485–1558. Rijks Geschiedkundige Publicaties 86. The Hague 1942

Snoy, Reyner *De rebus Batavicis libri XIII* ed Jacobus Brassica. Frankfurt, Daniel and David Aubriorum, Clemens Schleichius 1620. Copy at Yale University

Die Vadianische Briefsammlung der Stadtsbibliothek St. Gallen ed Emil Arbenz. Vol 3. St Gallen, Fenn 1893

Vivat Rex Carolus s.l., s.d. Copy in the Royal Library, The Hague

de Weert, Josse *Chronycke van Nederlant, besonderlyck der Stadt Antwerpen, 1097–1565* in Charles Piot, ed *Chroniques de Brabant et de Flandre* (Publications in 4⁰, Commission Royale d'histoire, Académie Royale de Belgique 21) Brussels 1879

SECONDARY SOURCES

Adams, Robert T. 'Pre-Renaissance Courtly Propaganda for Peace in English Literature' *Papers of the Michigan Academy* 32 (1946–8):431–6

– *The Better Part of Valor: More, Erasmus, Colet and Vives on Humanism, War and Peace* Seattle, University of Washington Press 1962

Ady, C.M. *The Bentivoglio of Bologna* Oxford, Oxford University Press 1937

von Albertini, Rudolf *Das florentinische Staatsbewusstsein in Übergang von der Republik zum Prinzipat* Bern, Francke 1955

Allen, P.S. 'Dean Colet and Archbishop Warham' *English Historical Review* 17 (1903):303–6

Augustijn, Cornelis *Erasmus en de Reformatie* Amsterdam, H. Paris 1962

Bainton, Roland 'The *Querela pacis* of Erasmus, Classical and Christian Sources' *Archiv für Reformationsgeschichte* 42 (1951):32–48

– 'Erasmus, Luther, and the Dialogue *Julius exclusus*' in *400 Jahre luthrischer Reformation: Festschrift für Franz Lau* Göttingen, Vandenhoek und Ruprecht 1967. Pp. 17–26.

– *Erasmus of Christendom* New York, Scribner's 1969

Baron, Hans *The Crisis of the Early Italian Renaissance* Princeton, Princeton University Press 1955

– *From Petrarch to Bruni* Chicago, University of Chicago Press 1968

Bayley, C.C. *War and Society in Renaissance Florence* Toronto, University of Toronto Press 1961

Bense, Walter F. 'Paris Theologians on War and Peace, 1521–1529' *Church History* 41 (1972):168–85

Bentley, Jerry H. 'Humanists and Holy Writ: A Comparison of the Pauline Scholarship of Erasmus and Lorenzo Valla' PH D dissertation, University of Minnesota 1976

Benz, Ernst 'Christus und die Sileni des Alcibiades' *Aus der Welt der Religion* new series, 3 (1940):1–31

Blok, P.J. *Geschiedenis eener Hollandsche Stadt* vol 2. The Hague, Nijhoff 1912

van der Blom, N. 'Fausto Andrelini Forlivensis, Poeta Regius' *Hermeneus* 42 (1971):256–65

Bohatec, Josef *Budé und Calvin: Studien zum Gedankenwelt des französischen Humanismus* Graz, Bohlau 1950

Brachin, Pierre '*Vox clamantis in deserto*: réflexions sur le pacifisme d'Erasme' in *Colloquia Erasmiana Turonensia* ed Jean-Claude Margolin. Toronto, University of Toronto Press 1972.

Brandi, Karl 'Die Wahl Karls V'*Gesellschaft der Wissenschaften zu Göttingen, philologisch-historische Klasse, Nachrichten* (1925)

– *The Emperor Charles V* trans C.V. Wedgwood. London, Jonathan Cape 1939

Braudel, Fernand *La Méditerranée et le monde méditerranéen* Paris, Colin 1949

Bridge, John S.C. *A History of France from the Death of Louis XI* 4 vols. Oxford, Clarendon 1921–9

de la Brosse, O. *Le Pape et le Concile: la comparaison de leurs pouvoirs à la veille de la Réforme* Paris, Cerf, 1965

Brown, Frieda *Religious and Political Conservatism in the Essays of Montaigne* Geneva, Droz 1963

Brugmans, H. *Geschiedenis van Amsterdam* 8 vols. Amsterdam, 'Joost van der Vondel' 1930–4

Brulez, W. 'Brugge en Antwerpen in de 15e en 16e Euwen: een Tegenstelling?' *Tijdschrift voor Geschiedenis* 83 (1970):15–37

Burckhardt, Jacob *The Civilization of the Renaissance in Italy*. 2 vols. New York, Harper 1958

di Caprariis, Vittorio *Francesco Guicciardini, dalla politica alla storia* Bari, Laterza 1950

– 'Il *Panegyricus* di Erasmo a Filippo di Borgogna' *Rivista Storica Italiana* 65 (1953):199–222

Cartellieri, O. *Am Hofe der Herzöge von Burgund* Basel, B. Schwabe 1925

Chabod, Federico *Machiavelli and the Renaissance* New York, Harper 1958

– *Storia di Milano nel Epoca di Carlo V* Turin, Einaudi 1961

Chambers, D.S. *Cardinal Bainbridge in the Court of Rome, 1509–1514* London, Oxford University Press 1965

Chantraine, Georges 'Mysterium et sacramentum dans le *Dulce bellum inexpertis*' in *Colloquium Erasmianum* Mons, Centre universitaire, 1968.

Chartrou, Joseph *Les Entrées solonelles et triomphes de la Renaissance* Paris, Presses universitaires de France 1928

Chevalier, B. 'Le Roi Louis XI et les bonnes villes: le cas de Tours' *Le Moyen Age* 70 (1964)

Chrisman, Miriam *Strasbourg in the Age of Reform* New Haven, Yale University Press 1967

Clutton, G. 'Ter Maximum, a Humanist Jest' *Journal of the Warburg and Courtauld Institutes* 2 (1939):266–8

Cochrane, Charles N. *Christianity and Classical Culture* Oxford, Clarendon 1941

Constantinescu-Bagdat, Elise *La 'Querela pacis' d'Erasme* Paris, Presses universitaires de France 1924

Cosenza, Mario *Biographical Dictionary of the Italian Humanists* 6 vols. Boston, G.K. Hall 1968

[de la Court, Pieter] *Historie van Holland onder de Gravelijke Regering* s.l., 1662. Copy in the Bell Collection, University of Minnesota Library

Courtenay, William 'Covenant and Causality in Peter d'Ailly' *Speculum* 46 (1971):94–119

Cruickshank, C.G. *Army Royal: An Account of Henry VIII's Invasion of France* Oxford, Clarendon 1969

van Dalen, J.L. *Geschiedenis van Dordrecht* 2 vols. Dordrecht, C. Morks 1931–3

Dansaert, G. *Guillaume de Croy, dit le Sage* Brussels, Vermaut [1949]

Daxhelet, Etienne *Adrianus Barlandus, Humaniste belge, 1486–1538* (Humanistica et Lovaniensa 6) Louvain, librairie universitaire 1938

Delaruelle, Louis *Guillaume Budé: les origines, les débuts, les idées maitresses* Paris, H. Champion 1907

Derwa, Marcelle 'Trois Aspects humanistes de l'épicurisme chrétien' in *Colloquium Erasmianum* Mons, Centre universitaire 1968

Duncker, Ludwig *Fürst Rudolf der Tapfere von Anhalt und der Krieg gegen Herzog Karl von Geldern, 1507/1508* Dessau, Dünnhaupt 1900

Egers, Paul 'Kardinal Matthäus Lang' *Mitteilungen, Gesellschaft für Salzburger Landeskunde* 46 (1906)

Enno van Gelder, H.A. 'Cornelius Aurelius te Lopsen' *Bijdragen voor Vaderlandsche Geschiedenis en Oudheidunde* 4th series, 7 (1909):385–8

– 'Een Noord-Hollandsche Stad, 1500–1540' *Bijdragen voor Vaderlandsche Geschiedenis en Oudheidkunde* 4th series, 8 (1910):419–39

Fernandez, J.A. 'Erasmus on the Just War.' *Journal of the History of Ideas* 34 (1973):209–26

Fredericq, Paul *De Nederlanden onder Keizer Karel* Ghent, Vuylstene 1885

Fruin, Robert 'De Verpandingen van 1496 en 1515 en haar Voorbereiding' in his *Verspreide Geschriften* The Hague, Nijhoff 1902. Vol 6:138–75

– 'De Samensteller van de zoogenaamde Divisie-Kroniek' in *Verspreide Geschriften* vol 7:66–77.

Füeter, Eduard *Geschichte des europäischen Staatensystems von 1492 bis 1559* (Handbuch der mittelalterlichen und neueren Geschichte) ed G. von Below and F. Meinecke. Vol 2. Munich, Oldenbourg 1919

Gaillard, Arthur *Le Conseil de Brabant* 3 vols. Brussels, Lebègue 1898–1901

de la Garanderie, Marie Madeleine 'L'Harmonie secrète du *De asse* de Budé' *Bulletin de l'association Guillaume Budé* (1968):473–86

Geldner, Ferdinand *Die Staatsauffassung und Fürstenlehre des Erasmus von Rotterdam* (Historische Studien 191) Berlin, Eberling 1930

Giono, Jean *The Battle of Pavia* London, Peter Owen 1963

ter Gouw, J. *Geschiedenis van Amsterdam* vols 3 and 4. Amsterdam, Scheltema and Holleman 1881–4

de Graaf, Bob 'Alardus Amstelredamus' *Folium* 4 (1954):29–118

– *Reyner Snoygoudanus: A Bio-Bibliographical Study* Nieuwkoop, De Graaf 1968

Griffiths, Gordon *William of Hornes, Lord of Hèze, and the Revolt of the Netherlands, 1576–1580* Berkeley, University of California Press 1954

– *Representative Government in Western Europe in the Sixteenth Century* Oxford, Clarendon 1968

Guenée, Bernard, and Lehoux, Françoise *Les Entrées royales françaises, de 1328 à 1515* Paris, CNRS 1968

Le Baron Guillaume *Histoire des bandes d'ordonnance des Pays-Bas* (Mémoires de l'Académie royale des sciences, des lettres et des beaux-arts de Belgique, Classe des Lettres 40) Brussels, Académie royale 1873

Gundolf, Friedrich *Caesar: Geschichte seines Ruhmes* Berlin, Georg Bindl 1924

Hale, J.R. 'Sixteenth-Century Explanations of War and Violence' *Past and Present* 51 (1971):3–26

– *Renaissance Europe, 1480–1520* New York, Harper 1973

Hauser, Henri *Débuts de l'âge moderne* Paris, Alcan 1929

Herding, Otto 'Isokrates, Erasmus, und die *Institutio principis christiani*' in *Dauer und Wandel der Geschichte: Festschrift für Kurt von Raumer* ed Rudolf Vierhaus and Manfred Butzenhart. Münster, Aschendorff 1966

Hillerbrand, Hans *Die politische Ethik des oberdeutschen Täufertums* Leiden, Brill 1962

Hirschauer, Charles *Les Etats d'Artois de leurs origines à l'occupation française, 1346–1640* 2 vols. Paris, Champion 1923

von Höfler, C. 'Kritische Untersuchungen über die Quellen der Geschichte Philipps des Schönen' *Sitzungsberichte der kaiserlichen Akademie* Vienna 1883, 1888

Holmer, Paul Leroy 'Studies in the Military Organization of the Yorkist Kings' PH D dissertation, University of Minnesota 1977

Hoogewerff, G. 'Erasmus te Rom in de Zomer van 1509' *De Gids* 122 (1959):22–30

d'Hoop, Alfred *Inventaire sommaire des archives des Etats de Brabant* Brussels, s.d.

de Hoop Scheffer, J.G. *Geschiedenis der Kerkhervorming in Nederland van haar Ontstaan tot 1531* Amsterdam 1873

de Hornedo, Rafael Maria, SJ 'Carlos v y Erasmo' *Miscellanea Comillas* 30 (1957):201–47

Hugenholz, F.W.N. 'Het Kaas- en Broodvolk' *Bijdragen en Mededelingen van het Historisch Genootschap gevestigd te Utrecht* 81 (1967):14–34

Huizinga, Johan 'Erasmus über Vaterland und Nationen' in *Gedenkschrift zum 400en Todestage des Erasmus* Basel, Braus-Riggenbach 1936

Jacob, E.F. *Henry V and the Invasion of France* New York, Collier 1966

Jansen, H.P.H. *Hoekse en Kabiljauwse Twisten* Bussum, van Dishoeck 1966.

Johnson, Roger N. *Aggression in Men and Animals* Philadelphia, Saunders 1972

de Jouvenel, Bertrand *On Power* (first published in French 1945) Boston, Beacon 1962

Kalkoff, Paul *Die Anfänge der Gegenreformation in den Niederlanden* 2 vols (Studien des Vereins für Reformationsgeschichte 79, 81) Halle, Verein für Reformationsgeschichte 1903

– *Erasmus, Luther und Friedrich der Weise* (Studien des Vereins für Reformationsgeschichte 132) Leipzig, Verein für Reformationsgeschichte 1919

– (ed) *Wormser Reichstag* Munich, Oldenbourg 1922

– 'Die Kaiserwahl Friedrichs des Weisen' *Archiv für Reformationsgeschichte* 21 (1924):133–40

– *Die Kaiserwahl Friedrichs IV und Karls V* Weimar, Bohlau's Nachfolger 1925
– 'Die Stellung Friedrichs des Weisen zur Kaiserwahl von 1519 und die Hildesheimer Stiftsfehde' *Archiv für Reformationsgechichte* 24 (1929):270–94
Kalma, J.J. *Grote Pier van Kimswerd* Leeuwarden, De Tille 1970
Keen, Maurice *The Laws of War in the Middle Ages* London, Routledge and Kegan Paul 1965
Kelley, Donald R. *The Foundations of Modern Historical Scholarship* New York, Columbia University Press 1970
Kerling, N.J.M. *Commercial Relations of Holland and Zeeland with England from the Late Thirteenth to the Close of the Fourteenth Century* Leiden, Brill 1954
de Keyser, Lucie 'Cornelius Grapheus, Humaniste Anversois, Etude bio-bibliographique' MA thesis, Louvain 1929 (typescript, Université catholique de Louvain)
Koch, A.C.F. *The Year of Erasmus' Birth* Utrecht, Dekker and Gumbert 1969
Kölker, A.J. *Alardus Amstelredamus en Cornelius Crocus, twee Amsterdamse Priester-Humanisten* Nijmegen, Dekker and van de Vegt 1963
von Koerber, Eberhard, *Die Staatstheorie des Erasmus von Rotterdam* Berlin, Duncker and Humblot 1967
Kommoss, Rudolf *Sebastian Franck und Erasmus von Rotterdam* (Germanische Studien 153) Berlin, Eberling 1934
Kossman, F. 'Een Vergeten Lofdicht van Erasmus op de Orde van het Gouden Vlies door Alvar Gomez, 1517' *Het Boek* 26 (1940–2):357–62
Krahn, Cornelius *Dutch Anabaptism* The Hague, Nijhoff 1968
Kuiper, E.T. 'Erasmus als Politiek Propagandist' *Tijdschrift voor Geschiedenis* 37 (1922):147–67
Larner, John *The Lords of Romagna* Ithaca, Cornell University Press 1965
Le Long, Isaac *Historische Beschryving van de Reformatie der Stad Amsterdam* Amsterdam, Van Septeren 1754
Lemonnier, H. *Les Guerres d'Italie: la France sous Charles VIII, Louis XII, et François I* (Histoire de France 5:1.) ed Ernst Lavisse. Paris, Hachette 1911
Lestoquoy, J. *Les Evêques d'Arras* Fontenay-le-Comte, Lussaud 1942
Lewis, P.S. *Later Medieval France* New York, St Martin's 1968

– (ed) *The Recovery of France in the Fifteenth Century* New York, Harper and Row 1971

Lorenz, Konrad *On Aggression* London, Methuen 1967

Lot, Ferdinand *Recherches sur les éffectifs des armées françaises, 1494–1562* Paris, SEVPEN 1962

Lutz, Heinrich *Ragione di stato und christliche Staatsethik im 16en Jahrhundert* Münster, Aschendorff 1961

– *Christianitas afflicta* Göttingen, Vanderhoek und Ruprecht 1964

Lyon, Bryce *From Fief to Indenture* Cambridge, Harvard University Press 1957

McConica, James K., CSB 'Erasmus and the "Julius"' in Charles Trinkaus, ed *The Pursuit of Holiness in Late Medieval and Renaissance Religion* Leiden, Brill 1974

McNeil, David O. *Guillaume Budé and Humanism in the Reign of Francis I* Geneva, Droz 1975

Maravall, José Antonio *Las Comunidades de Castilla* Madrid, Revista de Occidente 1963

Mattingly, Garret 'Some Revisions of the Political History of the Renaissance' in Tinsley Helton, ed *The Renaissance: A Reconsideration* Madison, University of Wisconsin Press 1961

Meilink, P.A. *Archieven van de Staten van Holland: Eerste Deel, voor 1572* The Hague, Algemene Landsdrukkerij 1929

Meinecke, Friedrich *Machiavellism: The Doctrine of Raison d'Etat and Its Place in Modern History* New York, Praeger 1965

Mesnard, Pierre *L'Essor de la philosophie politique au XVIe siècle* Paris, Boivin 1936

Molhuysen, P.C. 'Cornelius Aurelius' *Nederlands Archief voor Kerkgeschiedenis* new series 2 (1903):1–33; 4 (1907):54–78

– 'Nieuwe Bescheiden over Cornelius Aurelius' *Nederlands Archief voor Kerkgeschiedenis* new series 4 (1905–6):54–73

Nauwelaerts, M.A. 'Un Ami anversois de More et d'Erasme, Petrus Aegidius' *Moreana* 15 (1967):83–96

Nübel, Otto *Pompeius Occo* Tübingen, Mohr 1972

Overmeer, P.J. 'Het Staande Leger en de Huurbenden in de Nederlanden, 1471–1584' *Navorscher* 59 (1910):181–93, 425–40

Parker, Geoffrey *The Army of Flanders and the Spanish Road* Cambridge, Cambridge University Press 1972

Partner, Peter *The Papal State under Martin V* London, British School in Rome 1958

Pastor, Ludwig *A History of the Popes* 40 vols. St Louis, Herder 1910–68

Philips, Margaret Mann *The Adages of Erasmus* Cambridge, Cambridge University Press 1964
Pirenne, Henri *Histoire de Belgique* Vol 3. Brussels, Lamertin 1907
– *Early Democracies in the Low Countries* New York, Norton 1970
Pitti, Clemente *Un Amico di Erasmo: Andrea Ammonio* Florence, Le Monnier 1956
Poelhekke, J.J. 'Het Naamloze Vaderland van Erasmus' *Bijdragen en Mededelingen betreffende de Geschiedenis van de Nederlanden* 86 (1971):90–123
Pollard, A.F. *Wolsey* London, Longmans 1909
Post, R.R. 'Een Ontwerp van een Bischoppelijke Toespraak Gemaakt door Erasmus' *Archief voor de Geschiedenis van de Katholieke Kerk in Nederland* 9 (1967):322–30
Prims, Floris *Antwerpiensa, losse Bijdragen tot de Antwerpse Geschiedenis* Antwerp, De Vlijt 1936
Proyart, M. le Chanoine 'Nicholas le Ruistre, évêque d'Arras' *Mémoires de l'Académie des sciences, des lettres et des arts* 2nd series, 7 (1876):223–40
Rattner, Josef *Aggression und menschliche Natur* Freiburg, Walter 1970
von Raumer, Kurt *Ewiger Friede: Friedensrufe und Friedenspläne seit der Renaissance* Munich, Alber 1953
Rayment, Charles 'The *Tyrannicida* of Erasmus: Translated Excerpts with Introduction and Commentary' *Speech Monographs* 26 (1959):233–47
Reedijk, Cornelis 'Erasmus' Versen op het Overlijden van Hendrik van Bergen, Bisschop van Kamerijk' *Het Boek* 30 (1949/51):297–305
– 'Een Schimpdicht van Erasmus op Julius II' in *Opstellen aan F.K.H. Kossman* The Hague, Nijhoff 1958
Regout, Robert, SJ 'Erasmus en de Theorie van de Rechtvaardigden Oorlog.' *Bijdragen voor Vaderlandsche Geschiedenis en Oudheidkunde* 7th series, (1936):155–71
Reichling, D. *Johannes Murmellius: sein Leben und seine Werke* reprint of 1880 edition. Nieuwkoop, De Graaf 1963
Le Baron de Reiffenberg *Histoire de l'ordre de la toison d'or* Brussels, Imprimerie normale 1830
Reintges, Theo *Ursprung und Wesen der mittelalterlichen Schützengilden* (Rheinisches Archiv 58) Bonn, Rohrscheid 1963
Renaudet, Augustin *Erasme et l'Italie* Geneva, Droz 1954
– *Préréforme et Humanisme à Paris pendant les premières guerres d'Italie* 2nd ed. Paris, Librairie d'Argences 1954

Rice, Eugene F. Jr 'The Patrons of French Humanism, 1480–1520' in A. Molho and J. Tedeschi, eds *Renaissance Studies in Honor of Hans Baron* DeKalb, Northern Illinois University Press 1971

Richardson, Walter C. *Mary Tudor, the White Queen* London, Peter Owen 1970

Ritter, Gerhard *The Corrupting Influence of Power* London, Tower Bridge 1952

Romier, Lucien *Les Origines politiques des guerres de religion* 2 vols. Paris, Perrin 1913–14

de Romilly, Jacqueline *Thucydide et l'impérialisme athénien* Paris, 'Les Belles Lettres' 1947

Rose, Walther 'Die deutschen und italienischen Schwarzen (Grossen) Garden im 15en und 16en Jahrhundert' *Zeitschrift für historische Waffen- und Kostümkunde* 4 (1912/14):73–97

Rosenfeld, Paul 'The Provincial Governors from the Minority of Charles V to the Revolt' *Standen en Landen/Anciens Pays et Assemblées d'Etat* 17 (1959):3–27

Rosenthal, Earl '*Plus ultra, non plus ultra* and the Columnar Device of Emperor Charles v' *Journal of the Warburg and Courtauld Institutes* 34 (1971):204–28

Rottier, E. *La Vie et les travaux d'Erasme considérés dans leurs rapports avec la Belgique* (Académie royale des sciences, des lettres et des beaux-arts de Belgique, Mémoires couronnées 6) Brussels 1853–4

Russell, Jocelyne 'Wolsey and the Campaign for Universal Peace' *Bulletin of the Institute for Historical Research* (1971)

Sasso, Gennaro *Niccolò Machiavelli, storia del suo pensiero politico* Naples, Istituto Storico 1958

Scarisbrick, J.C. *Henry VIII* London, Eyre and Spottiswood 1969

Schanz, Georg *Englische Handelspolitik gegen das Ende des Mittelalters* 2 vols. Leipzig, Duncker and Humblot 1881

Schätti, Karl *Erasmus und die römische Kurie* Basel, Helbing and Lichtenhahn 1954

Schneller, Adelheid *Der brüsseler Friede von 1516* (Historische Studien 83) Berlin, Eberling 1910

Schottenloher, Otto 'Erasmus, Johann Puppenruyter, und die Entstehung des *Enchiridion militis christiani*' *Archiv für Reformationsgeschichte* 45 (1954):109–16

– 'Erasmus und die respublica christiana' *Historische Zeitschrift* 210 (1970):295–323

Schrocker, Alfred 'Maximilians I Auffassung von Königtum und das

ständische Reich' *Quellen und Forschungen aus italienischen Archiven und Bibliotheken* 50 (1971):181–204
Scribner, R.W. 'The Social Thought of Erasmus' *Journal of Religious History* 6 (1970):3–26
Seneca, F. *Venezia e il Papa Julio II* Padua, Liviana Editrice 1962
Setton, Kenneth M. 'Pope Leo X and the Turkish Peril' *Proceedings of the American Philosophical Society* 113 (1969):367–424
Simeoni, Luigi *I Signorie* 2 vols. Milan, Villardi 1950
Slavin, A.J. *The 'New Monarchs' and Representative Assemblies* Boston, Heath 1965
Slootmans, C.J.F. 'Erasmus en zijn Vrienden uit Bergen-op-Zoom' *Taxandria* 35 (1928):113–23
– *Jan metten Lippen, zijn Familie en zijn Stad* Rotterdam, Donker 1945
Solon, Paul D. 'Popular Response to Standing Military Forces in Fifteenth Century France' *Studies in the Renaissance* 19 (1972): 78–111.
Sorel, Albert *Europe in the Old Regime* New York, Harper 1972
Sowards, J.K. 'The Two Lost Years of Erasmus' *Studies in the Renaissance* 9 (1962):161–86
Stange, Carl *Erasmus und Julius II: Eine Legende* Berlin, Töpfelmann 1937
Struick, J.E.A.L. *Gelre en Habsburg, 1492–1528* Arnhem, Brouwer en Zoon 1960
Sturge, Charles *Cuthbert Tunstall* London, Longmans, Green 1938
Taylor, F.L. *The Art of War in Italy, 1494–1525* Cambridge, Cambridge University Press 1921
Telle, E.V. 'Le *De copia verborum* d'Erasme et le *Julius exclusus*' *Revue de la littérature comparée* 22 (1948):441–7
Terdenge, H. 'Zur Geschichte der holländischen Steuern im 15en und 16en Jahrhundert.' *Vierteljahrschrift für Wirtschafts- und Sozialgeschichte* 18 (1925)
de Tervarent, Guy *Attributs et symboles dans l'art profane, 1450–1600* (Travaux d'Humanisme et Renaissance 28) Geneva, Droz 1958
Theissen, J.S. *De Regering van Karel V in de Noordlijke Nederlanden* Amsterdam, Meulehoff 1912
Thompson, Craig *The Translations of Lucian by Erasmus and St Thomas More* Ithaca 1940
Thürlemann, Ines *Erasmus von Rotterdam und Juan Luis Vives als Pazifisten* Fribourg, St Paulus 1932

Tracy, James D. 'Erasmus Becomes a German' *Renaissance Quarterly* 21 (1968):281–8
– *Erasmus: The Growth of a Mind* (Travaux d'Humanisme et Renaissance 121) Geneva, Droz 1972
– 'Bemerkungen zur Jugend des Erasmus' *Basler Zeitschrift für Geschichte* 72 (1972):221–30
– 'On the Composition Dates of Seven of Erasmus' Writings' *Bibliothèque d'Humanisme et Renaissance* 31 (1969):355–64
Triwunar, Milosch *Guillaume Budés 'De l'Instituition du Prince'* Erlangen, Deichert 1903
Ullmann, Heinrich *Kaiser Maximilian I* 2 vols. Stuttgart 1891
– *Franz von Sickingen* Leipzig, Hirzel 1872
Valvekens, P.E. *De Inquisitie in de Nederlanden in de Zestiende Eeuw* Brussels, De Kinkoren 1949
Vaughan, Richard *Philip the Bold* Cambridge, Harvard University Press 1962
– *John the Fearless* London, Longmans 1966
– *Philip the Good* New York, Barnes and Noble 1970
– *Charles the Bold* London, Longmans 1973
Velius, Theodorus *Chronyck van Hoorn tot het Jaar 1630* ed Sebastian Centen. Hoorn, J. Duyn 1740
Vicens Vives, Jaimé *An Economic History of Spain* Princeton, Princeton University Press 1969
De Vocht, Henri *Jerome de Busleiden, His Life and Writings* (Humanistica et Lovaniensa 9) Turnhout, Brepols 1950
– *History of the Collegium Trilingue Lovaniense* 4 vols. Louvain, Publications universitaires 1950
Wagenaar, J. *Amsterdam in zijn Opkomst, Aanwas, Geschiedenis* 4 vols. Amsterdam, Isaak Tirion 1760
Waley, D.P. *The Papal State in the Thirteenth Century* London, St Martin's 1961
von Walther, Andreas *Die burgündische Zentralbehörden unter Maximilian I und Karl V* Leipzig, Dunker and Humblot 1909
– *Die Anfänge Karls V* Leipzig, Duncker and Humblot 1911
Wegg, Jervis *Antwerp, 1477–1559* London, Methuen 1916
– *Richard Pace, A Tudor Diplomatist* New York, Barnes and Nobles Reprint 1971
Wilcox, Donald *The Development of Florentine Humanist Historiography* Cambridge, Mass., Harvard University Press 1969
Willard, Charity Cannon 'The Concept of True Nobility at the Court of Burgundy' *Studies in the Renaissance* 14 (1967):33–48

Williams, Raymond *Culture and Society* New York, Columbia University Press 1969
Yates, Frances *Astraea: The Imperial Theme in the Sixteenth Century* London, Routledge and Kegan Paul 1975
Zilverberg, S.B.J. *David van Bourgondie, Bisschop van Terwaan en van Utrecht* Groningen, Wolters 1951

Index

Erasmus Studies

A Series of Studies Concerned with Erasmus and Related Subjects

1 *Under Pretext of Praise: Satiric Mode in Erasmus' Fiction*
Sister Geraldine Thompson

2 *Erasmus on Language and Method in Theology*
Marjorie O'Rourke Boyle

3 *The Politics of Erasmus: A Pacifist Intellectual and His Political Milieu*
James D. Tracy.